To Elizabeth, a cherished
friend, a prop
and the on
who can take a joke

C000000947

UNBROKEN

Unbroken

A HISTORY OF JEWISH-ROMAN RELATIONS FROM 168BCE TO 634CE

André Nice

André Nice

Dedicated to Patrick, for teaching me just about everything I know.

Contents

Introduction

Chapter 1- An Introduction Detailing the Hasmonean Dynasty

Chapter 2- Pompey's Invasion of Judea

Chapter 3- The Rise of Herod

Chapter 4- The Divisions of Hillel and Shammai

Chapter 5-The Fall of Herod

Chapter 6- The Tetrarchy

I. Herod Archelaus
II. Salome
III. Herod Antipas and Herod Philip

Chapter 7- Yehoshua and the Christians

I. Early Life
II. A Theory Regarding John the Baptist

III. Yehoshua's Downfall

IV. A Tainted Legacy

Chapter 8- The Origins of Herod Agrippa

Chapter 9- Mad Emperor Gaius

Chapter 10- The Redemption of Judea by Herod Agrippa I

Chapter 11- How the Julio-Claudians Met Their End

Chapter 12- The Destruction of Judea by Herod Agrippa II

Chapter 13- The Year of 4 Emperors

Chapter 14- The Fall of Jerusalem

Chapter 15- Flavian Rule and the Fate of the Jews

Chapter 16- The Kitos War

Chapter 17- Bar Kochba

Chapter 18- The Decline of Rome

Chapter 19- The Rise of Christian Antisemitism and the Third Temple

Chapter 20- How the Byzantines Lost the Holy Land

Introduction

A Jew and a Vicar's son walk into a bar...

I imagine this sounds like the setup for a joke, but in fact the idea for this book was born from my long-standing friendships with Christians.

Three of my closest friends are the children of Vicars so we always had a level of friendly debate. One thing I noticed was that we all had fundamentally different views about Jesus and who he really was.

I would often frequent their Church youth group, and they welcomed me even though I wasn't a Christian. I got on well with the Christians and often talked about Religion, Philosophy and my writing.

It was while I was there that I decided to do something about Herod, mostly because I felt like he was viewed in an excessively fictionalised way by most Christians.

I wanted to get past the fiction, I wanted to write something which was academic, informative and thought-provoking.

That desire for knowledge, that creative spirit in viewing the past was fostered by one of the best people I have ever known.

This book is dedicated to Patrick, my former RE teacher because of his unwavering belief in me.

In lessons I was often bored or felt like nothing we studied was particularly stimulating, so Patrick and I would share lunches together once a week. We'd use these lunches as a chance to talk about religion and philosophy.

I consistently disagreed with my teacher on a great number of issues but that never mattered to us. He saw potential in me, and I saw in him a real intellectual rival.

In hindsight I realised why we had those talks. Because he knew I needed to be thinking to be happy. I needed complicated Philosophical and Religious discussions to feel fulfilled.

That is ultimately a characteristic of mine which forced me to write this book. Because I am lost and bereft of hope when I am not doing something I consider meaningful.

To me re-examining Roman history from a Jewish perspective is meaningful because it is primarily taught from a Christian perspective or from a Roman one.

We are an integral part of Rome's history and Rome is an integral part of ours, so it is only right that we should have both sides of the story to observe.

Often, we are a footnote, a scapegoat. Most people believe New Testament narratives about Jewish history blindly because they have never seen the other side.

Patrick always encouraged me to get more in touch with my Jewish identity despite the fact that he was a Catholic. Instead of playing the evangelist my teacher always played the teacher. And he did so well enough that this book could happen in the first place.

His Irish-Catholic background was something I could relate to. I happen to be Irish on both sides and a large number of my relatives are Maronite Christians from Lebanon.

Needless to say, this mixed religious influence gave me a certain affinity for Jesus, even if I've never believed in his divinity.

Who was Jesus? I wanted to get to the bottom of this perplexing question, I wanted to figure out what he means to Jewish history.

The content later widened to a more general discussion of relations between the Jews and the Roman empire.

One of the main themes of this book involves the development of Christianity and how the Christians ultimately took up the mantle of the Romans when it came to terrorising the Jews.

So, it is no surprise that my debates with my wise and jovial RE teacher went a long way in inspiring the idea for this book.

Some may ask, why isn't a Christian telling this story? My answer is to remind the reader just how Jewish Jesus was.

He was born to a Jewish father (or stepfather if you subscribe to the view that he was conceived immaculately) and a Jewish mother. Jesus was then raised in the middle east and died there. He went to synagogue, was circumcised and spent most of his time with Jews.

Although he had gentiles in his inner circle most of the people, he would have interacted with were Jewish or at least of a similar origin so painting him as some sort of White-Western figure is something of a reduction of his character.

Conjecture on Jesus' skin colour seems to me like an identarian waste of time but what can be established is that he was at least brown.

The point I am making is that to understand a Jewish Middle Eastern man's life the world he was born in must be considered.

Most historical sources on Jesus are either incredibly white-washed or second-hand accounts.

In other words, their reliability is questionable, and they ignore Jewish history almost completely.

I could have simply ignored the Roman side of the story and entirely spent time on Judaism instead, but in doing so I would be guilty of the same historical revisionism used against the Jews.

When referring to the Roman province of Judaea I chose to use the 'aea' spelling, and when referring to the independent state of Judea I chose to spell it with 'ea' instead.

This may look confusing or lazy but is actually a very deliberate use of language. I wished to make the difference between the Romanized province and the sovereign Jewish state very clear because more often than not the line between these two separate entities is blurred.

I am in fact of Jewish-Italian extraction myself, so in a sense I am attempting to reconcile my two rival cultures which were at conflict for so long. A portion of my lineage is from the Italkim (the descendants of slaves brought to Italy from Judaea after the First Roman-Jewish War) and another portion is from the Greek-Cypriot Romaniote Jews.

Growing up in a household with mixed Greek, Italian, Egyptian, Lebanese, Cypriot and English heritage has given me a unique understanding of the Mediterranean style of living Jesus must have been accustomed to. Not just Mediterranean customs and world-views, but also the immense diversity of the Mediterranean rather than just one group.

I also understand some of the events of his life all too well. I understand what it is like to be a foreigner living in a foreign land.

My family originally lived in Egypt but left in 1956 due to anti-semitic policies including taking the property of Jews and expelling them en masse.

In speaking about the history of Egypt I speak of my own history. My grandmother was born in Alexandria and her parents were of Jewish-Italian and Lebanese-Cypriot extraction respectively.

When the Suez Canal came under national ownership in 1956 my family were forced out of Egypt having had their possessions taken by the Egyptian state because of their Jewish roots.

I do not grudge Egypt for this offence; on the contrary I look on at Alexandria across the Mediterranean Sea as my true home.

It is a dear place that lives on in the annals of memory, I still see the photos of my grandmother on a camel opposite the pyramids adorning the walls. I still yearn to smell the salt from the vast sapphire coast.

When I speak of Egypt, I speak of a place that I love, but which does not yet love me in turn.

But I have faith that in time Egypt will come to love the Jews as it used to do. That old rivalries will blossom into friendships.

I grew up in a house where Arabic was the lingua franca, and in my own cooking I've married Jewish and Lebanese foods.

Jesus had to move to an unknown country with very little to his name and make something of himself. Jesus wanted to enfranchise the poor and weak, yet his messages have largely been corrupted by people who see him as an easy avenue for avoiding criticism and garnering support.

Affluent Christians in Western countries simply cannot fully understand who he was without the personal knowledge of what that is like.

I am a third-generation immigrant, so my suffering is as nothing compared to my ancestors, but even observing my elderly relatives and hearing their stories about coming here has given me a window into the life of a refugee.

Another reason I wrote this book was to fiercely oppose Conservative Christians, particularly American ones who despite their immigrant origins seem to have forgotten their origins.

It is people like Mike Pence who use Jesus as their reference for personal morality, yet if he came back today, they would probably view him with contempt.

The paradox of being a KKK member and burning a Cross in the garden of a black family is something I wanted to address by rediscovering Jesus' identity.

Any true follower of Jesus would support the rights of the poor (because Jesus was poor) and the rights of minorities (because Jesus would be considered a minority in most countries) and would support immigrants and asylum seekers (because Jesus was both).

The hypocrisy of loving a proto-Socialist, Jewish refugee and being on the Far-Right Politically is something I will never agree with, but fortunately something that I understand.

It is the exact same trick Roman Christians pulled when they needed someone to blame for the death of Jesus other than themselves.

In their fear and desire for someone to hate they chose to target the very same ethnic group Jesus himself came from.

They blamed the Jews for the death of their prophet and persecuted them, going against every single moral principal Jesus ever stood for.

Jesus was a political dissident who died fighting for a cause he believed in, he was an anti-establishment figure, but his modern followers have also become the very same establishment they swore to destroy.

The Jews never stooped to this. Radicalism and freedom are core principles of Judaism both in theory and in practice.

Even in the face of the horrors of persecution, slavery and genocide the Jews kept fighting, they kept rethinking their identity and adapting just enough to continue in their fight.

The beauty of Judaism's evolution is that rather than abandoning its most basic ideals it never changed so rapidly that it got lost in the change.

When their temple was taken, they didn't quit, they just learned to live and worship without a temple.

Rather than wallowing in sorrow they learned to celebrate life's joys and process grief in a healthy way.

Rather than relying on divine redemption or an afterlife they learned to do good things in this life and to redeem themselves by striving to learn from their mistakes.

Judaism is healthy because it doesn't fetishize surrender or hold grudges. Judaism can forgive oppression but never forgets it.

Their rebellion, their defiance, their sacrifice may have failed but it was not in vain. It lives on to this very day. It reminds us that even if we lose our lives, we live on in those we leave behind.

No matter where a Jew may wander, he holds the souls of his forefathers deep within. The legacy of the Jews is freedom, the revenge of the Jews on the Romans is that we outlived them, and that unlike them we shall live forever.

Our triumph is in our defeats, our greatest sorrows bring out the greatest joys. Suffering fuels us, injustice angers us. Our oppression reminds us to do what is right, to lend a hand to all who suffer what we suffer.

> *"He has shown you, O mortal, what is good.*
> *And what does the Lord require of you?*
> *To act justly and to love mercy*
> *and to walk humbly with your G-d."*
> *-Micah 6:8*

The Jews possess the profoundest of empathy because we have suffered so profoundly. The answer to our history with the Romans is not to forget it, or to lament it, but to hold our heads high at the thought that we defended ourselves with such dignity against such an overwhelming foe.

When the Lord called us, we picked up our swords. When the Romans came knocking, we always fought back.

If all else is forgotten, then let that be what is remembered about the history of the Jews and the Romans.

1

Chapter 1- An Introduction Detailing the Hasmonean Dynasty

The Hasmoneans reigned over Judea from 140BCE to 37BCE. At this time the Greeks had ruled the Jews for many years. In the early days of Seleucid occupation, the Jews were tolerated far better than under the Ptolemaic Egyptians previously. This resulted in Jewish communities popping up all over the empire which stretched as far as Babylon. Due to the Greek tradition of exercising naked in public many of these Jews in diaspora abandoned the tradition of circumcision to fit in better with their Greek counterparts. This created a long-term religious rift between the Jews and the Greeks.

The tradition of the Hellenistic Seleucids had been to allow the Jews to worship in peace, only interfering in their affairs to extract tributary taxes.

This policy was changed by Antiochus IV of the Seleucid empire. Antiochus had initially entered conflict with the Egyptians but in a legendary display of Roman authority a Senator stopped him in his tracks. The Emperor of the Seleucids rode to Alexandria but was blocked on the sands of the Mediterranean coast by a certain Gaius Popillius Laenas.

Laenas had been sent as the Roman ambassador to force Antiochus to cease his campaign against Egypt. The old Roman seemed unassuming to Antiochus and Laenas drew a circle with a stick made of vine in the sand around him.

"Before you leave this circle, give me a reply that I can take back to the Roman Senate."[1]

Innocuous as this may sound it was tantamount to blackmail. In layman's terms Laenas was saying 'If you do not agree to leave Egypt the Romans will declare war on you'. The threat was more than enough to pressure Antiochus into agreeing. He left Egypt with a good number of spoils but was humiliated by this foreign-policy defeat.

To gain the funds needed to pay his men Antiochus decided to sack the poorly defended Jewish temple.

In the year 168BCE Antiochus had unleashed his fury on the city of Jerusalem. His supporters in the city let him in without a fight, but he chose to make one. The High Priest Menelaus allowed Antiochus to enter the city and handed the treasures of the temple over to him.

This is detailed in the Christian book of Maccabees.

"Raging like a wild animal, he set out from Egypt and took Jerusalem by storm. He ordered his soldiers to cut down without mercy those whom they met and to slay those who took refuge in their houses. There was a massacre of young and old, a killing of women and children, a slaughter

of virgins and infants. In the space of three days, eighty thousand were lost, forty thousand meeting a violent death, and the same number being sold into slavery.[2]

With this atrocity Antiochus sparked the Maccabean revolt. This conflict would bring about the independence of Judea under the Hasmonean dynasty.

Beyond the attack against the Jerusalemites Antiochus also began to erode Jewish autonomy in 168BCE by undermining the religious rites and cultural practices of the Jews. The rebellion was not only a battle between oppressor and oppressed, but also a battle between Hellenism and Judaism.

Judaism is and has always been a slowly adapting body. It responds to the changes the world forces upon it, but it does so in its own time. This was no less true in Hasmonean Judea.

Modernisation slowly entered and there were key reforms to the High Priesthood, which became an appointed position rather than a purely hereditary one. A duopoly between the monarchy and the Priesthood formed and the pair ruled Judea in a measure of harmony.

This was mostly because the monarch could veto, remove or kill any High Priest who defied them such as Alcimus who was opposed to the Maccabean revolt.

The Great Sanhedrin had always enjoyed governmental authority but in the Hasmonean age independence redoubled this and cemented the Sanhedrin's position as both the Supreme Court and legislature of Judea.

This was a perfect arrangement considering the fact that Rabbis also acted as lawyers.

Religious law and secular law were one in the same and as a result interpreting the Torah was how the Rabbis came to judicial rulings.

This legalistic approach made the Judean system a very judicious one by the standards of the day.

With the formation of the Yeshivot (Rabbinical schools) schooling became more formalised and many of the greatest Rabbis ever to live were moulded at these institutions.

Another important consideration in viewing this period is that the majority of Jews in the world lived in Persia, Alexandria and other regions. A minority of Jews in fact lived in Judea and most of the money that entered the temple came from foreign Jews who could not travel that far for religious holidays.

The temple was an easy target for plunder because it was poorly defended and during key festivals its coffers swelled with coins.

Opportunistic foreigners saw this as an invitation to steal the funds from there and this led to Jerusalem having a seasonal target on its back.

Needless to say, Judea had a progressive form of government and a great deal of money, they were inevitably going to be attacked at some point.

The Greeks wished to convert the Jews to their way of living[3] and began repressing Jewish culture at a similar time. This sort of folly would not stand, not least for the Maccabees.

The occupiers set up an idol to Zeus on the temple mount itself and this forced Mattathias ben Johanan to action. Being a descendant of the High Priesthood and a Kohen made it possible for Mattathias to reconsecrate the Jewish temple.[4]

This key detail would make Mattathias and his five sons very important in the battle against the occupying Hellenists. Mattathias was sick, so he called his sons to Modin. He kept going for a number of years despite his sickness.

Judah Maccabee, Eliezer Avaran, Simeon Thassi, John Gaddi, and Jonathan Apphus attended their father. The mood was solemn, both because of their father and because of the ruin that had come to the Jews of Jerusalem. Matthew cried out at those who obeyed Antiochus.

"If anyone be zealous for the laws of his country, and for the worship of G-d, let him follow me."[5]

Many chose to follow him, including his sons. Their initial campaign which began in 166BCE did not go well because the Jews refused to fight on Shabbat. This allowed the enemy an essential tactical advantage.

The battle for Jewish identity raged on with Mattathias at its head until eventually Mattathias grew too ill to keep going and summoned his sons one last time.

"O my sons, I am going the way of all the earth; and I recommend to you my resolution, and beseech you not to be negligent in keeping it, but to be mindful of the desires of him who begat you, and brought you up, and to preserve the customs of your country, and to recover your ancient form of government, which is in danger of being overturned, and not to be carried away with those that, either by their own inclination, or out of necessity, betray it, but to become such sons as are worthy of me; to be above all force and necessity, and so to dispose your souls, as to be ready, when it shall be necessary, to die for your laws; as sensible of this, by just reasoning, that if G-d see that you are so disposed he will not overlook you, but will have a great value for your virtue, and will restore to you again what you have lost, and will return to you that freedom in which you shall live quietly, and enjoy your own customs. Your bodies are mortal, and subject to fate; but they receive a sort of immortality, by the remembrance of what actions they have done. And I would have you so in love with this immortality, that you may pursue after glory, and that, when

you have undergone the greatest difficulties, you may not scruple, for
such things, to lose your lives. I exhort you, especially, to agree one with
another; and in what excellency any one of you exceeds another, to yield
to him so far, and by that means to reap the advantage of every one's own
virtues. Do you then esteem Simon as your father, because he is a man of
extraordinary prudence, and be governed by him in what counsels he
gives you. Take Maccabeus for the general of your army, because of his
courage and strength, for he will avenge your nation, and will bring
vengeance on your enemies. Admit among you the righteous and
religious, and augment their power."[6]

With these words Mattathias left the world, knowing full well that his sons would take these words with them in the war to come. In effect this made Judah Maccabee the leader of the army and Simon the spiritual leader of their movement.

This was a wise choice and served the Jews well. From 167BCE this rebellion turned into a guerrilla war. Judah Maccabee saw multiple victories such as the Battle of the Ascent of Lebonah in 167 BCE and the Battle of Beth Horon in 166BCE.

Antiochus built the Acra fortress in Jerusalem which was manned by the Greeks and their allies among the Jews. As well as this circumcision was banned, Jews were forced to work on Shabbat and were forced to eat pork.

The Seleucid generals were fractious and more focussed on self-advancement than any unified goals, this meant that the Maccabees were able to face them one at a time and defeat their armies with ambush tactics.

The Jewish army grew massively due to liberalisation. Jews who were forced to break their laws by the Greeks were welcomed into the army and the Jewish army fought on the Sabbath.

This breach of the Torah's laws allowed the Jews to fight back. Judah gave a speech when times were desperate that rallied his troops and strengthened their resolve.

"Many are easily hemmed in by a few; in the sight of Heaven there is no difference between deliverance by many or by few; for victory in war does not depend upon the size of the army, but on strength that comes from Heaven. With great presumption and lawlessness they come against us to destroy us and our wives and children and to despoil us; but we are fighting for our lives and our laws."[7]

Eventually the Maccabees triumphed, and Judah reconsecrated the temple in the name of G-d.

By 164BCE Jerusalem was retaken. Judah and his brothers entered the temple and saw that it had been defiled, the meat of pigs littered the Holy place, and the sacred menorah was put out.

Judah declared himself High Priest and made the temple Holy again. He ignited each light of the menorah for eight days and this gesture became the inspiration of Hannukah. At the same time, Antiochus IV fell off his horse and died.[8]

The story later adopted into Jewish culture was that Judah found one small container of sacred oil and G-d allowed this to be used to light the menorah for 8 days. Hannukah is unique in that it is the only Jewish holiday not directly mentioned in the Hebrew Bible.

This fable was likely formulated as a justification for the continued celebration of the holiday, which many Rabbis of the day would have seen as unnecessary if it was not a holiday directly dedicated to G-d. Purim had a similar origin in that it was a reimagined version of a Persian holiday which the Jews happened to enjoy.

There was some contention regarding the Maccabees attaining the High Priesthood. As warriors these brothers had come into contact with dead bodies and were considered ritualistically unclean.

In many ways their departure from religious rituals was what made the Maccabees so successful, but it must be said that their breaking of the rules was controversial as well.

Antiochus' successor was but a child, so the Seleucid administration became even less functional than it had been before. Lysias was the regent for the young new Emperor and led a vast army of 55,000 men as well as war elephants to retake Jerusalem.

With half of these numbers at hand Judah fought the enemy at Beit Zecharia and lost, his brother Eliezer was killed in the fighting. This was the first defeat for the Jews in the war.

Just as the siege of Jerusalem was set to begin a rival claimant for the Seleucid throne Demetrius had taken Antioch (the Capital of the empire). This forced Lysias to flee despite having the upper hand.

The Romans had kept Demetrius as a hostage and used the threat of his release to keep the Seleucids in line. Now that he was free, he made efforts to take the throne for himself.

After becoming the Seleucid Emperor Demetrius offered Judah Maccabee peace if he stepped down from the High Priesthood and gave it to Alcimus instead. Alcimus was from the Oniad branch of the Priestly tradition.[9]

These were the pro-Greek faction who had allowed the temple to be desecrated. Despite this Judah accepted peace to spare his country any further conflict.

When a rebellion began far from Judea the Maccabees deposed Alcimus and prepared to fight the Seleucids yet again.

In light of this the Maccabees made an alliance with Rome against the Seleucids. This benefitted Rome because it gave them another vector for expansion, and it benefitted the Jews because they needed Roman aid to secure autonomy.[10]

In discussing Jewish-Roman relations it must first be said that there are obvious parallels between the development of Jewish autonomy and the development of Rome's status as a superpower.

A superpower can best be characterised by its ability to exert authority over other states.
Rome exemplified this with its use of client Kings and tributary vassalage.

The fact that the Romans could intercede on behalf of their allies and could intimidate other states into doing their bidding shows the extent to which Rome dominated the Mediterranean by this time.

This initially helped the Jews because it gave them a protector on the world stage, but in the end, it led to Judea's total and utter annexation by the Romans. Roman protection was something of a Faustian deal, it gave the Jews protection, but it also gave the Romans the ability to meddle in their affairs.

The Jewish people were mercantile and made money through the use of trade routes between Asia and the Mediterranean.

This trade made them a useful ally in the Middle East but eventually the Romans would come to realise that a trade partner was not as useful as a territory, and they chose to take the wealth of Judea for themselves.

Beyond this economic side of the relationship the Jews were unwilling to accept Roman religious ideas. The Romans favoured a materialistic religious culture with idolatry being the norm, but the Jews detested this.

For places like Gaul or North Africa adopting Roman religion was not a stretch, the Romans usually incorporated the deities of conquered people into their own pantheon.
With the Jews and later the Christians the Romans were unable to accomplish this.

Hashem the G-d of Israel is a monotheistic deity and any attempt to worship idols or undermine the Jewish religion was met with fierce resistance and violent opposition.

The Jews would not go quietly, and the Romans would not go either. Despite being opposites, they shared this degree of religious obstinacy to the last.

When the Maccabees first made alliances with the Romans, they did not imagine it leading to conflict, Rome was a distant power and had no ambitions to expand that far east.

Rome was getting bigger, but no one could have imagined how big it ended up being. For the Maccabees the nature of what unfolded would have come as a surprise.

The Romans gave a decree to the Seleucids informing them of the alliance and their willingness to defend the Jews.

"The decree of the Senate concerning a league of assistance and friendship with the nation of the Jews. It shall not be lawful for any that are subject to the Romans to make war with the nation of the Jews, nor to assist those that do so, either by sending them corn, or ships, or money; and if any attack be made upon the Jews, the Romans shall assist them, as far as they are able; and again, if any attack be made upon the Romans, the Jews shall assist them. And if the Jews have a mind to add to, or to take away any thing from, this league of assistance, that shall be done with the common consent of the Romans. And whatsoever addition shall thus be made, it shall be of force."

By the time Roman aid came Judah and his brother John had died in battle. Alcimus was briefly allowed to return to his office after this, but as he approached the temple it is alleged that he died of a sudden illness which took him in a matter of days.[11]

Many attribute this sudden death as an act of divine retribution.

Jonathan Apphus, the youngest of the Maccabees became High Priest in 160BCE as the war finally came to an end. Jonathan gained influence by aiding Seleucid imperial claimants in a series of civil wars, but this resulted in his murder by one of these men in 143BCE.[12]

The final surviving son of Mattathias Simeon declared himself both to be High Priest and the Prince of Judea. This formally began the Hasmonean dynasty which would last until 37BCE.[13]

The Jews had not had independence since the fall of the Davidic line in 605BCE to the Babylonian conquest of Jerusalem. The notion of an independent Jewish state had not existed in living memory for 500 years, yet Simeon brought it back to life.

The reason Simeon had not taken the title of King was that there were still living claimants to the Kingdom of David.

In Exodus 4:14-17 when Moshe (Moses) refused to take the role of High Priest to honour his brother Aaron, G-d was furious as this implied his brother's honour was more important than the Lord.

G-d then explicitly prevented Moshe from taking the role of High Priest.

This set the precedent in Judaism that the secular ruler of the Jews and the spiritual one would be separate. Simeon knew of this and to avoid controversy and impiety only took the relatively humble title of Prince.

His successors would ignore this and become Kings and Queens anyway. They were a more established dynasty by then so could afford to make some enemies.

In 135BCE Simeon and his sons Mattathias and Judah met their end at a feast in Jericho. By the deceit of Simeon's son-in-law, they were lured to the fabled city and killed.[14]

The success of the Maccabees came down to an increase in toleration. Whilst Mattathias Maccabee had persecuted Jews who broke the laws of the Torah Judah realised that these people were not to blame for their misdeeds.

These people had been forced by an occupying power to do abhorrent things such as eating pork and making sacrifices to foreign deities. Judah welcomed these people into his ranks and so his ranks swelled.

It must be said that alienating people is far less likely to gain your cause support than acceptance. Judah was willing to bend the rules when it served his interests.

This cost him some popularity but from the fact that Hannukah is celebrated today and from the fact that the Hasmonean dynasty gained Judea its independence it can be inferred that he won the argument in the end.

Whilst I believe in the importance of Jewish rituals and the laws of the Torah, I do not put either of these above the basic survival of the Jewish people. We are meant to live by Jewish laws, not die by them.

Because Mattathias had been so obstinate, he lost many men and almost lost the war. Not fighting on Shabbat was completely impractical. There is no point in following the Law only to be killed. A greater sin than fighting on Shabbat is to let Judaism be wiped out because of an unwillingness to compromise.

There is a point where pragmatism comes before idealism, and in some ways, I think old Mattathias saw this when he appointed Judah as his successor. He knew Judah could be the reformer he had failed to be in his life.

Judah's successors Jonathan and later Simeon were both decent in their office, but they failed to see their enemies in plain sight.

Simeon was too big for his boots. Although he had a similar pragmatism to Judah, he failed to use it when he unwittingly met his death at Jericho. He was fatally arrogant and excessively trusting.

The last surviving heir of the Hasmoneans, Sir
Hyrcanus took up his father's mantle and became
ejected the murderers from Judea and laid siege to tł
To discourage John the defenders brought out his mother as a
hostage, she had other ideas.

"And as he thought that so far as he relaxed as to the siege and taking of
the place, so much favor did he show to those that were dearest to him by
preventing their misery, his zeal about it was cooled. However, his mother
spread out her hands, and begged of him that he would not grow remiss
on her account, but indulge his indignation so much the more, and that he
would do his utmost to take the place quickly, in order to get their enemy
under his power, and then to avenge upon him what he had done to those
that were dearest to himself; for that death would be to her sweet, though
with torment, if that enemy of theirs might but be brought to punishment
for his wicked dealings to them."[15]

With this show of defiance John's mother was brutally murdered
before his very eyes. The siege lasted many months, but John's resolve continued until the murderers were forced to flee the country
in disgrace.

So, at an immense cost John Hyrcanus won. Seeing the Jews
in disarray Antiochus VII, the Emperor of the Seleucids made
war with John. Antiochus laid siege to Jerusalem for a year[16] and
eventually overpowered the Jewish forces there.

John Hyrcanus made peace with Antiochus, giving him money
and general support.

Antiochus in turn respected Jewish autonomy and allowed religious
observances to continue unimpeded.

John would also aid Antiochus in military campaigns, John was gifted in the ways of war and had defeated Antiochus many years prior in a separate conflict. As High Priest John's absence from his people made him a very unpopular figure.

People were angry that their chief religious official was on the other side of the world fighting for another country.

John returned eventually in 128BCE and took many lands from Idumea and Samaria. Samaria encompassed parts of Lebanon and northern Israel whilst Idumea included parts of the West Bank and Southern Israel.[17]

The Samaritans were descendants of the breakaway Kingdom of Israel and shared much of their culture and religious practices with their southern counterparts. The only distinct difference was that the Samaritans had their own temple situated near Samaria and they had their own Priesthood.

The Idumeans meanwhile were the dubious descendants of Jacob's brother Esau. Their culture was entirely different to that of the Jews so their conversion was far more of a challenge which would have long-term impacts on Judaism (notably the matrilineal nature of Jewish heritage).

John's conquests increased the size of the Jewish state massively and the people living in these areas were forced to adopt Judaism. As well as this John renewed his alliance with Rome and used political intrigues in the Seleucid empire to declare Judea fully independent.

Hyrcanus' draconian religious policies set him at odds with the predominantly religious Pharisee movement.

The Great Sanhedrin was the legislative and representative body of the Jewish people. The main factions within it were the Pharisees and the Sadducees.

The Pharisees were more religiously inclined but also more liberal because their members were often from areas with a larger non-Jewish population. The Pharisees opposed the idea of having a High Priest and secular leader as one person because of the precedent set by Moshe who appointed Joshua and Eleazar as his two successors.

"So the Lord said to Moses, "Take Joshua son of Nun, a man in whom is the spirit of leadership, and lay your hand on him. Have him stand before Eleazar the priest and the entire assembly and commission him in their presence. Give him some of your authority so the whole Israelite community will obey him. He is to stand before Eleazar the priest, who will obtain decisions for him by inquiring of the Urim before the Lord. At his command he and the entire community of the Israelites will go out, and at his command they will come in."[18]

It was religiously important to have a High Priest and secular leader be separate and equal.

These figures were supposed to keep balance and govern the main aspects of Jewish life in peaceful separation.

The Sadducees meanwhile were the more Conservative pro-Aristocratic faction which preserved the interests of the ruling elite.

Initially John Hyrcanus had been a supporter of the Pharisees, but when they attempted to get him to make his son Aristobulus High Priest instead John defected to the Sadducees.[19]

To reconcile these divisions John gave his High Priesthood to Aristobulus and his secular leadership to his wife. Aristobulus resorted to an act of cruelty that would never be forgotten.

He had his own mother locked in a cell and starved to death and took his father's Princely title for himself. [20]

Most of Aristobulus' brothers shared their mother's imprisonment, save for Antigonus who was held in high regard by his older brother.

During the festival of Sukkot, or the Feast of Tabernacles Aristobulus fell ill and was bedridden.

Eventually Antigonus was assassinated on returning from a campaign in Galilee by his brother.[21] The explanation for this offered by Flavius Josephus is somewhat questionable and it could be argued that it was a contrivance used for narrative effect.

"But when Antigonus was once returned from the army, and that feast was then at hand when they make tabernacles to [the honor of G-d,] it happened that Aristobulus was fallen sick, and that Antigonus went up most splendidly adorned, and with his soldiers about him in their armor, to the temple to celebrate the feast, and to put up many prayers for the recovery of his brother, when some wicked persons, who had a great mind to raise a difference between the brethren, made use of this opportunity of the pompous appearance of Antigonus, and of the great actions which he had done, and went to the king, and spitefully aggravated the pompous show of his at the feast, and pretended that all these circumstances were not like those of a private person; that these actions were indications of an affectation of royal authority; and that his coming with a strong body of men must be with an intention to kill him; and that his way of reasoning was this: That it was a silly thing in him, while it was in his power to reign himself, to look upon it as a great favor that he was honored with a lower dignity by his brother. Aristobulus yielded to these imputations, but took care both that his brother should not suspect him, and that he himself might not run the hazard of his own safety; so he ordered his guards to lie in a certain place that was under ground, and dark; [he himself then lying sick in the tower which was called Antonia;] and he commanded them, that in case Antigonus came in to him unarmed, they should not touch any body, but if armed, they should kill him; yet did he send to

Antigonus, and desired that he would come unarmed; but the queen, and those that joined with her in the plot against Antigonus, persuaded the messenger to tell him the direct contrary: how his brother had heard that he had made himself a fine suit of armor for war, and desired him to come to him in that armor, that he might see how fine it was. So Antigonus suspecting no treachery, but depending on the good-will of his brother, came to Aristobulus armed, as he used to be, with his entire armor, in order to show it to him; but when he was come to a place which was called Strato's Tower, where the passage happened to be exceeding dark, the guards slew him; which death of his demonstrates that nothing is stronger than envy and calumny, and that nothing does more certainly divide the good-will and natural affections of men than those passions."[22]

Antigonus was a rival, and Aristobulus had shown no scruples when dispatching members of his family before. It is therefore not a stretch to say that he simply murdered his brother out of a desire to secure his power.

In fact, Aristobulus did not take his father's title. He elevated himself as Aristobulus I, King of the Jews. The last King of the Jews Zedekiah had been deposed in 586BCE, blinded and taken in chains to Babylon to live out the rest of his days in ignominious slavery.[23]

"Zedekiah was twenty-one years old when he became king, and he reigned in Jerusalem eleven years. His mother's name was Hamutal daughter of Jeremiah; she was from Libnah. He did evil in the eyes of the Lord, just as Jehoiakim had done. It was because of the Lord's anger that all this happened to Jerusalem and Judah, and in the end he thrust them from his presence. Now Zedekiah rebelled against the king of Babylon. So in the

ninth year of Zedekiah's reign, on the tenth day of the tenth month, Neb-
uchadnezzar king of Babylon marched against Jerusalem with his whole
army. They encamped outside the city and built siege works all around it.
The city was kept under siege until the eleventh year of King Zedekiah.
By the ninth day of the fourth month the famine in the city had become
so severe that there was no food for the people to eat. Then the city wall
was broken through, and the whole army fled. They left the city at night
through the gate between the two walls near the king's garden, though the
Babylonians were surrounding the city. They fled toward the Arabah, but
the Babylonian army pursued King Zedekiah and overtook him in the
plains of Jericho. All his soldiers were separated from him and scattered,
and he was captured. He was taken to the king of Babylon at Riblah in the
land of Hamath, where he pronounced sentence on him. There at Riblah
the king of Babylon killed the sons of Zedekiah before his eyes; he also
killed all the officials of Judah. Then he put out Zedekiah's eyes, bound
him with bronze shackles and took him to Babylon, where he put him in
prison till the day of his death."

Aristobulus was by no means a successor of David, and there
were a multitude of these, so his title was a controversial one
indeed.

The death of Antigonus was possibly partly caused by Aristobulus' wife Salome Alexandra.
Alexandra was a wily political operator and had immense influence
over her husband. When he had his brother murdered the King's
health worsened rapidly. The stress and guilt he felt caused his
health to plummet.

On his death bed the King named his brother Alexander Jannaeus as his heir. He died in 103BCE.[24]

Before the saga of the Hasmoneans can be resumed the general governance of Judea must be discussed and given ample context.

The hybrid secular-religious government the Hasmoneans formed was very complex and enshrined many important religious beliefs of the Jews in how the state was organised.

Firstly, Jewish law did not recognise the relevance of private land ownership. The land of Eretz Yisrael was seen as G-d's land and as a result could not be owned by human beings.

People could own things such as houses and tools which were used on the land, so this did not stop an economic hierarchy from existing.

Taxation was based upon income rather than on land ownership. Judea was a mercantile and agricultural state so taxation could only be reliably measured by income. Later, during the Roman occupation of Judea this difference would create rifts that formed antisemitic canards that continue to this day.

Synagogues meanwhile were used more generally as local courthouses for local issues. If a divorce was taking place or there was some sort of pecuniary dispute the local rabbinate would be responsible for coming to a resolution.

During the Hasmonean period Yeshivot were established for educating Rabbis instead of the former apprenticeship system. This meant that Rabbis acted more as lawyers who would interpret the Torah and apply it to cases they were met with. The combination of legalism and religiosity is very much a quintessential element of the Jewish faith.

Local Sanhedrim were courts that dealt with issues that the synagogues could not manage.
These also chose representatives who would sit in the Great Sanhedrin which was a national body.

Though this was not a democratic society by any means it was the closest thing to a Parliamentary democracy that the world had ever seen. It represented local issues in a larger, national setting and essentially governed in the interests of an electorate (albeit a limited, male, wealthy one).

Uniquely the Great Sanhedrin also governed judicial affairs. The Av Beit Din was chosen from the minority party and served over judicial affairs. The Nasi came from the majority party and served functionally as a head of government, something not too dissimilar to a Prime Minister.

A lot of essential areas of government including taxation, war and justice were administered by the Sanhedrin.

As well as this because death sentences could only be issued by the Great Sanhedrin (which only presided over a small number of cases). This indicates that for the most part the death penalty was abandoned in Judea.

During the Hasmonean era a sort of duopoly developed. The Zugot 'the era of pairs' was a time in which the Nasi and Av Beit Din were from rival factions. Their disputations and debates formed much of modern Jewish law and practice. By fiercely debating the meaning of Jewish law the Sanhedrin codified Jewish law.

The most notable of these pairs was the Pharisee Rabbi Hillel and the Sadducee Rabbi Shammai who will be discussed at length later.

In some ways these changes and reforms were used to emulate Rome. Ironically the Maccabees who had fought to preserve Jewish culture ended up embracing Greek notions of governance and culture anyway.

Alexander Jannaeus took his Greek name and embraced it. He wedded his brother's widow, and she was poised to effectively rule for him. Salome Alexandra was an intelligent woman and much older than her new husband.

Her brother Simeon ben Shetach was a prominent Pharisee. This was significant because Alexander could be King with Simeon as High Priest. This would have resumed the separation of the High Priesthood and the monarchy.

Shockingly, Salome fell pregnant and was taken out of the political scene for years to come.

In the early days of Alexander's reign, he went to war with Ptolemy Lathyros and the galilee was occupied by the Seleucid forces. Alexander later turned this failure around and increased Judea's territory.

The expansion of Judea was summarised by Josephus.

"Now at this time the Jews were in possession of the following cities that had belonged to the Syrians, and Idumeans, and Phoenicians: At the seaside, Strato's Tower, Apollonia, Joppa, Jamhis, Ashdod, Gaza, Anthedon, Raphia, and Rhinocolura; in the middle of the country, near to Idumea, Adorn, and Marissa; near the country of Samaria, Mount Carmel, and Mount Tabor, Scythopolis, and Gadara; of the country of Gaulonitis, Seleucia and Gabala; in the country of Moab, Heshbon, and Medaba, Lemba, and Oronas, Gelithon, Zorn, the valley of the Cilices, and Pollo; which last they utterly destroyed, because its inhabitants would not bear to change their religious rites for those peculiar to the Jews. The Jews also possessed others of the principal cities of Syria, which had been destroyed."[25]

In 93BCE due to his conquest of Gaza Alexander earned the ire of the neighbouring Nabateans who defeated him and forced him into a humiliating peace.

On returning to Jerusalem during Sukkot Alexander was pelted by jeering angry crowds who threw their Etrogim at him.

With both his body and his ego bruised Alexander had these rioters executed.

As well as this Alexander declared war on the Pharisees which sparked a civil war in Judea.

The Pharisees gained help from Demetrius the Seleucid Emperor and defeated Alexander. But due to chaos in the Seleucid lands the Pharisees were left on their own.[26]

Without any help left the Pharisees fled the country. Those who could not escape were taken to Jerusalem and endured a horrid end.

First their wives and children were murdered in front of them, then as Alexander watched the 800 unfortunate Pharisees were crucified for his amusement.

After this Simeon Ben Shetach returned to Judea because the King's sons had reached adulthood, and as a result their mother the Queen was again able to exert her authority over King Alexander.

Salome Alexandra and Simeon ruled Judea from then on, Alexander merely oversaw military affairs.

The disgraced, hated and powerless King's drinking soon caught up to him and he died in 76BCE.

On his deathbed he was not met with love or warmth, but hate and enmity from all he had slain, maimed and attempted to suppress. Among these Salome Alexandra chastised her husband for leaving his family after causing such uproar among the population.

"To whom dost thou thus leave me and my children, who are destitute of all other supports, and this when thou knowest how much ill-will thy nation bears thee?"[27]

She knew that her position would always be precarious because of how poorly her husband had ruled the Kingdom. She was not merely the consort to the King, but the reigning monarch of Judea in her own right. Alexander had left the Kingdom to his capable wife.

When Salome Alexandra became Queen her brother Simeon ben Shetach became Nasi. With this the Pharisees became dominant again.

Instead of making Simeon High Priest Alexandra chose to give the role to her eldest son Hyrcanus.

At this time the Seleucid empire finally fell to Armenia. To avoid possible invasion Salome Alexandra sent gifts and ambassadors to King Tigranes of Armenia.

He was impressed by Alexandra and promised her his protection.[28]

Salome Alexandra's younger son was supported by the Sadducees, and this set him at odds with his mother and his brother Hyrcanus.

Around this time the Kingdoms of Pontus and Armenia were absorbed into Rome and as a result the two largest threats to Judea were too busy repelling invasions to invade Judea.

In 67BCE Salome Alexandra died. Her death marked the end of a golden age for the Jewish people. Without her steadfast and unifying leadership, the Kingdom of Judea would never reach the same heights again. Her sons would not be united and civil war would continue for many years thereafter.

As far as the successors of John Hyrcanus go Salome Alexandra was among the best.

John Hyrcanus was a capable General but spent little time on domestic affairs. He made the same mistake as so many other Hasmoneans. He took on two of the most important roles in the country and couldn't manage both.

He was better than others who managed to fail at both (notably Alexander Jannaeus) to the detriment of Judea.

His successor Aristobulus I was both cruel and easily swayed. His wife Salome Alexandra controlled his administration behind the scenes, and she was likely responsible for the death of Aristobulus' brother in some degree.

Although it is also possible that Aristobulus I saw his brother Antigonus as a threat or just had a falling out with him. Either way the cruel King defiled the laws of his country by adopting a title that was not his.

Aristobulus was somewhat capable in military affairs and somewhat capable in religious ones. In this sense he could be seen as a mediocre King and a mediocre High Priest.

The King died in terrible pain and regret over the loss of his brother. His wife married his younger brother Alexander.

Alexander was a poor general and a catastrophic High Priest. His rule can best be described as a series of poorly waged wars and a fledgling administration kept together by his wife.

Alexander would somehow create a new problem for each one his wife solved.

The mark of a good monarch was the ability to unite the political factions in Judea. Instead of attempting to do this Alexander simply declared war on the faction that he happened to dislike and viciously murdered them when he had the good fortune of defeating them.

Thankfully his wife took the reins again and did good works to repair the damage. Alexander died a drunk and a fool, he is potentially the worst of the Hasmoneans.

Salome Alexandra at least attempted to resolve the rifts in Judean politics by giving the High Priesthood to one of her sons and the Crown to another. What she failed to account for was the treachery of her son Aristobulus who she ended up disinheriting before she died.

Failure sometimes cannot be avoided, but at least Alexandra gave it her all.

2

Chapter 2- Pompey's Invasion of Judea

Aristobulus had been disinherited because of his alignment with the Sadducees and so John Hyrcanus II became both King and High Priest of Judea in 67BCE.

This immediately set the brothers at odds and many politicians took advantage of this for their own ends.

Chief among these was Antipater the Idumean.

Antipater was a descendant of the Edomites who had been converted by force to Judaism in the reign of John Hyrcanus I. Though he was Jewish religiously he was ethnically foreign.

Antipater made use of his foreignness by using it to gain the support of his armies, which were largely filled with non-Judeans.

Antipater decided to encourage Aristobulus in rebellion against John Hyrcanus II because he was seen as more hard-line and stronger than the comparatively merciful Hyrcanus.[29]

The brothers who arguably destroyed their own Kingdom were complete opposites but shared core values. John was a pious and moral man who favoured peace above war. His softness also made him a perfect puppet for those with more gumption.

Only 3 months into John Hyrcanus II's reign he was forcibly deposed with a siege of Jerusalem. Contrary to what Antipater advised and to what he expected of Aristobulus the new King of the Jews set his brother free.

When the brothers met in the Holy temple, they clasped hands and John Hyrcanus II swore an oath renouncing his Kingship and promising to live out his days in peaceful retirement.

Aristobulus II ignored his chief adviser who wanted John Hyrcanus II killed and in doing so compelled him to move to John Hyrcanus II's side.[30]

Antipater now saw the malleable and peaceable John Hyrcanus II as his ticket to political relevance and supreme authority.

This gambit paid off for Antipater and in 64BCE he laid siege to Jerusalem again with an army of Nabatean (Arab) soldiers. Aristobulus II was caught in the siege and had little chance of surviving.

By pure luck a sandstorm hit which forced the fighting to be halted. Eventually the Romans sided with Aristobulus II because he was in control of the temple. This meant that he was more likely to pay them money for their help.

The Romans had taken Syria so had a direct border with Judea from which they could send forces in aid of Aristobulus II.

Oddly however when Pompey Magnus did not answer the diplomats sent by Aristobulus he took this as an indication of war and began moving against the Romans. This forced the Romans to side with John Hyrcanus.

Pompey was a notable Roman General at this time and had a string of successes from his campaign against the Armenian King Tigranes.[31]

In Alexandrium Pompey sieged Aristobulus and ordered his men not to attack on Shabbat.

This act made the Romans seem respectful of Jewish customs and gained Pompey a great deal of support from the local Jewish population.

Aristobulus II was compelled to surrender to Pompey and allowed him to take Jerusalem on behalf of his brother Hyrcanus.

The Sadducees who were loyal to Artistobulus continued to hide out in the temple mount and the Acra fortress and refused to let Pompey enter.

When Antipater used Hyrcanus to further his ambitions he was able to extract whatever he wanted and so too were the Roman occupiers who saw him as the more servile candidate.

It was such mercy that compelled Hyrcanus to willingly surrender to his brother and go in peace from Jerusalem previously.

Aristobulus II meanwhile was headstrong and rash, initially Antipater saw this as a sign that he would be a good King, but it did not change the fact that he loved his brother and set him free when it would have been more expedient to put him to death.

His rashness caught up with him when he naively assumed he could fight off the Romans and his innate goodness came into play again when he surrendered to Pompey, knowing that a prolonged war would mean the deaths of many more Jews.

Both of these brothers clearly cared for each other and in some measure wanted what was best for the public.

12,000 of the temple's most loyal defenders were killed when Pompey broke through their defences in 63BCE.

Pompey was magnanimous in victory and refused to plunder the city. But he entered the temple, having slaughtered its defenders. The Roman General entered the holy of holies and in doing so earned the ire of the Jews.

In fairness to him he did this without awareness, and when informed of his error was greatly ashamed and ordered the temple to be ritualistically cleansed.

"No small enormities were committed about the temple itself, which, in former ages, had been inaccessible, and seen by none; for Pompey went into it, and not a few of those that were with him also, and saw all that which it was unlawful for any other men to see but only for the high priests. There were in that temple the golden table, the holy candlestick, and the pouring vessels, and a great quantity of spices; and besides these there were among the treasures two thousand talents of sacred money: yet did Pompey touch nothing of all this, on account of his regard to religion; and in this point also he acted in a manner that was worthy of his virtue."[32]

Pompey had never set out to conquer Judea, the perception he wanted to emanate was that he was simply a friend of the Jews who had come to resolve a deeply divisive political dispute.

For the most part his grace in victory and respect for Jewish customs made him a popular figure.

There have been many books with a larger and more in-depth focus on Pompey than this one, but there are some essential points of contextual information that explain in very clear terms Pompey's motivations for invading Judea.

One is simply the use of 'The Great' as an epithet. As Mary Beard posits in her book *'SPQR A History of Ancient Rome'* the battle between Mithridates VI of Pontus and Pompey was a battle between two men who wanted to paint themselves as successors of Alexander the Great.

In simpler terms, Pompey invaded Judea because it was what Alexander the Great did.

Another important point Beard makes which explains Pompey's motivations is that although he was defending the Roman Republic from the ambitions of Julius Caesar, he was in fact the one who began the culture of pomp and central authority that the Roman empire is known for.

In simpler terms, Pompey invaded Judea because he saw himself as an Emperor and knew that a successful campaign in the east would cement his status and authority.

By this time Rome saw itself as the ruler of the Mediterranean, those who were not formally provinces of the Roman empire were still expected to perform the functions of a vassal. Judea was not different in the slightest.

Pompey Magnus (the Great) bore no obvious hatred for the Jews, and in fact went to great lengths to accommodate their religious customs when he invaded. His motivations for war were far more cynical than any ideological desire to expand Rome or convert the Jews.

He simply knew Judea was too unstable to be a useful ally in the region and saw the sacrifice of his men as a good chance to gain glory and to expand Roman influence.

When the war was done, he proved this by occupying a large portion of Judea, especially along the coast. He also demoted John from King to Ethnarch. This was part of the way Rome often tried to gradually absorb new lands.

It was far easier to install puppets and form tributary relations than it was to invade and occupy a region. The Romans took advantage of their size and influence to force the leaders of smaller Kingdoms to acquiesce to their desires.

By making John and Ethnarch Pompey implied that he was of a lesser status than the previous Kings and that he was beholden only to Rome. It also gave the Romans a valid excuse for later invasions.

If John was deposed or attempted to reclaim his power Rome could invade from Syria and simply take Judea by force. More often than not client Kings saw the writing on the wall and just willed their lands to Rome to avoid a pointless war they knew they could never hope to win.

The King of the Iceni Prasutagus chose to do this in an attempt to avoid war with Rome.

Despite the failure of this attempt and the infamous rebellion led by his wife Boudica it is a piece of evidence that conveys just how impossible defeating Rome would have seemed to the Judeans.

Pompey used this fear to extract terms that suited Rome and his Judean campaign is regarded as a resounding success. In the words of Mary Beard, he used a *"judicious mixture of diplomacy, bullying and well-placed displays of Roman force."*[33]

The Roman General had Hyrcanus reinstated as High Priest and set about fixing the damage the civil war had caused to Judean government institutions.

Pompey did however restrict Judean independence, occupying much of the north and relegating Hyrcanus back to merely a head of state and not a King.

Antipater increased his power vastly because of his closeness with Pompey and in effect he ran Judea on Hyrcanus' behalf.

To avoid a dynastic dispute John Hyrcanus' daughter Alexandra married Aristobulus' son Alexander and their daughter Mariamne being a descendant of both brothers was the designated heir set to resolve their dispute.

Relations between Rome and Judea soured when Marcus Licinius Crassus sacked the temple and stole its wealth on the way to a campaign in Parthia.

"Now Crassus, as he was going upon his expedition against the Parthians, came into Judea, and carried off the money that was in the temple, which Pompey had left, being two thousand talents, and was disposed to spoil it of all the gold belonging to it, which was eight thousand talents. He also

took a beam, which was made of solid beaten gold, of the weight of three hundred minae, each of which weighed two pounds and a half. It was the priest who was guardian of the sacred treasures, and whose name was Eleazar, that gave him this beam, not out of a wicked design, for he was a good and a righteous man; but being intrusted with the custody of the veils belonging to the temple, which were of admirable beauty, and of very costly workmanship, and hung down from this beam, when he saw that Crassus was busy in gathering money, and was in fear for the entire ornaments of the temple, he gave him this beam of gold as a ransom for the whole, but this not till he had given his oath that he would remove nothing else out of the temple, but be satisfied with this only, which he should give him, being worth many ten thousand [shekels]. Now this beam was contained in a wooden beam that was hollow, but was known to no others; but Eleazar alone knew it; yet did Crassus take away this beam, upon the condition of touching nothing else that belonged to the temple, and then brake his oath, and carried away all the gold that was in the temple."[34]

Following on from this the first triumvirate of Pompey, Crassus and Gaius Julius Caesar collapsed because of Crassus' death.

After a successful campaign in Gaul Caesar and Pompey went to war. When Pompey lost this war Antipater was forced to switch sides and gave military aid to Caesar.

Julius Caesar's rise was a complicated affair and is hotly debated today. He gained prominence by acting as a buffer between Crassus and Pompey in his capacity as consul and pontifex maximus.

The pontifex maximus was the Roman equivalent of the High Priest in Judea, though far less powerful in the day-to-day running of the state.

The consuls were elected annually and acted as short-term heads of the army and Senate.

When Caesar's term as consul ended Pompey had him given three governorships north of Italy as a reward for his services.

This was what Roman politicians often did to get their rivals away from the capital.

Instead of letting himself fall into irrelevance Caesar chose to invade Gaul and successfully took it for Rome.

In doing this he committed an unfathomable genocide and almost lost his glory, his power and his life. In risking it all Caesar managed to cement his authority.

The Senate was not pleased, however. They saw his unilateral choice to go to war as a signal that he would one day attempt to destroy the republic.

This was not helped by the fact that he came back to Rome with an army (an action which was illegal). In the end Pompey and Caesar fought a civil war for the soul of Rome and Caesar won.

When he won Caesar had himself made Dictator for ten years and then for life. A Dictator was more of a temporary leader who was to deal with a particular crisis then retire from their supreme authority than the demagogic meaning the term is given today.

Cincinnatus for instance was Dictator of Rome twice in 458BCE and 439BCE respectively and retired from both Dictatorships once he had dealt with the crises at hand.

In the end Caesar's power got to his head and his Senatorial colleagues killed him in the chamber. The conspirators then had their own civil war with Caesar's friend Mark Anthony and his adopted son Octavian (Augustus).

Caesar had a penchant for pardoning his rivals and incorporating them into his administration. When Pompey was defeated many of his allies were willingly taken in by Caesar.

Mercy ended up killing Julius Caesar when these same men stabbed him over 20 times in the Senate chamber.

After this when Caesar was the Dictator of Rome, Antipater gave his son Herod command over some military affairs in the Galilee. Herod ended up slaughtering a bandit named Hezekiah and all of his men. This war crime earned him the hatred of much of the country.

Herod was ordered to stand trial in the Great Sanhedrin and probably would have been sentenced to death were it not for the intercessions of his father Antipater.

"The mothers also of those that had been slain by Herod raised his indignation; for those women continued every day in the temple, persuading the king and the people that Herod might undergo a trial before the Sanhedrim for what he had done. Hyrcanus was so moved by these complaints, that he summoned Herod to come to his trial for what was charged upon him. Accordingly he came; but his father had persuaded him to come not like a private man, but with a guard, for the security of his person; and that when he had settled the affairs of Galilee in the best manner he could for his own advantage, he should come to his trial, but still with a body of men sufficient for his security on his journey, yet so that he should not come with so great a force as might look like terrifying Hyrcanus, but still such a one as might not expose him naked and unguarded [to his enemies.] However, Sextus Cæsar, president of Syria, wrote to Hyrcanus, and desired him to clear Herod, and dismiss him at his trial, and threatened him beforehand if he did not do it."[35]

Due to a direct threat from Rome John Hyrcanus II was compelled to let Herod go free. He was allowed to attend his trial with armed guards which essentially meant that if he were to be found guilty, he could simply kill the members of the Sanhedrin. Because the Sanhedrin was still willing to sentence Herod to death, Hyrcanus sent him to Damascus as to avoid a fight.

John's sense of justice was so strong that he was willing to provoke Antipater by putting Herod on trial. This shows without a doubt that where competency may not have resided a sense of righteousness certainly did.

Unsurprisingly Herod did not face any punishment and was allowed to go freely in the end.

Antipater was a foreigner in a foreign land, and he had a mixed reputation. He was a cunning politician and used his influence to run the country in his own right.

His habit of switching sides in conflicts had left him with a reputation of being something of a turncoat.

In fairness to him he only did this at integral moments where he was threatened, when Aristobulus ignored his advice and let John Hyrcanus go free he became a marked man in a sense.

If he had stayed with Aristobulus he would have probably been killed or side lined over time.

All in all, when the going got tough, Antipater got going.

In 44BCE Julius Caesar was betrayed by a rabble of Senators who killed him in the Senate chamber itself.

And when Julius Caesar died, he had little choice but to defect to the Liberators, they had control in the eastern empire and would have killed or replaced Antipater if he had not nominally switched to their side.

Antipater was later killed for betraying the Caesarians after Caesar's assassination. He had done this to ensure that the

Republican factions in Rome would not kill him so it could be said that his submission to Caesar's killers was an insincere gesture made for political survival.

When Antipater was murdered his legacy was secured by the favour Mark Anthony threw on Phaesel and Herod. Despite being the eldest of Antipater's sons Phaesal was taken captive and died in prison, this was what ultimately gave Herod the chance to rise to prominence.

Any commentator of the day would have probably told you that Mariamne would be Queen one day, but Antipater's son Herod had other plans.

3

Chapter 3- The Rise of Herod

As a boy Herod was leaving school when he was stopped in the street by Menachem the Essene. Menachem was a Jewish nobleman who was notorious for his gift at divination.

He told the young Herod that he would be King of the Jews for at least 30 years. This prophecy would one day come true, and Menachem would be given the role of Av Beit Din for his enduring loyalty to Herod. This moment was the start of a long and storied life.

The tale of a reign which involved reform, love, death, political intrigue and especially towards the end was characterised by heinous acts of violence.

Antipater's son Herod was betrothed to Mariamne. He had been married and had a son from this marriage, but his father forced him to banish his wife Doris and his son Antipater II.[36]

Herod's mother was an Arab noblewoman, and his father was of Edomite ancestry. This meant that on both sides Herod was ethnically not a Jew. His primary claim to legitimacy was his engagement to Mariamne.

In 41 BCE John Hyrcanus II was overthrown by Aristobulus II's son Antigonus II Mattathias.

When Parthia invaded the eastern regions of the Roman Republic in the wake of Caesar's death, they also took Judea and installed Antigonus II as their puppet.

Herod and Mariamne fled the country in search of aid from the Romans. They would have probably been killed if they stayed.

Herod's brother Phaesel was taken as a hostage by the Parthians and eventually killed himself in prison to avoid giving the enemy a useful hostage.

By this time Herod was so despised that he could not even flee through Jewish territory, so he went south to the fortress of Masada. At first the pair tried to escape through Nabatea but this Kingdom was also under Parthian rule, so they eventually took refuge with Cleopatra VII of Egypt.

This is the same Cleopatra who is so notorious today. She urged Herod to stay in Egypt, but he attempted to sail to Rome anyway. The voyage was already dangerous because of Sextus Pompey (Pompey Magnus' son) who had taken over the Italian islands and was launching a campaign of piracy to hamper his enemies in Rome.

Herod was shipwrecked on the island of Rhodes and from there conveyed messages to Mark Anthony his chief ally in Rome. Once he heard from Herod Anthony sent for Herod and the couple soon arrived in Italy to gain Roman support against Antigonus II.

At this time Mariamne was only 14 and Herod was a great deal older. Mariamne valiantly put forward her case and tried to convince the Romans to aid her, but they would not listen.

Then Anthony reminded them of Antipater's loyalty to Rome and the chamber crowned Herod the King of the Jews. This surprised

Herod just as much as it did everyone else, he had expected his wife to become Queen instead.

He had been chosen instead of his wife because the Romans knew very well that he would remain loyal to them, Mariamne would have been less predictable.

Herod landed in Acre with a Roman force to remove Antigonus II Mattathias and take the Judean throne for himself. The new King encircled Jerusalem and took much of the country in a matter of months.

In 37BCE Herod married Mariamne and was now able to claim legitimacy as the husband of the true heir to the Hasmonean monarchy.

The siege of Jerusalem was slow and brutal. Antigonus used Herod's lack of Jewish ancestry as a propaganda tool to keep morale up. Herod was greatly offended by this and in a show of his piety he allowed sacrifices to continue in the temple.[37]

In the end Antigonus was defeated and Sosius the Roman General who had been sent with Herod had to be bribed to stop him from looting the temple. He still looted the other parts of the city and there was little Herod could do to stop it.

Herod strongly condemned Sosius to Anthony and had Antigonus II Mattathias killed before he could flee and potentially mount a counterattack.[38]

Had Herod only been characterised by his early reign he would have probably been known as 'Herod the Builder'. He built the Antonia fortress north of the temple and fortified the city of Jerusalem.

He also built many large and lavish palaces for himself at the expense of the taxpayer. A part of this was vanity, and another part was the fact that he was so unpopular among the Jews that he essentially needed fortresses all over the country to protect him from their ire.

The most notable of these was Masada which had elaborate defences and pleasure palaces within. He would only need a fortress in the heart of his own country for one thing, to defend himself from the ire of his own people. He spent the tax money of the Jews lavishly on himself and moreover on defences he could use against his own subjects.

He Romanised a lot of the city of Jerusalem and his new structures featured Roman architectural styles rather than the old, Jewish ones. He was catering to the people who kept him in power (the Romans) rather than the people who wanted him gone (the public and Hasmonean elite).

It should not be assumed that Herod was all-powerful yet. His Kingship relied on support from the Hasmoneans and his wife, brother-in-law and mother-in-law. They still had serious influence in the affairs of the state.

Alexandra was a clever woman and used her position to further the interests of her family, she was suspicious of Herod and Herod was in turn suspicious of her.

Mariamne also plied Herod and influenced his government, she did this largely in the interests of her brother Aristobulus, who Herod made High Priest to appease his wife's family.

Aristobulus was young, younger than the legal requirement to take this office, but Herod saw that if he did not concede to the Hasmoneans, he could lose their vital support.

Herod had appointed Ananelus as High Priest but was forced to remove him in favour of the teenager Aristobulus.

This did not hamper Herod's power for long because Aristobulus soon drowned. It is highly likely and widely agreed that Herod had his wife's brother killed.

"Now the nature of that place was hotter than ordinary; so they went out

in a body, and of a sudden, and in a vein of madness; and as they stood
by the fish-ponds, of which there were large ones about the house, they
went to cool themselves [by bathing], because it was in the midst of a hot
day. At first they were only spectators of Herod's servants and acquain-
tance as they were swimming; but after a while, the young man, at the
instigation of Herod, went into the water among them, while such of
Herod's acquaintance, as he had appointed to do it, dipped him as he was
swimming, and plunged him under water, in the dark of the evening, as
if it had been done in sport only; nor did they desist till he was entirely
suffocated. And thus was Aristobulus murdered, having lived no more in
all than eighteen years, and kept the high priesthood one year only;
which high priesthood Ananelus now recovered again.[89]

After the death Herod had Ananelus appointed to the High
Priesthood once again and Alexandra wrote to Cleopatra VII demanding justice.

Because of her intimate relationship with Mark Anthony Cleopatra was able to get him to demand that Herod stand trial. Mark
Anthony's summons was absolute, and Herod could not simply
escape it like he had escaped his last trial.

Herod was a paranoid and often vindictive figure. He left his
uncle Joseph in charge of the government while he was gone and
gave him a very strange order.

If Herod was found guilty and killed his wife Mariamne was to
be killed as well, as to avoid the chance that she could remarry.

Even though Joseph was of no relation of Mariamne he
stubbornly refused to carry out Herod's orders and confessed the
plot to Mariamne who was horrified.

Herod was wily and managed to convince Anthony to spare
him, though he couldn't produce much evidence of his innocence.

Herod found out what his uncle had done and killed him for disobeying him.

Relations between Herod and his Hasmonean counterparts began to sour after this incident, and they would not soon improve.

Herod's love for his wife was great, but his desire to own and control her was even greater. In his moral sickness he perceived the threat of another man having what was his as worse than the thought of killing his own wife.

The King was obsessive and demanding and never trusted the woman he claimed to adore, his style of love was toxic and unhealthy and ultimately drove the people around him to hate him. Even his own family.

Herod was always suspicious and paranoid, and because of his perceived lack of legitimacy he never felt truly secure about the position he was in.

No matter how many people he killed he was never safe.

If Herod had not suffered from some form of clinical depression, it is likely that his natural intelligence would have made him an excellent King of the Jews.

And in terms of his ability to lead he was excellent. In the simplest of terms Herod was bad at being good and good at being bad.

Herod had two faces. Not so much because he was overtly deceptive, but because he was unstable.

The best way I can describe Herod is that he was good at domestically ruling his Kingdom, but that in his personal affairs he was harsh, paranoid and cruel.

Because of the Christian penchant for painting Herod as a mad tyrant and villain I am going to say, controversial as it is, that Herod was not as bad as he is portrayed to be with the caveat that he was still fairly bad.

He kept his country stable during crises, succeeded in war and in peace. And whether we like it or not he built the Judea of his day, even if he did leave a track of dead bodies in his wake.

I also say this because in later passages when Jesus Christ is discussed it is important to remember that Herod had no interactions (with any historicity to back them up) with Jesus or his followers. Herod died a number of years before Jesus was even born.

So, to attack Herod from a Christian perspective as many often do is to reduce and forget the man Herod was, and the crimes he is known to actually be responsible for.

In 32BCE Mark Anthony married Cleopatra VII of Egypt and gave his eastern holdings which stretched from Greece to North Africa to his new wife and their heirs in his will.

The Roman people could not accept this, it would have given the wealthiest provinces of the empire to a foreign power and the general perception of Anthony was that he had been swayed by Cleopatra's womanly charms.

Roman society was patriarchal and viewed excessive sexual intercourse as feminine, so Anthony was perceived as treacherous and feminine.

This perception was carefully utilised by Anthony's main opponent Augustus, who used propaganda to disseminate information within the population.

Before this point of collapse the second triumvirate had been fairly stable. Mark Anthony administered the eastern provinces, Marcus Lepidus administered North Africa (but was clearly an inferior buffer between the two main triumvirs) and Augustus administered the Iberian Peninsula, Italy and Gaul.

This system was reliable for a time because Augustus and Anthony shared common goals and interests, and through the marriage of Anthony and Augustus' older sister Octavia the triumvirs were forced to work together and be civil.

Most of their enemies had been removed either at the battle of Philippi in 42BCE or in the proscriptions that came after their collective rise to power. Cicero for instance was slaughtered and his severed hands were nailed to the doors of the Senate.

With the enemies of the Caesarians dead or scared into submission the only natural opponents they had left were one another.

Herod was loyal to Anthony and chose to side with him in the civil war, this was a risky move considering that if he lost Herod would probably be killed and replaced.

All of this brewing conflict culminated in the battle of Actium in 31BCE. This sea battle was a disaster for Anthony, and he was forced to flee with Cleopatra back to Alexandria, where he was soundly beaten again the following year.

The triumvirate was always somewhat unstable, and Anthony probably knew this. During the civil war he cut off grain supplies from Egypt in the hopes that the people of Rome would starve.

Egypt was a wealthy nation with a vast agricultural base, the grain dole was an essential supply of grain from Egypt that kept the bustling Roman population fed. As soon as the grain stopped coming in Augustus knew that he had to get it back again.

In the Roman world suicide when you had been beaten was considered honourable. It saved your soldiers a prolonged war and was considered an act of heroism.

So, when Mark Anthony fell on his own sword in 30BCE he was doing one last service to the Roman Republic.

He had been led to believe that his wife Cleopatra had committed suicide, when he learned the truth, he was carried to her side and died in her arms.

Cleopatra initially thought she could sway Augustus in the same way she had swayed Caesar and Anthony before him, but it simply didn't work.

She was not conventionally attractive by today's standards. She had a large nose and Greek-Semitic features because the Ptolemaic royal family she hailed from was of Greek origin.

In the wake of Alexander the Great's conquest of much of the known world his general Ptolemy took control of the Egyptian portion of his empire and became the first head of the new Ptolemaic dynasty.

This dynasty was characterised by incest. In fact, Ptolemy XIV Cleopatra's younger brother had been married to her at one point. Seeing that she was the senior partner in this union Ptolemy's advisers conspired to drive Cleopatra out which eventually led to the Egyptian civil war.

Caesar chose to side with Cleopatra and gave her Roman support so she could take the throne for herself.

The Ancient Egyptian culture and society that used hieroglyphics and built Pyramids was as old to Cleopatra as Cleopatra is to us. By the time of the civil war Egypt had been firmly Hellenised and many Egyptian cities were given Greek names.

Cleopatra was itself a Greek name. The Ptolemies did not even speak the common tongue of the Egyptian populace, who had much darker skin and a very different ethnic makeup.

In fact, Cleopatra (who was a polyglot) was the first Greek ruler of Egypt who even spoke Egyptian.

Augustus was far less susceptible to Cleopatra's charisma and used his natural intelligence to see through her glib flirtations.

When she realised there was no hope in her efforts, she decided to kill herself too. She would rather be dead than endure the humiliation of being dragged through the streets of

Rome in chains for the jeering crowds to see.

When she was dead Augustus annexed the Egyptian state as a part of Rome to secure the supply of grain that the city of Rome sorely needed.

Egyptian independence was largely dead from here on. First the Romans held Egypt until the crisis of the third century which saw Egypt along with most of the Roman east break away into the Palmyrene empire under Zenobia in 270CE.

Emperor Aurelian reclaimed the east including Egypt and had Zenobia beheaded. It was next the Byzantine empire which controlled Egypt long after the collapse of the Western portion of Rome in 476CE.

Eventually Emperor Heraclius lost Egypt to the Islamic Rashidun Caliphate in 639CE. This Caliphate too ended up falling to the Umayyad Caliphate which itself dissolved into a series of smaller entities including the Abbasid Caliphate which controlled Egypt.

In 1250CE the Mamluk Sultanate formed and included the majority of Egypt.

Finally, in 1517CE the Ottoman empire under Selim I took Egypt, and it was only after a brief French occupation and multiple 19th century wars in the region that Egypt under Muhammad Ali Pasha was given independence.

Even with this Egypt came directly under British influence and didn't enjoy a large degree of autonomy.

It would not be until 1955CE when Gamal Abdel Nasser nationalised the Suez Canal and forced the British to leave that Egypt achieved full, undisputed sovereignty over its own affairs.

What this illustrates is just how monumental the defeat of Cleopatra and Anthony really was, and how the legacy of this defeat can be felt today.

It is likely that Herod truly loved Anthony, he implored him to take a different path in his letters and even when he ignored the advice he was given Anthony could rely on Herod.

Herod played into Augustus' vanity and lavished him with praise and gifts when his benefactor Anthony lost the war and killed himself.

Moreover, he showed courage in defending Anthony's legacy. Most of Anthony's friends ended up dead, Herod survived because he was upfront about his intentions and made no apologies.

Herod stood by his friend and for that he must be admired in that isolated case. Herod's other offences are a different matter.

After Actium Herod saw that Anthony would not win the war, and his paranoia began to intensify. He began to see old John Hyrcanus II as a threat, for he could be reinstalled as King or Ethnarch if Herod was killed.[40]

He had initially honoured John Hyrcanus and gave him every respect, but after Actium he began to see him more as a rival than an old friend and benefactor.

Herod got an excuse to finish John off when he intercepted a letter, he had sent to Malchus the governor of Syria which allegedly contained conspiratorial material. Poor old Hyrcanus was put to death by the Sanhedrin, which by now was well and truly the property of Herod.

"And this was the fate of Hyrcanus; and thus did he end his life, after he had endured various and manifold turns of fortune in his lifetime. For he was made high priest of the Jewish nation in the beginning of his mother Alexandra's reign, who held the government nine years; and when, after his mother's death, he took the kingdom himself, and held it three months, he lost it, by the means of his brother Aristobulus. He was then restored by Pompey, and received all sorts of honor from him, and enjoyed them forty years; but when he was again deprived by Antigonus, and was maimed in his body, he was made a captive by the Parthians, and thence returned home again after some time, on account of the hopes that Herod had given him; none of which came to pass according to his expectation, but he still conflicted with many misfortunes through the

whole course of his life; and, what was the heaviest calamity of all, as we have related already, he came to an end which was undeserved by him.

His character appeared to be that of a man of a mild and moderate disposition, and suffered the administration of affairs to be generally done by others under him. He was averse to much meddling with the public, nor had shrewdness enough to govern a kingdom. And both Antipater and Herod came to their greatness by reason of his mildness; and at last he met with such an end from them as was not agreeable either to justice or piety."[41]

At the same time Augustus defeated Mark Anthony handily and he was forced to kill himself in disgrace.

When Herod heard of his he mourned his lost friend but decided to meet Augustus at Rhodes to secure his position.

He spoke emphatically to Augustus of the fact that he had been loyal to Anthony and would have made the same choice again. Herod lamented that he had not done more in aid of his friend. He is claimed to have made this speech to Augustus.

"for if a man owns himself to be another's friend, and knows him to be a benefactor, he is obliged to hazard every thing, to use every faculty of his soul, every member of his body, and all the wealth he hath, for him, in which I confess I have been too deficient. However, I am conscious to my-self, that so far I have done right, that I have not deserted him upon his defeat at Actium; nor upon the evident change of his fortune have I transferred my hopes from him to another, but have preserved myself, though not as a valuable fellow soldier, yet certainly as a faithful counselor, to Antony, when I demonstrated to him that the only way that he had to save himself, and not to lose all his authority, was to slay

Cleopatra; for when she was once dead, there would be room for him to retain his authority, and rather to bring thee to make a composition with him, than to continue at enmity any longer. None of which advises would he attend to, but preferred his own rash resolution before them, which have happened unprofitably for him, but profitably for thee. Now, there-fore, in case thou determinest about me, and my alacrity in serving Antony, according to thy anger at him, I own there is no room for me to deny what I have done, nor will I be ashamed to own, and that publicly too, that I had a great kindness for him. But if thou wilt put him out of the case, and only examine how I behave myself to my benefactors in general, and what sort of friend I am, thou wilt find by experience that we shall do and be the same to thyself, for it is but changing the names, and the firmness of friendship that we shall bear to thee will not be dis-approved by thee."[42]

Augustus was impressed with Herod's courage, honesty and integrity. He forgave the King of the Jews for siding with his enemy and lavished Herod with the truest praise and respect.

It was in this way that two true enemies became even truer friends and allies.

When he was only a teenager the young Octavian (great-nephew to Julius Caesar) was adopted by Caesar in his will and given all his lands and money. Octavian used these funds to pay the dues Caesar had promised the people rather than keeping it for himself.

Giving this money to the people had a more cynical motive in Roman politics. People started seeing Octavian the same way they had seen his uncle, as their friend, master and benefactor.

Besides, who doesn't want free money?

With the help of Agrippa his friend and ally Octavian was able to defeat Mark Anthony and the Senators in a series of civil wars.

In 27BCE Octavian became Augustus 'The August' and claimed the honorary title of Senatus Princeps 'The First Senator'. With this the Roman Republic became an empire, albeit with some vestiges of the old Senatorial system.

In this early phase of imperial Rome, the Senate was still very powerful and the absolute monarchy we imagine today when thinking of imperial Rome developed gradually over time.

Diocletian was the first Emperor to abandon Augustus' title and instead called himself the Dominus or 'Master'.

The Senate was only formally done away with when the Byzantine Emperors took on the title of Autokrator and the absolute monarchical authority that came with it.

It was easier for Augustus to do away with the Senate's powers and leave it in place, Rome was a place that took changes slowly as well as reluctantly.

Augustus respected Herod's loyalty and integrity in sticking with Anthony to the last. He would sooner have an ally who backed his friends than someone who switched sides at a whim.

For all his faults Herod stuck by his friend knowing it would probably cost him his life.

Augustus saw Herod's shameless defence of Anthony as a sign of good character, and in the end, he would sooner have a client King of good character than some opportunist who stabbed, maimed and betrayed his way to the top.

In some ways Augustus' motivations were much less pure than this. Herod had shown success in fighting off the other Kingdoms that bordered Rome, and Judea linked Syria with

Egypt which made it an important trade outpost for the Romans. Apart from small foreign policy concessions Herod continued to rule without restriction.

It is hard to tell whether it was pragmatism, admiration or some mix of both of these which compelled Augustus to leave Herod in his position.

4

Chapter 4- The Divisions of Hillel and Shammai

After Herod was spared by Augustus, he continued his works. He built the Herodium palace, and he continued to renovate the cities of Judea. This palace was to the south of Jerusalem.

Herod had a lot of wealth to go around, he extracted salt from the dead sea and had a great deal of natural resources to trade and utilise. King Herod also invested in modern (by his standards) water supplies to the biggest cities in Judea, these emulated the Roman aqueducts and borrowed heavily from Roman engineering.

The King of the Jews erected a vast port city on the coast of Judea which he named Caesarea in honour of his friend and benefactor Imperator Caesar Augustus. From this city Rome could expand its trade, this undoubtedly made Judea a wealthier province.

One thing Herod understood very well was that you have to spend money to make money.

Investments in architecture and modernisation generated a meaningful increase in state revenue because whilst they cost an arm and a leg, they also sprouted even more limbs for the state to exploit.

As well as this state spending was and is an important job creation method. By building cities and palaces Herod gave his people honest work and in doing so stimulated the economy.

For this principle to work reliably the investments which are made have to be effective, and the mark of a good administrator both in ancient times and today is the degree to which public money can be invested effectively.

Herod's investments were sometimes vain but often generated more than enough revenue to make up the cost.

What he wasted on pleasure palaces and self-preservation he made up for in public works.

The most ambitious and memorable work Herod undertook was to renovate the Temple Mount in 19BCE and its surroundings.[43]

He altered the holy building to include marble and gold and levelled up the structure from the foundation stone. There were a few reasons for this mammoth task to be undertaken.

Chief among these however was a deep insecurity in Herod that he was not a 'real Jew'.

Although I feel it is important to clarify that there is no such thing as a 'real Jew' and that the Jewish identity is diverse and welcoming to everyone, the Judaism of Herod's contemporaries was not as tolerant as the Judaism I embrace today.

In fact, Rabbi Akiva one of the most prominent Rabbis of all time was the son of Jewish converts. The point I am making is that Judaism is about belief and adherence to the law.

Values and actions speak louder than your family tree or last name.

Because of the Edomite ancestry of both Herod's mother and his father he was not regarded as legally Jewish and was therefore looked at in a negative light by his subjects.

He was compensating for this fact when he enacted public displays of his piety. A cynical analyst would claim this was because he wanted to appease his Jewish subjects. A less cynical one would attribute his choices to the fact that he was a convinced Jew and believed in the morality of exalting the temple's magnificence.

A wary analyst would accept that it was probably some combination of both that underpins Herod's motivations.

On top of the temple itself being improved Herod also saw the utility in building a Roman-style marketplace outside of the temple called the Royal Stoa. There was already a sort of cash exchange outside the temple.

The need for a means of financial exchange surrounding the temple was long-standing and there was an important reason for it.

In the early days of the Jewish people nearly all Jews lived in or near Jerusalem. During the festivals it was commanded in Deuteronomy that the Jews would offer sacrifices at the temple.

"Three times a year shall all your men appear before the Lord your G-d in the place that G-d will choose [referring presumably to the Temple in Jerusalem], on the festivals of Pesah (Passover), Shavuot (the Feast of Weeks), and Sukkot (the Festival of Booths). They shall not appear empty handed. Each shall bring his own gift, appropriate to the blessing which the Lord your G-d has given you"[44]

After the fall of the tribes of Israel and Judah to the Babylonians the majority of Jews ended up living in Iran, Egypt and other far-off regions from the home of their ancestors.

Because they could no longer bring personal sacrifices to the temple the faithful Jews in diaspora had to send money in place of their dues.

The money they sent was obviously from a range of currencies with differing exchange rates so outside of the temple a currency exchange popped up. Herod developed this into a full marketplace which increased the temple's revenues and made the system more efficient.

Having a monument to the excesses of human greed outside of the holiest place in the world was to say the least controversial and it brings up a much more serious set of questions about Judaism that will be discussed later at length.

In summation, the market stood against all that Judaism taught and acted as a symbol of the materialistic decline in Jewish values under the Herodians. Rabbi Hillel and later Jesus Christ would preach bitterly against this marketplace and what it represented.

Herod's public works were a success overall even if some of them ended up tainting his legacy a great deal.

What he did not spend on public works Herod was forced to spend on securing his regime.

He is alleged to have used a form of secret police to monitor public feeling towards him. As well as this he had a bodyguard of 2000 men modelled after Emperor Augustus' own guard.[45]

In the end it is evident that a lot of Herod's people didn't like him all that much, and as a result he was forced to suppress their contempt with the use of all the powers available to him.

This is not to say that Herod forgot his people in times of need. He did in fact help provide aid to the public during the famine of 25BCE[46] which ended up saving Judea from near ruin.

Herod's second marriage was initially good, he and Mariamne had 2 sons, Alexander and Aristobulus and 2 daughters, Salampsio and Cypros.

His relationship with Mariamne was for a time strong, he undoubtedly had great affection for her. But in many ways his fixation on her was driven by a form of clinical or manic depression.

Salome, Herod's beloved sister told him that Mariamne had been unfaithful to him. He refused to believe this probable lie and confronted Mariamne, offering her his forgiveness.

When Mariamne told him that Joseph had revealed Herod's order to her, he became convinced that Joseph had slept with his wife. For this Joseph was killed.

Herod's suspicions varied and went away for moments, but they kept coming back and nothing Mariamne said or did would assuage them. In the end he put her on trial before the Sanhedrin.

In 29BCE the woman who had been expected to be Queen was sent in chains to be tried for treason and adultery. The Sanhedrin was largely loyal to their Hasmonean princess and would likely have voted to acquit her were it not for Menachem the Essene.

The Essenes were an ascetic sect of Judaism who believed in living an austere and almost Epicurean lifestyle. Menachem was on the other hand a corrupt politician who used his status to live a life of luxury.

Because the Essenes were the minority of the Sanhedrin Menachem was given the role of Av Beit Din (Chief justice). He used his role and probably also a measure of bribery and intimidation to force the Sanhedrin to convict Mariamne on all her false charges.

The Queen of Judea was beheaded soon after. Both Hillel and Shammai were united in the view that this was immoral and used their positions to speak on Mariamne's behalf, but it came to no use.

Mariamne's mother Alexandra tried to declare herself Queen but was captured and killed as well.

After Mariamne was slain Herod married multiple women both for his personal pleasure and for all the political benefits these unions afforded him.

There was no explicit opposition to polygamy in Jewish Law, but it was frowned upon by this time and considered an excessively Hellenistic practice.

His new wives Mariamne Boethus (Not to be confused with Herod's second wife), Cleopatra of Jerusalem and Malthace of Samaria bore him 13 other children including Herod Philip, Herod Antipas and Herod Archelaus.

In 20BCE Herod's sons were sent to be educated in Rome. This would give them connections in Rome and also allow them to communicate better with the Romans if they ever inherited Herod's position.

Herod's dream was for Judea to remain a strong and independent country with expanded borders and modern, Romanesque works all about. This dream was quite unrealistic, and Herod ended up giving into his desire for power just as he had given into his paranoia when it came to Mariamne.

Unfortunately, Rabbi Hillel the Nasi of the Sanhedrin was unable to stop the savage execution of Queen Mariamne. Once Menachem the Essene left the Sanhedrin the Pharisees regained control and quickly split into rival factions.

The new Av Beit Din was Rabbi Shammai, the major rival of Hillel. The two often argued but their administration was civil at its core and united in preventing anything like what had happened to Mariamne from happening ever again.

A Rabbi often held a day job on top of being a Rabbi, or it can be more aptly described as a family trade seeing as they earned no fixed wage from Torah study or from their work as the legislators of the state.

Rabbi Shammai was a builder by trade and Rabbi Hillel was a carpenter. When Jesus Christ is discussed in later passages this acts as an important piece of evidence supporting the view that he was in fact a Rabbi.

The origins of Hillel can be traced to the Babylonian Jewry in around 110BCE, he moved to Judea to make something of himself and attempted to study under Shemaya and Avtalyon, arguably the two most prominent Rabbis of the time.

Much of Hillel's belief system has entered public consciousness today, albeit in subtle forms that aren't very easy to trace unless you remember the history of the Jews.

The similarities between Hillel and Jesus Christ for instance must not be forgotten. Hillel came from humble beginnings and was not quick to anger. Hillel admonished wealth and unjustified power, he exalted the poor and weak, he preached social justice, peace and help for those who could not help themselves.

He worked as a carpenter by day and as a rabbi as well. It is more than likely therefore that the Jesus we know today was either a student of or an amalgamation of Hillel's character and teachings.

Hillel's background and teachings are best exemplified in this Talmudic passage.

תָּנוּ רַבָּנַן: עָנִי וְעָשִׁיר וְרָשָׁע בָּאִין לַדִּין, לֶעָנִי אוֹמְרִים לוֹ: מִפְּנֵי מָה לֹא עָסַקְתָּ בַּתּוֹרָה? אִם אוֹמֵר: עָנִי הָיִיתִי, וְטָרוּד בִּמְזוֹנוֹתַי, אוֹמְרִים לוֹ: כְּלוּם עָנִי הָיִיתָ יוֹתֵר מֵהִלֵּל?

אָמְרוּ עָלָיו עַל הִלֵּל הַזָּקֵן שֶׁבְּכָל יוֹם וָיוֹם הָיָה עוֹשֶׂה וּמִשְׂתַּכֵּר בִּטְרַפָּעִיק, חֶצְיוֹ הָיָה נוֹתֵן לְשׁוֹמֵר בֵּית הַמִּדְרָשׁ, וְחֶצְיוֹ לְפַרְנָסָתוֹ וּלְפַרְנָסַת אַנְשֵׁי בֵיתוֹ. פַּעַם אַחַת לֹא מָצָא לְהִשְׂתַּכֵּר, וְלֹא הִנִּיחוֹ שׁוֹמֵר בֵּית הַמִּדְרָשׁ לְהִכָּנֵס. עָלָה וְנִתְלָה וְיָשַׁב עַל פִּי אֲרוּבָה כְּדֵי שֶׁיִּשְׁמַע דִּבְרֵי אֱלֹהִים חַיִּים מִפִּי שְׁמַעְיָה וְאַבְטַלְיוֹן.

אָמְרוּ: אוֹתוֹ הַיּוֹם עֶרֶב שַׁבָּת הָיָה, וּתְקוּפַת טֵבֶת הָיְתָה, וְיָרַד עָלָיו שֶׁלֶג מִן הַשָּׁמַיִם. כְּשֶׁעָלָה עַמּוּד הַשַּׁחַר אָמַר לוֹ שְׁמַעְיָה לְאַבְטַלְיוֹן: אַבְטַלְיוֹן אָחִי, בְּכָל יוֹם הַבַּיִת מֵאִיר וְהַיּוֹם אָפֵל, שֶׁמָּא יוֹם הַמְעוּנָּן הוּא? הֵצִיצוּ עֵינֵיהֶן וְרָאוּ דְּמוּת אָדָם בָּאֲרוּבָה. עָלוּ וּמָצְאוּ עָלָיו רוּם שָׁלֹשׁ אַמּוֹת שֶׁלֶג. פֵּרְקוּהוּ, וְהִרְחִיצוּהוּ וְסָכוּהוּ, וְהוֹשִׁיבוּהוּ כְּנֶגֶד הַמְּדוּרָה. אָמְרוּ: רָאוּי זֶה לְחַלֵּל עָלָיו אֶת הַשַּׁבָּת

עָשִׁיר, אוֹמְרִים לוֹ: מִפְּנֵי מָה לֹא עָסַקְתָּ בַּתּוֹרָה? אִם אוֹמֵר: עָשִׁיר
הָיִיתִי וְטָרוּד הָיִיתִי בִּנְכָסַי. אוֹמְרִים לוֹ: כְּלוּם עָשִׁיר הָיִיתָ יוֹתֵר מֵרַבִּי
אֶלְעָזָר? אָמְרוּ עָלָיו עַל רַבִּי אֶלְעָזָר בֶּן חַרְסוֹם שֶׁהִנִּיחַ לוֹ אָבִיו אֶלֶף
עֲיָרוֹת בַּיַּבָּשָׁה, וּכְנֶגְדָּן אֶלֶף סְפִינוֹת בַּיָּם. וּבְכָל יוֹם וָיוֹם נוֹטֵל נֹאד שֶׁל
קֶמַח עַל כְּתֵיפוֹ וּמְהַלֵּךְ מֵעִיר לְעִיר וּמִמְּדִינָה לִמְדִינָה לִלְמוֹד תּוֹרָה.

"Apropos the great wealth of Rabbi Elazar ben Harsum, the Gemara cites that which the Sages taught: A poor person, and a wealthy person, and a wicked person come to face judgment before the Heavenly court for their conduct in this world. To the poor person, the members of the court say: Why did you not engage in Torah? If he rationalizes his conduct and says: I was poor and preoccupied with earning enough to pay for my sustenance and that is why I did not engage in Torah study, they say to him: Were you any poorer than Hillel, who was wretchedly poor and nevertheless attempted to study Torah?

They said about Hillel the Elder that each and every day he would work and earn a half-dinar, half of which he would give to the guard of the study hall and half of which he spent for his sustenance and the sustenance of the members of his family. One time he did not find employment to earn a wage, and the guard of the study hall did not allow him to enter. He ascended to the roof, suspended himself, and sat at the edge of the skylight in order to hear the words of the Torah of the living G-d from the mouths of Shemaya and Avtalyon, the spiritual leaders of that generation.

The Sages continued and said: That day was Shabbat eve and it was the winter season of Tevet, and snow fell upon him from the sky. When it

was dawn, Shemaya said to Avtalyon: Avtalyon, my brother, every day at
this hour the study hall is already bright from the sunlight streaming
through the skylight, and today it is dark; is it perhaps a cloudy day?
They focused their eyes and saw the image of a man in the skylight. They
ascended and found him covered with snow three cubits high. They
extricated him from the snow, and they washed him and smeared oil on
him, and they sat him opposite the bonfire to warm him. They said: This
man is worthy for us to desecrate Shabbat for him. Saving a life overrides
Shabbat in any case; however, this great man is especially deserving.
Clearly, poverty is no excuse for the failure to attempt to study Torah.

And if a wealthy man comes before the heavenly court, the members of
the court say to him: Why did you not engage in Torah? If he says: I was
wealthy and preoccupied with managing my possessions, they say to him:
Were you any wealthier than Rabbi Elazar, who was exceedingly wealthy
and nevertheless studied Torah? They said about Rabbi Elazar ben
Harsum that his father left him an inheritance of one thousand villages
on land, and corresponding to them, one thousand ships at sea. And each
and every day he takes a leather jug of flour on his shoulder and walks
from city to city and from state to state to study Torah from the Torah
scholars in each of those places."[47]

The point made with these words is simply that Jews are the
same in the eyes of G-d, regardless of their status in life or their
possessions. We should all strive to be thoughtful, and we should
bring relief to the poor and the needy.

You could be a Jew no matter where you came from or what
you had to your name.

Hillel was tremendously respected despite being cripplingly poor, as was Jesus Christ. Both men found a certain glory in being poor and did not blame the poor for their poverty. The only problem for which a person could be blamed in the eyes of Hillel was to ignore and forget the laws of the Torah.

And as he said, the only rule of the Torah that mattered was *'love your neighbour as yourself'.*

According to the Talmud Hillel was more patient than Shammai and this ultimately made him a better Rabbi. There is an iconic case mentioned in the Talmud which illustrates the core differences of faith and temperament that marked the divisions between Hillel and Shammai.

The Talmud can best be described as a text which enshrines the intellectual progress of Rabbis in interpreting Jewish law. Though it does not have the same authority as the Torah it is regarded as very important for Jewish thought.

שׁוּב מַעֲשֶׂה בְּגוֹי אֶחָד שֶׁבָּא לִפְנֵי שַׁמַּאי. אָמַר לוֹ: גַּיְּירֵנִי עַל מְנָת שֶׁתְּלַמְּדֵנִי כָּל הַתּוֹרָה כּוּלָּהּ כְּשֶׁאֲנִי עוֹמֵד עַל רֶגֶל אַחַת! דְּחָפוֹ בְּאַמַּת הַבִּנְיָן שֶׁבְּיָדוֹ. בָּא לִפְנֵי הִלֵּל, גַּיְּירֵיהּ. אָמַר לוֹ: דַּעֲלָךְ סְנֵי לְחַבְרָךְ לָא תַּעֲבֵיד – זוֹ הִיא כָּל הַתּוֹרָה כּוּלָּהּ, וְאִידַּךְ פֵּירוּשַׁהּ הוּא, זִיל גְּמוֹר.

"There was another incident involving one gentile who came before Shammai and said to Shammai: Convert me on condition that you teach me the entire Torah while I am standing on one foot. Shammai pushed him away with the builder's cubit in his hand. This was a common measuring stick and Shammai was a builder by trade. The same gentile came before Hillel. He converted him and said to him: That which is hateful to you do not do to another; that is the entire Torah, and the rest is its interpretation. Go study."[48]

What this rather whimsical scene shows is that Hillel saw Jewish law as something to be interpreted rather than strictly followed. He could compress complex ideas into simple terms which people could follow adaptively.

Shammai meanwhile was more conservative and concerned with taking Jewish law literally.

The importance of the debates between Hillel and Shammai cannot be overstated, their arguments set the modern standards of Jewish practice. In modern practice Hillel is widely regarded to have been the winner of these disputes.

Beit Hillel (The House of Hillel) and Beit Shammai (The House of Shammai) would never be reconciled, but their inability to reconcile would reconcile, codify and transform the Jewish religion.

The one thing that seemed to unite the opposing Pharisee factions was a mutual distaste for Herod and all that he did. Both men put their differences to one side when it came to doing all that was in their worldly power to defeat Herod in his every effort.

The greatest act of rebellion Hillel mounted against Herod's rule took the form of a new law which he had passed in the Sanhedrin.

An issue had risen for Rabbinic authorities and for the Mediterranean world more generally in the form of people born to Jewish mothers, but who had non-Jewish fathers.

There is a comedy bit in Monty Python's Life of Brian that features a reference to this genuine social issue.

BRIAN: Bloody Romans.

MANDY: Now, look, Brian. If it wasn't for them, we wouldn't have all this, and don't you forget it.

BRIAN: We don't owe the Romans anything, Mum.

MANDY: Well, that's not entirely true, is it Brian?

BRIAN: What do you mean?

MANDY: Well, you know you were asking me about your, uh...

BRIAN: My nose?

MANDY: Yes. Well, there's a reason it's... like it is, Brian.

BRIAN: What is it?

MANDY: Well, I suppose I should have told you a long time ago, but...

BRIAN: What?

MANDY: Well, Brian,... your father isn't Mr. Cohen.

BRIAN: I never thought he was.

MANDY: Now, none of your cheek! He was a Roman, Brian. He was a centurion in the Roman army.

BRIAN: You mean... you were raped?

MANDY: Well, at first, yes.

Life of Brian is by no means a historically accurate film, but in this scene, it did touch upon a genuine issue facing the Jews at this time.

Due to a series of wars and proxy wars many Jewish women had been sexually assaulted by foreign soldiers and the offspring were raised Jewish but could not be legally designated as such because they did not have a Jewish father.

This meant that a subset of the Judean population belonged to no ethno-religious group and therefore lacked any sort of place in society. This was vaguely similar to modern Mixed-Race people during American segregation who couldn't quite be designated as either Black or White.

Hillel decreed that Jewish heritage would from that day on be matrilineal. This is still the law of the Jewish people today.

Because Herod's mother was a gentile, he would not have been considered Jewish by the new law.

This rule couldn't be applied retroactively so Herod was still a Jew, but it was still a very direct attack on him. It also made a lot of his children including Herod Archelaus and Herod Antipas non-Jews because their mother was a Samaritan woman.

But the mere fact that by the new matrilineal standard Herod wouldn't have been seen as a Jew infuriated him and acted as a huge political win for his critics.

Admittedly Hillel probably didn't radically change Jewish Law for as petty a reason as angering Herod, but I like to think that he enjoyed the knowledge that he had at least upset Herod.

It is with the dubious and era-specific reasoning behind the matrilineal rule that I consider it to be outdated and unworkable in a modern context. There is no inherent or intrinsic difference between Jewish men and Jewish women, and therefore Jewish identity cannot be pegged to one parent.

This is especially problematic in a modern context where families are becoming more diverse and complicated.

It is understandable that Hillel chose his course, but it is not so easy to understand why modern Rabbinic authorities keep to it seeing as it isn't very relevant anymore. It was very much a time-specific measure, so it seems to be redundant.

Another unfortunate consequence for King Herod was that he lost any claims to regnal legitimacy above his oldest sons, who now outranked him in the succession of Judea legally speaking and in the eyes of the Jewish people.

At certain points it is claimed that the Sanhedrin even plotted Herod's assassination, true or not these rumours would have unfortunate consequences for Herod's sons.

5

Chapter 5- The Fall of Herod

In his last years Herod became intensely paranoid, changeable, angry and tyrannical. He began to use contrived political tricks and acts of sedition against his own family, because he started seeing them as his enemies just like everyone else.

This was not helped by the fact that a great number of his relations were just as bad as he was and used his insanity to their advantage. He pitted people against each other and used bizarre methods to undermine everyone in his family.

In many ways the only ones he ended up trusting were the vilest ones. His sister Salome who had plotted the downfall of all her enemies kept Herod under her thumb because she knew how to exploit his mental illness. If she was unhappy with someone (such as Mariamne) she could simply start telling Herod that they were a traitor, and the King would soon after deal with them to bring about a moment of ease before the cycle of terror started over again.

Herod had always been a violent man, but now he was a violent man without the ability to judiciously use his violence, he was a danger to all those close to him. At least in his early days he used some form of self-control to limit the scope of what he did, now he had killed or silenced anyone with the ability to stop him.

One of the wily courtiers who manipulated Herod in his last days was his first son Antipater, who returned to court on instruction from his father. A huge reason for this was his complete distrust of the children Mariamne bore him, he saw them as baring the same guilt as their mother.

"As he was thus disturbed and afflicted, in order to depress these young men, he brought to court another of his sons, that was born to him when he was a private man; his name was Antipater; yet did he not then indulge him as he did afterwards, when he was quite overcome by him, and let him do every thing as he pleased, but rather with a design of depressing the insolence of the sons of Mariamne, and managing this elevation of his so, that it might be for a warning to them; for this bold behavior of theirs [he thought] would not be so great, if they were once persuaded that the succession to the kingdom did not appertain to them alone, or must of necessity come to them. So he introduced Antipater as their antagonist, and imagined that he made a good provision for discouraging their pride, and that after this was done to the young men, there might be a proper season for expecting these to be of a better disposition; but the event proved otherwise than he intended, for the young men thought he did them a very great injury; and as Antipater was a shrewd man, when he had once obtained this degree of freedom, and began to expect greater things than he had before hoped for, he had but one single design in his head, and that was to distress his brethren,

and not at all to yield to them the pre-eminence, but to keep close to his
father, who was already alienated from them by the calumnies he had
heard about them, and ready to be wrought upon in any way his zeal
against them should advise him to pursue, that he might be continually
more and more severe against them. Accordingly, all the reports that were
spread abroad came from him, while he avoided himself the suspicion as
if those discoveries proceeded from him; but he rather chose to make use
of those persons for his assistants that were unsuspected, and such as
might be believed to speak truth by reason of the good-will they bore to
the king; and indeed there were already not a few who cultivated a
friendship with Antipater, in hopes of gaining somewhat by him, and
these were the men who most of all persuaded Herod, because they
appeared to speak thus out of their good-will to him: and with these joint
accusations, which from various foundations supported one another's
veracity, the young men themselves afforded further occasions to
Antipater also; for they were observed to shed tears often, on account of
the injury that was offered them, and had their mother in their mouths;
and among their friends they ventured to reproach their father, as not
acting justly by them; all which things were with an evil intention
reserved in memory by Antipater against a proper opportunity; and
when they were told to Herod, with aggravations, increased the disorder
so much, that it brought a great tumult into the family; for while the king
was very angry at imputations that were laid upon the sons of Mariamne,
and was desirous to humble them, he still increased the honor that he had
bestowed on Antipater, and was at last so overcome by his persuasions,
that he brought his mother to court also. He also wrote frequently to
Cæsar in favor of him, and more earnestly recommended him to his care
particularly. And when Agrippa was returning to Rome, after he had

finished his ten years' government in Asia. Herod sailed from Judea; and
when he met with him, he had none with him but Antipater, whom he
delivered to Agrippa, that he might take him along with him, together
with many presents, that so he might become Cæsar's friend, insomuch
that things already looked as if he had all his father's favor, and that the
young men were already entirely rejected from any hopes of the king-
dom."[49]

Antipater returned in large part because Herod wanted to reduce the influence of his sons after they overtook him in the succession. He saw them as a threat to his rule and even though he was an old man, his spite made him prefer taking down the whole country with him rather than surrendering the throne peacefully.

Herod would have sooner seen the Romans take his Kingdom than his opponents at home.

He feared betrayal so severely that he was willing to give up his legacy to avoid it.

In 12BCE Aristobulus and Alexander came home from Rome and were acclaimed by the people. These young men were the heirs to the throne and obviously better than Herod in the eyes of the public. People adored and cherished the sons of Mariamne for they were seen as fresh blood with the same air of legitimacy and moral dignity as their mother.

When they brought the Roman style, they had learned home Herod was angry, he loathed them for becoming what they had been forced to be.

He loathed the fact that they conducted themselves the way they had been forced to during the education he subjected them to. He saw it as a sign that they were more modern than him.

And more to the point, he saw their rapport with Rome as a threat to his authority. If the Romans liked his sons more than him, they could always replace him.

Antipater stroked Herod's ego and made him see Alexander and Aristobulus as enemies, in 13BCE he ended up making Antipater his heir instead of the sons of Mariamne.

Herod wanted to humble Alexander and Aristobulus by showing them that he had another option in the form of their older half-brother. This ended up doing the opposite and made the brothers deeply hateful and suspicious of their father.

Many of the less brave survivors of Herod's early reign tolerated him in the hopes that when he died his sons would succeed him and be the righteous rulers the Jews desired.

Herod was more than aware of this and probably saw it as an incentive to kill him, the removal of his sons from the succession was originally aimed at putting them in their place so they wouldn't get too big for their boots and make an attempt at rebellion or sedition.

Alexander and Aristobulus both had good marriages and fathered multiple children, their line had already been established and this first change to Herod's will was a shock to Judean society and had serious destabilising impacts on the state even before Herod died.

Alexander's son Tigranes V of Armenia founded a Herodian dynasty of Armenian Kings who would unwittingly preserve the legacy of Herod far longer than Judea would.

Herod still bore affection for his boys but at the same time he knew that his son Alexander was prideful and popular with the people. His sister Salome convinced him that Alexander was plotting his downfall. When Antipater joined the whisperings, it only confirmed what Herod had feared.

Most people would think carefully before acting on accusations that their son had betrayed them, but Herod's severe paranoia never let him have peace unless he ruthlessly purged anything and everything which he perceived as a threat.

He jailed his son Alexander on charges of treason and made him give a defence. His son went against all odds and gave such a convincing defence that it bought him his freedom, albeit only for a while.

"O father, the benevolence thou hast showed to us is evident, even in this very judicial procedure, for hadst thou had any pernicious intentions about us, thou hadst not produced us here before the common savior of all, for it was in thy power, both as a king and as a father, to punish the guilty; but by thus bringing us to Rome, and making Cæsar himself a witness to what is done, thou intimatest that thou intendest to save us; for no one that hath a design to slay a man will bring him to the temples, and to the altars; yet are our circumstances still worse, for we cannot endure to live ourselves any longer, if it be believed that we have injured such a father; nay, perhaps it would be worse for us to live with this suspicion upon us, that we have injured him, than to die without such guilt. And if our open defense may be taken to be true, we shall be happy, both in pacifying thee, and in escaping the danger we are in; but if this calumny so prevails, it is more than enough for us that we have seen the sun this day; which why should we see, if this suspicion be fixed upon us? Now it is easy to say of young men, that they desire to reign; and to say further, that this evil proceeds from the case of our unhappy mother. This is abundantly sufficient to produce our present misfortune out of the former; but consider well, whether such an accusation does not suit all such young men, and may not be said of them all promiscuously; for nothing can hinder him that reigns, if he have children, and their mother be dead, but the father may have a suspicion upon all his sons, as intend-

*ing some treachery to him; but a suspicion is not sufficient to prove such
an impious practice. Now let any man say, whether we have actually and
insolently attempted any such thing, whereby actions otherwise incredible
use to be made credible? Can any body prove that poison hath been prepared? or prove a conspiracy of our equals, or the corruption of servants,
or letters written against thee? though indeed there are none of those
things but have sometimes been pretended by way of calumny, when they
were never done; for a royal family that is at variance with itself is a
terrible thing; and that which thou callest a reward of piety often
becomes, among very wicked men, such a foundation of hope, as makes
them leave no sort of mischief untried. Nor does any one lay any wicked
practices to our charge; but as to calumnies by hearsay, how can he put an
end to them, who will not hear what we have to say? Have we talked with
too great freedom? Yes; but not against thee, for that would be unjust, but
against those that never conceal any thing that is spoken to them. Hath
either of us lamented our mother? Yes; but not because she is dead, but
because she was evil spoken of by those that had no reason so to do. Are
we desirous of that dominion which we know our father is possessed of?
For what reason can we do so? If we already have royal honors, as we
have, should not we labor in vain? And if we have them not, yet are not
we in hopes of them? Or supposing that we had killed thee, could we
expect to obtain thy kingdom? while neither the earth would let us tread
upon it, nor the sea let us sail upon it, after such an action as that; nay,
the religion of all your subjects, and the piety of the whole nation, would
have prohibited parricides from assuming the government, and from
entering into that most holy temple which was built by thee But suppose
we had made light of other dangers, can any murderer go off unpunished
while Cæsar is alive? We are thy sons, and not so impious or so thought-*

less as that comes to, though perhaps more unfortunate than is convenient for thee. But in case thou neither findest any causes of complaint, nor any treacherous designs, what sufficient evidence hast thou to make such a wickedness of ours credible? Our mother is dead indeed, but then what befell her might be an instruction to us to caution, and not an incitement to wickedness. We are willing to make a larger apology for ourselves; but actions never done do not admit of discourse. Nay, we will make this agreement with thee, and that before Cæsar, the lord of all, who is now a mediator between us, If thou, O father, canst bring thyself, by the evidence of truth, to have a mind free from suspicion concerning us let us live, though even then we shall live in an unhappy way, for to be accused of great acts of wickedness, though falsely, is a terrible thing; but if thou hast any fear remaining, continue thou on in thy pious life, we will give this reason for our own conduct; our life is not so desirable to us as to desire to have it, if it tend to the harm of our father who gave it us."[50]

After this Herod was reconciled with his son for a while, this was in part because Augustus had witnessed the display and executing his son would have been embarrassing.

The issues were still there, and eventually Herod's hatred and contempt outweighed his love and mercy. A series of skirmishes between Herod and his sons resulted in their final imprisonment.

In 7BCE Alexander and Aristobulus were jailed on false charges of treason by the bidding of Antipater and Salome.

Tero, King Herod's barber willingly testified (untruthfully) that Herod's sons had tried to kill him in cold blood.

The friends and allies of the princes tried to save them at any cost. Many men good and bad, loyal and disloyal to King Herod intervened to save his sons and gave impassioned defences at the greatest risk to their own lives.

Many people who loved Herod and loathed his enemies stood up for Alexander and Aristobulus, no one with any ounce of moral credit to his name could stand there and allow the slaughter of the two remaining Hasmonean princes of Judea.

No one with integrity or a sense of justice could stand there without saying something, and even some of Herod's most ardent defenders were included in that bloc.

Herod had all these brave men killed and purged anyone who supported his sons. Once he had received permission from Augustus to treat his sons as he saw fit, he decided to have them strangled in their dingy prison cells like common criminals.

So it was that Herod's sons and the Hasmonean heirs to the throne were viciously strangled with chords until the life left them.

Augustus was shaken by this incident and according to Macrobius Ambrosius Theodosius he is reported to have said this.

"Melius est Herodis porcum esse quam"[51]

'It is better to be Herod's pig than one of his sons.'

This was of course in reference to Herod's strict adherence to Kashrut (Kosher eating) and the fact that any pig Herod had would end up living longer than his children.

What this proved to nearly everyone who observed it was that Herod was ruthless, not just in the traditional sense but to the point of being utterly destructive of himself and all others.

He had just killed the only two people in the world who could reconcile the Herodian line with the Hasmoneans (for now at least).

After this evil act even the sycophants who fawned over Herod were frightened of his ire and wanted him gone. He was too old and too mad; he was in his seventies in fact.

Herod was now so remote from any form of a moral or logical compass that neither his enemies nor his friends could predict what he would do next.

Despite his contempt for his sons Herod spared their children and was known to be fond of them. Aristobulus' son and daughter Herod Agrippa and Herodias were sent off for a Roman education.

The way he doted on his grandchildren seems to point so a certain amount of guilt. In his rare moments of clarity Herod wanted to do something that would atone for his sins.

The blame for the deaths of the princes was laid mostly at the feet of Herod and his allies but the same brush that smeared the Herodians also smeared Antipater, he was seen as the chief instigator of the downfall of his brothers.

People knew Herod was mad, and they knew he was prone to rage. But they also knew that the people he was intimate with were the ones who fed his insanity and weaponised it, so they saw Antipater over Herod's shoulder and figured it out for themselves. He was almost seen as worse than his father because he was fully lucid and still allowed such horrid things to happen.

There was probably at least a nugget of truth behind that claim. Antipater had been an outsider for many years, in some ways Herod would have probably felt guilty for banishing the boy by order of his grandfather Antipater the elder and compensated for this by letting him do and say what he wanted.

Antipater was also clean of the general problems his rivals had for Herod when it came to being trustworthy, unlike the Hasmonean princes he had no claim to the throne beyond what his father offered. And unlike his younger half-siblings he had not spent long in Herod's court and neither had a great number of enemies or allies.

Having no allies made him need Herod for protection and favours, having no enemies made him seem more objective and less ambitious.

These factors all meant that he required Herod's patronage for any hope at achieving authority, so Herod kept him close in the knowledge that he was the only relative (on paper) that wasn't a direct threat to his rule.

Though Antipater was not extremely important to the Herodian dynasty he has received importance in some theories regarding the history of the Jews at the time.

One rather outlandish theory is put forward by Robert Graves in his book 'King Jesus'.[52] The passage in question recounts how Herod's son Antipater was married in secret by the High Priest Simon Boethus to Miriam, a Davidic claimant.

This Miriam would be the mother of Jesus, and Antipater would be his father. They had to be married in secret because their children would be the true heirs to the throne of Judea, which would probably incur Herod's wrath.

Mary was said to be a descendant of Eli one of the judges of Israel from the historical sections of the Tanakh. Though there is little to no evidence that this is true.

When Antipas died, Miriam was said to have married an old carpenter called Joseph to protect her unborn baby (Jesus).

As well as this the revisionism which took hold in Judea after Herod's death popularised the notion of a Davidic claimant taking the Judean throne. Before the rise of Judas of Gamala and the Zealots a Davidic King had not ruled Judea in over 600 years and most people considered the Hasmonean dynasty to have more legitimacy.

This was in large part because there were just so many people who could prove through their surnames and Rabbinic records that they were descendants of the Davidic line.

By the rules of human genetics if you doubled your number of ancestors going back 20 or more times you would have at least a million ancestors in a region of the world that had less than half that in the time of David.

Therefore, you must have the same ancestors on different sides of your family converging over time.

In fact, by the rules of human genetics we are all related to each other at least twice over.

The point I am trying to make is that being a Davidic claimant wasn't as much of an achievement as many people think it was, and as a result it wasn't seen as an automatic reason to be given the crown of Judea.

It is an interesting hypothesis that Graves made but it seems to ignore these important pieces of information.

Legally speaking Antipater wasn't even the natural heir after Herod's sons by Mariamne, it was in fact the middle-child Herod Boethus. Boethus was married to Herodias the daughter of his half-brother Aristobulus and seeing as she was a descendant of the Hasmonean dynasty through her grandmother Mariamne, her husband was the highest-ranking claimant at the time.

Forms of incest like this were common in royal families in the region but were considered a moral stain by the Jewish people and were only allowed at all to avoid non-Jews entering the royal succession.

It was regarded as impious, but it served the important purpose of restricting access to the line of succession and awkwardly forced the siblings to work together. If they were all intermarried, it was not as easy to kill each other in civil wars.

Herod the Great ignored the law and chose Antipater as heir anyway because he believed (correctly) that Boethus was opportunistic and would try to overthrow him.

The only thing Herod's paranoia could not foresee is blindingly obvious in hindsight.

Antipater and Boethus worked together to plot the death of their father. This plot was ironically the only one that was actually true. In 5BCE they were discovered and Boethus was banished.

Of the two Boethus got off lightly, for Antipater was the one Herod chose to kill. Publius Quinctilius Varus, the governor of Syria found Antipater guilty of conspiracy and sent him to Herod, who ended up having him killed just 5 days before his own end came.

Herod urgently made a new will after the fall of Herod Boethus and Antipater to consolidate his power and ensure that none of his children ever got any big ideas again.

In this new will his youngest son Antipas was made the new heir, this was mainly out of contempt for Archelaus who he was upset with at the time.

He eventually got over his distress and named Herod Archelaus as his chief heir, giving Antipas and Herod Philip dominion over smaller regions of Judea as Tetrarchs.

Antipas and Archelaus were brothers from the same mother, Malthace the Samaritan.

Because their mother wasn't a Jew the pair were considered non-Jews by Law, so they were arguably even less legitimate than Herod himself.

Herod's death was a long, drawn out and torturous experience to say the very least. The disease in question is unknown but was likely some severe form of kidney disease paired with putrid gangrene.

He was paranoid, mad, severely ill and developed gangrene of the genitals which is said to have included worms or maggots in his penis.

"Herod's distemper greatly increased upon him after a severe manner, and

this by G-d's judgment upon him for his sins; for a fire glowed in him slowly, which did not so much appear to the touch outwardly, as it augmented his pains inwardly; for it brought upon him a vehement appetite to eating, which he could not avoid to supply with one sort of food or other. His entrails were also ex-ulcerated, and the chief violence of his pain lay on his colon; an aqueous and transparent liquor also had settled itself about his feet, and a like matter afflicted him at the bottom of his belly. Nay, further, his privy-member was putrefied, and produced worms; and when he sat upright, he had a difficulty of breathing, which was very loathsome, on account of the stench of his breath, and the quickness of its returns; he had also convulsions in all parts of his body, which increased his strength to an insufferable degree. It was said by those who pretended to divine, and who were endued with wisdom to foretell such things, that G-d inflicted this punishment on the king on account of his great impiety; yet was he still in hopes of recovering, though his afflictions seemed greater than any one could bear. He also sent for physicians, and did not refuse to follow what they prescribed for his assistance, and went beyond the river Jordan, and bathed himself in the warm baths that were at Callirrhoe, which, besides their other general virtues, were also fit to drink; which water runs into the lake called Asphaltiris."[53]

Herod's evil was so painful and unbearable that he even attempted suicide, only to be stopped at the last second by his faithful cousin.

It is hard to say what Herod actually suffered from, but I would speculate that it was some form of severe kidney infection that spread to other parts of his body over time and ended up giving him bodily sepsis and gangrenous flesh.

The worms in his genitals could have also been a result of some form of sexual infection, but this wouldn't explain the other obvious symptoms of a bodily infection.

When he knew he was at death's door the King rewarded his friends and went to the city of Jericho to live out his final days.

He summoned Archelaus (who by now was the person he relied on to help him perform acts of violence) and Salome to his death-bed and made one last request to them.

This being that they have the highest-ranking men of the San-hedrin murdered so that their mourners would mourn at the same time as Herod died.

Herod was indeed so hated that he needed to rob grief meant for others. Although Archelaus and Salome promised to do as he asked, they secretly refused to, it was too insane even for them.

Between 1 and 4BCE (depending on if you believe Emil Schürer or W.E. Filmer) Herod finally died. This was likely a relief for him after his unendurable suffering.

Emil Schürer's argument was that Herod's successors backdated their accessions from 1BCE to 4BCE to imply that Herod had given them power even before he died.[54]

Herod's heirs came to power in 4BCE according to the dates provided by historical records. It is said that Herod Philip reigned over his dominion for 37 years and died in the 20th year of Tiberius' reign which would imply that he had become a Tetrarch in 4BCE instead of 1BCE.

In Josephus' account of Herod's death, it is said that there was a lunar eclipse before Passover when Herod died, which would go against the notion that he had died in 4BCE according to the calculations of W.E. Filmer.

Filmer posited that it was impossible for all the events that took place before Herod's death to happen during the time between the eclipse and Passover.[55]

Though I am more sympathetic to Schürer's view, and his work was a huge inspiration for my own research, it is true that the eclipse is a slight contrivance and was probably just used for dramatic purposes.

That is to say, I agree that Herod died in 4BCE but disagree fervently that an eclipse preceded this.

Herod dying in 4BCE also aligns better with other events of the time which make far more sense when viewed in the context of Herod's death being in this year.

No matter when he died Herod died infamous, wretched and hated by all. He hated his people just as much as they hated him. The only people he seemed to hate more than his people were his family, who he chose to victimise until the very end.

Even in death he found the cleverest ways to make their lives horrible.

6

Chapter 6- The Tetrarchy

When Herod died a strange sense of unity developed among the Jewish people. All factions and creeds shared in their relief that he was gone.

So many people had spent their lives trying to unite the Pharisees and Sadducees, it was only Herod's death that finally did it.

These factions realised that however much they disagreed with each other they hated Herod and his lackies far more.

Herod gave exorbitant sums of money to Augustus and Livia his wife in the will and also split his Kingdom into several smaller entities.

It was almost as if Herod's will was perfectly arranged to make Judea as weak as possible, it cut the hamstrings of all his successors.

Some of his relatives ended up with much more than they imagined, and others ended up with less.

Salome for instance ended up with Jericho, Ashkelon and Ashdod as well as the surrounding land which made up Gaza. As well as this she received a lot of money.

Antipas meanwhile received Perea and the Galilee. Both were wealthy provinces but were only connected by the Jordan river. Perea also bordered foreign Kingdoms which placed a serious burden on Antipas in times of war.

Herod Philip received control of Batanea which was situated to the east of the Galilee and encompassed the Golan Heights as well as Southern Syria.

Herod's chief successor was Archelaus who received control of Judea's heartland, most of its coast and its capital city.

This split was completely shambolic in nature. None of these low-grade officials could do anything to expand Jewish power and liberty, they were utterly splintered and distended.

In many ways Herod's confusing and chaos-generating will was a final act of scorn for the family he so distrusted. He decided to wilfully disinherit all his heirs of the Kingdom of Judea and in doing so left everyone disappointed.

He would rather watch his Kingdom burn than go through the humiliation of giving it away to a family he barely considered worthy of having it. Alternatively, he could also have done it with the intention of avoiding a conflict with Rome, which precedent shows would probably have been inevitable if Judea had been united under one ruler.

In creating this tetrarchy Herod made it clear to the Romans that Judea would willingly be absorbed into the empire, but it would do so in good time and with respect for Jewish customs. If this had been Herod's motivation rather than spite it would have made him the finest statesman of his age.

Another possibility is that he was so severely ill that Herod simply lost the ability to think critically and did something rash and out of character. For all his faults Herod spent all his life working to improve Judean power, to throw it all away after he died could only be an act of madness or an act of spite so severe that it is beyond the scope of reasonable thinking.

The fact that his will changed so often and so wildly would in today's legal tradition be considered grounds to declare him unsound of mind, but in this case, Augustus knew full well that it had given him every advantage.

Augustus opportunistically exploited Herod's will to consolidate Roman control of Judea.

This was why he immediately rejected Herod Boethus' petition to have Herod's will annulled.

The will would stand, and its contents would be honoured by the Roman state and its client tetrarchs.

That was what they were now, not Kings and Queens, merely Tetrarchs. Nominal heads of state who served under Roman administration.

None of the Tetrarchs would be Kings or Queens, and more importantly as Tetrarchs they were subject to Roman laws. When a Tetrarch died, were removed from or resigned their post they would be replaced by a Roman administration and their holdings would be claimed by the Roman state.

In other words, Judea would soon be annexed into the Roman empire, Herod's will had only bought the Jewish people a generation of freedom at most.

Judea's freedom was now a ticking timebomb, the lifetime of the Tetrarchs was the only force keeping the Jews from being subjugated by the Romans.

As well as this the Tetrarchs followed the rulings of the Great Sanhedrin. On paper this sounds like it would only enhance Jewish autonomy, but in practice it actually gave the Romans far more power.

This section will be split into smaller sections about each Tetrarch and their time in office for the sake of clarity and effectiveness.

I

Herod Archelaus

Of all the people Herod the Great could have chosen as his main successor, he went for a man who was notoriously violent and impious (mostly from carrying out the evil deeds his father ordered) as well as a man who was (legally speaking) not Jewish.

Archelaus had helped Herod to purge all known male descendants of the Hasmonean dynasty some years prior and was therefore actively associated with Herod's tyranny.

In a lot of ways, he was like his father, he shared the same harsh virtues and neurotic behaviour that seemed to mark his family out for indignity and injustice.

The only difference was that people weren't nearly as afraid of him. There was clamour in the streets and the people demanded a new High Priest and for Herod's enforcers to be brought to justice.

Archelaus appointed a new High Priest and set off for Rome to be confirmed in his office by Augustus. While he was gone, he sent his men to confront the crowds and tell them that the deaths Herod ordered were justified.

The men Herod Archelaus sent were stoned to death and the crowds began seeming more rebellious. The rebels took over the temple mount and so Archelaus blockaded them in and cancelled Passover observances in the city of Jerusalem.

While he was dealing with this his brother Antipas was trying to make the case for gaining dominion over Judea. Most of the Herodian family had contempt for one another, but they were largely united in the view that Archelaus was worse than Antipas.

For all his faults Antipas was more agreeable and less likely to make the entire population of his country furiously angry at him. He was something of a compromise candidate.

Archelaus didn't help his case when he massacred 3000 of the temple's occupants for their sedition against him. Antipas tried to use this incident as an indication that his older brother was too rash and self-assured to lead the Jews.

Nicholaus of Damascus who had served Herod for many years argued persuasively for Archelaus to the Romans.

"That what had been done at the temple was rather to be attributed to the mind of those that had been killed, than to the authority of Archelaus; for that those who were the authors of such things are not only wicked in the injuries they do of themselves, but in forcing sober persons to avenge themselves upon them. Now it is evident that what these did in way of opposition was done under pretense, indeed, against Archelaus, but in reality against Cæsar himself, for they, after an injurious manner, attacked and slew those who were sent by Archelaus, and who came only to put a stop to their doings. They had no regard, either to G-d or to the festival, whom Antipater yet is not ashamed to patronize, whether it be out of his indulgence of an enmity to Archelaus, or out of his hatred of virtue and justice. For as to those who begin such tumults, and first set about such unrighteous actions, they are the men who force those that punish them to betake themselves to arms even against their will. So that

Antipater in effect ascribes the rest of what was done to all those who were of counsel to the accusers; for nothing which is here accused of injustice has been done but what was derived from them as its authors; nor are those things evil in themselves, but so represented only in order to do harm to Archelaus. Such is these men's inclination to do an injury to a man that is of their kindred, their father's benefactor, and familiarity acquainted with them, and that hath ever lived in friendship with them; for that, as to this testament, it was made by the king when he was of a sound mind, and so ought to be of more authority than his former testament; and that for this reason, because Cæsar is therein left to be the judge and disposer of all therein contained; and for Cæsar, he will not, to be sure, at all imitate the unjust proceedings of those men, who, during Herod's whole life, had on all occasions been joint partakers of power with him, and yet do zealously endeavor to injure his determination, while they have not themselves had the same regard to their kinsman [which Archelaus had]. Cæsar will not therefore disannul the testament of a man whom he had entirely supported, of his friend and confederate, and that which is committed to him in trust to ratify; nor will Cæsar's virtuous and upright disposition, which is known and uncontested through all the habitable world, imitate the wickedness of these men in condemning a king as a madman, and as having lost his reason, while he hath bequeathed the succession to a good son of his, and to one who flies to Cæsar's upright determination for refuge. Nor can Herod at any time have been mistaken in his judgment about a successor, while he showed so much prudence as to submit all to Cæsar's determination."[56]

Herod Archelaus' act of depravity sent a clear message to everyone. Any form of opposition would result in retribution.

It also rubbed Augustus the wrong way, by using the Kingly power of massacring his own people Archelaus implied that his power was derived from a source other than Augustus. He overstepped and it soured relations with Rome.

It wasn't that he had sullied the temple with the blood of 3000 people, it was that he didn't ask the Romans first.

Fortunately for Archelaus Nicholaus' defence compelled Augustus to keep Herod's will as it stood and give Archelaus his inheritance.

Archelaus also fell at the Emperor's feet when he arrived at Rome which undoubtedly stroked his ego.

As the new ethnarch of Judea Archelaus was more powerful than any of his relatives, and he used his position to resume his cruelties.

From 4 BCE to 6CE Archelaus ruled Judea with an iron first. This angered his people but what ended up undermining him more fatally was love.

Archelaus chose to marry his deceased half-brother Alexander's wife Glaphyra. Marrying your brother's wife was not seen as immoral by the Jews, it was the fact that she had divorced Juba II of Mauritania to be with him.

Remarrying whilst your former partner was alive was considered impious among the Jews and the Sanhedrin would not stand for it.

She was also non-Jewish so at this point any pretence of the Herodians being legitimate was gone.

The Jews began to call for Archelaus' abdication and in 6CE he was removed.

The two were evidently in love. So much so that Archelaus was willing to resign all his power and live out his days in the Gallic city of Vienna (south of Lyons, not to be confused with Vienna, Austria).

He cared more for Galphyra than for himself or for his throne. Dignity and authority seemed like vacuous and distant things when he looked at her, so when I imagine him leaving Judea for the last time, I imagine him doing so with something of a wry smile.

All of his holdings became the Roman province of Judaea. Though the Sanhedrin had valiantly stood up for the laws of Judaism by removing Archelaus in doing so they had also deprived the Jewish people of a united, independent state.

They wiped Judea from the world faster than they had put it up. This was exactly why Augustus had honoured Herod's will, he knew it was easier to absorb Judea naturally than to take it by force.

\#

The worst thing that came from all this was that the Sanhedrin commanded the independent parts of Judea, and so the Romans used it as a means of controlling even the parts of Judea that hadn't yet been annexed.

Publius Sulpicius Quirinius was placed in control of Judea from his other posting in Syria.

Quirinius began a census of the new Roman holdings so they could be taxed in the Roman way.

When Rome taxed its subjects, it measured the capacity of the land owned to produce income and set the rates of tax accordingly. This was effective because it forced people to use their land for as much revenue as possible.

Their rate of tax was fixed, so the more they produced the more money they would have after tax. The only problem with this model is that it required a great deal of state interference and observation.

The Jews used a simple income tax as they obviously couldn't tax each other based on land that they did not claim to own.

Judea was especially hostile to the new system because the Jews did not recognise private land ownership as valid. In a sense, the act of having your land registered implied that you owned it.

In this sense participation in the census was seen as an act of religious impiety. Many people outright refused to engage with it.

It was so damaging to Judean society in fact that it caused another split among the Pharisees.

Judas of Gamala[57] is described by Flavius Josephus as a Pharisee who went rogue after the census was launched and began the "fourth sect" of 2nd temple Judaism. The first three sects were of course the Pharisees, the Sadducees and the Essenes.

The new 'Zealots' as they are known believed in a form of theocratic nationalism which favoured G-d as the only true ruler of Judea. Judas of Gamala was a descendant of the Davidic royal family and claimed that he was the messiah and would liberate the Jews from the Romans.

He left the Sanhedrin and began a life of open rebellion and banditry in the countryside. He told people not to participate in the sin of the Roman census, those who did were subject to having their land and livestock burned and stolen.

The influence of the Zealots grew with time. They were the only political faction proposing meaningful opposition to Roman rule and as a result the Judeans began to see the other factions in the Sanhedrin as 'old news' and saw the political order of the day as an enabler for Roman oppression.

It was reminiscent of all the cultural attitudes the Jews remembered from their days in Babylonian captivity and Seleucid occupation.

In a lot of ways, the Zealots had the same problem as old Mattathias Maccabee, they victimised their own people for doing things they had been coerced into doing rather than being conciliatory and tolerant.

Burning down the farms of people who disagree with you is not a quick way of gaining allies.

The notion of a Davidic claimant being the messiah was not common in Judea at this time, it was not widely accepted that a royal house with a multitude of claimants and which had not held power in almost a millennium would save the Jews now.

Being a descendant of King David was not widely viewed as a vector of legitimacy, it was in a way a form of revisionism which the Zealots carefully cultivated because by this stage the Hasmoneans were seen as unable to oppose Roman rule.

Without Archelaus a power vacuum developed, and it only got worse when political factions started fighting each other more fervently than the Romans.

II

Salome I

Salome I was exorbitantly rich and had holdings in modern Gaza and around the city of Jericho.

Unlike the others Salome was allowed to refer to herself as a Queen. She was wise and wily and always had a strong influence over her brother Herod.

Her husband Costobarus married her in 34BCE and when he caught the ire of Herod for trying to have the lands of Edom given to Salome instead of Herod it was only the intervention of Salome that stopped his execution.

Around 25BCE Costobarus was executed after having been divorced illegally by his wife.

She was assertive and strong-willed, so much so that she could break the law with impunity to divorce a man she no longer desired to be with.

Her death came around 10CE and her holdings were taken peacefully into Roman influence.

She was the oldest of the tetrarchs, so it is unsurprising that her rule came to an end fairly fast.

In the same year as Salome died so too did Hillel. It is said that he lived to be 120 years old like Moshe, although this is a questionable claim, and he was probably born later than is recorded. He was replaced as Nasi by his son Simeon ben Hillel who failed to maintain the delicate balance of stability in the Sanhedrin.

III

Herod Antipas and Herod Philip

Herod Antipas and Herod Philip were much younger and less changeable than Archelaus and Salome, so their reigns were longer-lasting and more stable.

They had long lives which kept them in control for far longer than the rest.

In 14CE Augustus finally met his end and was replaced by his adopted son Tiberius. Tiberius was the son of Augustus' wife Livia from her first marriage with Tiberius Claudius Nero and had become heir because his many rivals to that rank had died in dubious circumstances.

Among them were Augustus' two grandsons and his nephew Marcellus. Tiberius was not charming, charismatic or quite as capable as his predecessor and his general cruelty made him a figure of fear and loathing.

But the most concise and meaningful summary of Tiberius is that he was good enough. He did his job and kept the empire under some semblance of stable government.

The Galilee which was controlled by Antipas was agriculturally wealthy, filled with natural resources and contained the most religiously devout subset of the population. It was the support base for the Pharisees because of this.

Perea the region to the south was on the border of Nabatea which made it very vulnerable to attack.

Since Antipas had control of both of these, he was essentially given the best and worst territories to have together.

Herod Philip was married to Salome, the daughter of his half-niece Herodias and his half-brother Herod Boethus. His region was also reasonably fortunate and so the brothers chose to work together.

They ran their holdings together and essentially shared them in common. They doubled their holdings by halving their egos.

When Antipas was in Rome, he fell for his niece Herodias, and she divorced her husband Herod Boethus for his half-brother.

This brought on the ire of the Jews in a similar way to Archelaus, but in this case Antipas was able to use his good relations with Emperor Tiberius to get him to make it go away. He built a new capital city in the north called Tiberias in honour of the Emperor.[58]

The city was built on a Jewish graveyard which meant that the only people who were willing to occupy it either had to through lack of money or wanted to through lack of care for Jewish law.

In this way he bribed the Emperor's ego and was able to utilise his full support against the Sanhedrin and the Jews.

The scandal never died in the hearts and minds of his people however, and John the Baptist called the marriage impious and began having his followers ritualistically cleansed in the river Jordan.

The marriage was not legal by Jewish standards because Herod Boethus was still alive when Herodias left him for his brother.

Because Antipas had divorced the daughter of Nabataea's King, he swiftly declared war, easily occupying Perea and winning the conflict after years of fighting.[59]

This was the sort of loss that no one could come back from. It was a resounding defeat and cost the Jewish people dearly. The war is said to have occurred in 36CE. It ended in 37CE when Emperor Tiberius died. It had started going terribly wrong when Herod Philip died, and Antipas lost access to his brother's Batanean troops.

In the same year Antipas had John the Baptist put in prison and killed. Herodias' daughter Salome was said to have blamed the Baptist for the war with Nabataea, and as a result had his head sent to her on a platter.

Before John's death a similar figure gained even more prominence, Jesus Christ.

Valerius Gratus was appointed in 15CE as prefect of Judea. He wasn't in his position for very long, but one important precedent he set was through repeatedly changing the High Priest (almost annually).

Apart from being absurdly petulant and difficult this also meant that the High Priesthood would be appointed by Rome rather than by the Jews themselves.

Eventually in 26CE Gratus was replaced by Pontius Pilate. Pilate as you will read was an opportunist at the core and used his power to influence the Jews to do Rome's bidding.

7

Chapter 7- Yehoshua and the Christians

Before the exploration of Christianity begins two things must be made clear. Firstly, that this book is entirely dedicated to the Jewish perspective and in no way derives any sort of influence from the Christian religion beyond the use of some Christian sources and scholarly contributions.

Secondly, because Jesus was a Jew and because Jesus is a transliteration of the name from multiple languages, I do not consider it to be his legitimate name. I instead refer to him in this work by the name Yehoshua, because this is the true Hebrew name he used.

Jesus is more than just a name; it comes with a pile of identarian and religious issues. Jesus is (whether you believe in his divinity or not) a character and by using that name I would be associating this very human tale with a supernatural one.

Associating a Jew from ancient Judea with a whitewashed religious symbol does a disservice to him. It would be the ultimate form of colonialism and a poor choice for someone trying to write about who Yehoshua really was.

Portraying Yehoshua, the dark-skinned Jew as a blue-eyed white man called Jesus is a form of historical ignorance I simply cannot abide by.

We are prone to look for adventurous, theatrical answers to questions about Yehoshua but more often than not the answers are boring.

Often, he is simply a man doing what any man would do, living as any man would.

I don't reproach Yehoshua with this badge, quite the opposite in fact. To do what Yehoshua did and impact as many people as he did as a divine being would not be too difficult, but as a man it shows that he was one of the most moving, fascinating people the world has ever witnessed.

I

Early Life

The first mentions of Yehoshua by Josephus begin in Book 18 of the Antiquities of the Jews.

"Now there was about this time Jesus, a wise man, if it be lawful to call him a man; for he was a doer of wonderful works, a teacher of such men as receive the truth with pleasure. He drew over to him both many of the Jews and many of the Gentiles. He was [the] Christ. And when Pilate, at the suggestion of the principal men amongst us, had condemned him to the cross, those that loved him at the first did not forsake him; for he appeared to them alive again the third day; as the divine prophets had foretold these and ten thousand other wonderful things concerning him. And the tribe of Christians, so named from him, are not extinct at this day."[60]

It is highly likely that this excessively Christianised passage was altered by later Christian writers to enhance their standing in the text, but the mere fact that he is mentioned at all shows at the very least that he existed and that he was enough of an influence on contemporary Judaism for it to matter to Josephus.

I refer to Christianity as a sect because it was not created by Yehoshua himself, but by his disciples. In some ways they diluted his words so severely that they lost most of their value.

Yehoshua should be admired for his wisdom and radical anti-establishment perspectives. The best way to admire one of the finest Jews who ever lived is to tell his story authentically enough that it is relevant to the time he lived in and the realities of his life.

It does not matter if Yehoshua was born of a virgin, what matters is that he grew up as a refugee in a region full of chaos, war and bitter division. He saw the wanton corruption of the Sadducees, the Romans and the Herodian royal family and knew he had to act.

His death on the cross was not some supernatural event, and he did not (in the literal sense) rise again. A man who dies for the poor and mistreated is a hero even if he is not divine. And Yehoshua never claimed divinity of any kind, it was thrust upon his legacy by the opportunists who followed him and used his misery to maintain their own interests.

Rather than repeating the dubious claims of early Church Fathers I will strive to focus on what Jesus was really saying. He spoke and acted like the minor prophets of the latter part of the Tanakh. He repeated the cries of Ezekiel, Micah and Hosea that Israel had lost its way and was putting materialism before G-d.

It is the duty of any G-d fearing Jew to help the poor, to observe the Torah and to fight oppression. Yehoshua rejected the Roman virtues of shallowness, violence and war for a better world, a Kingdom beyond the vanity of humankind.

This does not make him the son of G-d, but it shows us that we are all children of G-d.

Yehoshua's life and death are a lesson to Jews and Gentiles alike, that we must never abandon the weak or forget that to G-d we are all equals.

Yehoshua must be respected as a Jew and his life must be analysed from his entirely Jewish perspective.

Many people of all walks of life seem to have forgotten this. It is not the lesson of one religion or one people, it is the lesson of a man (or deity depending on how you see it) who died for the one thing we can all devote ourselves to. Compassion.

Before discussing the New Testament is must be said that the Gospels and writings of this text were not codified until over a century after the events took place. They were passed down orally among early Christians and a lot of their original contents were lost.

I take to the view of John Crossan who believed that all sources written more than 30 years before or after Yehoshua's death should be viewed sceptically. Since the gospels were written outside of this timeframe, I will discuss them with the caveat that they probably aren't historically accurate or universally relevant.

One of the first things we hear about Yehoshua's life in the gospel of Matthew is that 'Herod' (the New Testament doesn't often specify which Herod they are referring to at any given time) tried to have Yehoshua killed by massacring all children below the age of 2.

"Then Herod, when he saw that he was mocked of the wise men, was exceeding wroth, and sent forth, and slew all the children that were in Bethlehem, and in all the coasts thereof, from two years old and under, according to the time which he had diligently inquired of the wise men. Then was fulfilled that which was spoken by Jeremiah the prophet, saying,

In Rama was there a voice heard, lamentation, and weeping, and great mourning, Rachel weeping for her children, and would not be comforted, because they are not."[61]

I am sceptical that this event happened, and I think it is clear that there are more rational explanations which can be derived from the gospel.

The mention of the prophecy from Jeremiah seems to match the common trend in Matthew of trying to insert Yehoshua into old Jewish texts as a way of showing that he was the true messiah.

The main issue with the notion that Herod slew the innocents is that a claimant to the Davidic line being born would not have been a unique or concerning issue for him. There were so many people who could claim to be related to the Davidic line that it almost deprived that distinction of any meaning.

If it were true, that Herod had killed all children aged 2 or below surely there would be some historical evidence for this?

Another thing that seems to point to it being a contrivance of the narrative is that it is reminiscent of the massacre of the innocents during the time of Moshe.

It is therefore far more likely that Matthew made up this event to represent the Hasmonean purge and to create a link between Yehoshua and the Old Testament as Matthew so often did.

Many of the Hasmonean claimants Herod slew were children so this small alteration is by no means a stretch. The notion of all Hasmoneans under the age of 2 being slain is far more feasible as there weren't nearly as many of these as there were people of the Davidic line.

Since Herod had died in 4CE and Yehoshua was born in 6CE it is probable that Yehoshua's family went to Egypt as political refugees.

My theory regarding this is that they actually left Judea because Joseph was a Pharisee who felt it would be safer to flee the country for political reasons.

Rabbinic training was often hereditary, so it is highly likely that Yehoshua's father Joseph was a Rabbi or at least from a Rabbinic family.

As of yet I can find no direct proof that Joseph sat in the Sanhedrin but considering his storied heritage it is highly possible that he was in the Sanhedrin, and this would explain why Yehoshua was taken to Egypt as an infant.

It would also explain the choice of Egypt, Yehoshua's sympathies for the opinions of the Pharisees, his connections with the Sanhedrin and why Yehoshua spoke multiple languages.

Alexandria was a Jewish city at this time, and it was the chief city for Yeshivot. If Yehoshua was a Rabbi, then being educated in Alexandria would have been the standard.

In modernity we often assume that the use of the term 'Rabbi (teacher)' to describe Yehoshua was some sort of colloquialism when in fact I think that it was a direct description of his profession.

A Rabbi often held a day job which was similar to a family trade, much like Rabbi Hillel Yehoshua was a carpenter by trade and learned this skill from his father Joseph.

This strongly suggests that Yehoshua was a Rabbi because it perfectly aligns with the general prerequisites of being one at the time. It also explains why he was both of a storied heritage and relatively poor, as Rabbis did not earn a wage for their religious work.

The reason I assume Yehoshua's father was a Pharisee will be expounded on later but in summation it is because of Yehoshua's strong belief in religious piety and social justice. His worldview generally aligned with Pharisaic teachings.

Although it must be said that he also shared a lot of his views with the Zealots, the Pharisees were ultimately the group that did the most to help him whereas the Zealots even voted to put him to death.

Yehoshua is known to have spoken Hebrew, Greek and Aramaic as well and considering that the only formal education institutions in Judea were the Yeshivot this points to the fact that Yehoshua at the very least attended the Yeshiva.

It is also pretty unlikely that Yehoshua was born in the town known as Bethlehem. When the Galilee was settled by the people of Judah (southern Israel) they often named towns after the ones in the south.

A town named after Bethlehem 'Bethlehem in the Galilee' happens to sit only a short distance from Yehoshua's hometown of Nazareth. It seems far more likely therefore that he was actually born here rather than in a town many miles to the south of the country which also sat in the Roman controlled province of Judaea.[62]

So, if Yehoshua was in a line of work we were led to believe he wasn't in, and born in a different town to the one we believed, and left his homeland for alternate reasons to the ones we are led to believe then at what point do we begin to accept that Yehoshua and Jesus are so different from each other that it is impossible to reconcile them?

At what point do we accept that the myth is just too far-flung from the reality?

I think that point is now. Even before we venture into the life he led as an adult the differences between fact and fiction are just too great. I am sure someone of the Christian faith would have a different answer but for the purposes of this book I must throw in the towel.

The best I can do is portray reality in the most authentic and engaging way possible in the hopes that for non-Christians this story can enhance their understanding of the world Christianity created.

And for Christians also I hope to bring about a better understanding of the world Yehoshua occupied and how he changed it forever.

What seems to be the case is that Yehoshua was a member of the House of Hillel, but that he held certain radical views of the Zealot party. He was too extreme for the Pharisees and too soft for the Zealots so they both ended up disavowing him to varying degrees.

Often when you try to please multiple groups you end up making them all angry, and as we will observe when it comes to Yehoshua's trial this was the case.

This is a view given tenuous support even by Vatican sources. Father Joseph Sievers wrote at length about Jewish historical sources and how these were entirely essential for a rounded view of Yehoshua's life.

There are several important excerpts from the work of Sievers. The one below explains the significance of analysing Yehoshua by the standards and conditions of his time for a rounded Christian perspective.

> *"It was noted quite a while ago that Judaism and Christianity have a great reluctance in common: fully and openly accepting that Jesus was a Jew. We Christians often create for ourselves an image of a Christ uprooted from his land, from his time, and from his people. Instead for the Jews, for many centuries, Jesus was he in whose name they were persecuted and therefore it was difficult to consider him one of them."[63]*

Sievers is a Catholic Priest which lends legitimacy to the Jewish identity of Yehoshua even from those who would probably derive greater benefit from denying this. He also correctly points out the difficulty of understanding Yehoshua from a Jewish perspective when Christians were largely responsible for oppressing the Jews.

That is another important reason for analysing Yehoshua in this way, because even if people oppressed the Jews in his name, he was still one of us and we have to come to terms with that reality in a healthy and informed way.

Sievers then mentions Schalom Ben-Chorin and Martin Buber in his analysis and quotes both scholars. This excerpt is quoting Sievers' quotation of Ben-Chorin who in turn was quoting Buber so in a sense I am quoting all three at once.

"Even Schalom Ben-Chorin has the same anxiety to promote a better understanding between Jews and Christians. Born and raised in Germany, from 1935 he lives in Jerusalem. He has now written more than twenty books (in German, some also translated in other languages), in which the relationship between Jews and Christians is the fundamental aspect. Above all, he wants to make Christians understand the roots in Judaism. Here we are particularly interested in one of his first books, on the figure of Jesus of Nazareth. The author begins with the presupposition that Jesus was a Jew of his time, to understand - and to rediscover - only in his Jewish context, even if he was an exceptional person.

Ben-Chorin takes from the already famous words of Martin Buber:

"Since my youth I noticed the figure of Jesus as that of my great brother. That Christianity should consider, has considered him and considers him as G-d and Redeemer, has always seemed to me a fact of great serious-ness, that I must try to understand for his love and for my love...My openly brotherly relationship with him always got stronger and got purer more than ever. And for me, it's more certain than ever that he will have an important place in the history of faith in Israel and that this place cannot be circumscribed with any of the usual categories of thought."[64]

In the attempt to place Jesus more precisely in his context, Ben-Chorin affirms:

"In this sense, we believe not to err in letting Jesus be amongst the Pharisees, naturally in the middle of a lower group of opposition. Jesus himself taught like a Rabbi Pharisee, and with a high level of authority, whose excessive emphasis must then be without doubt considered like a kerigmatic tradition"[65]

The best translation of the word 'kerygma' is message, it essentially refers to the teachings of Yehoshua and how he spread these to a wider audience through the revelation of his supposed divinity in the form of parables and miracles.

The fact that Jewish and non-Jewish sources (however different their conclusions may be) all agree that Yehoshua was Jewish and that his teachings came from this Jewish context is a further source of proof for my view that Yehoshua was and is a Jewish figure.

Irrespective of how likely it is that Yehoshua was a Pharisee, it must be said that his views were similar enough to them for it to be fairly easy to argue that he was either inspired by them or trying to appeal to them intellectually.

"Instead, the work of David Flusser is much more different, he is an emeritus professor at the Hebrew University in Jerusalem, and is famous for his works on the Manuscripts of the Dead Sea and other Jewish texts, as well as on the New Testament. His first book on Jesus was a great editorial success, with translations in various languages. In it Flusser attempted to make the figure of Jesus better understandable, he sees Jesus as a representative of genuine Judaism, close to the Pharisees but critical

of him. Flusser argues on two fronts: on the one hand he wants to liberate
Christians from what they consider a skepticism which is too much ex-
plained by the exegists, especially caused by the influence of Bultmann; on
the other side, between the lines, in making certain criticisms on Jesus and
the Pharisees, he also wants to criticize some modern Jewish currents.
Therefore he sees Jesus as an important character not only for his time but
also for our time.[66]

When referencing Flusser Sievers is trying to illustrate the point that whether or not Yehoshua was a Pharisee, he was certainly sympathetic to them, and they were sympathetic back to him with a certain level of healthy criticism.

David Flusser himself directly tried to remind us of how valuable a Jewish context is for understanding Yehoshua.

"we understand the parables of Jesus in the right way only when we con-
sider them belonging to the literary style of the Rabbinical parables."[67]

Yehoshua's style of storytelling and promotion of Jewish apoc-alypticism are oddly reminiscent of the latter apocryphal books of the Tanakh.

The theme of Tikvah (hope) in the Book of Ezekiel is similar to Yehoshua's beliefs. This excerpt from the book of Ezekiel is a metaphor for the resurrection of Israel as an independent state and the perseverance of the Jewish people.

"The hand of the Lord was on me, and he brought me out by the Spirit of
the Lord and set me in the middle of a valley; it was full of bones. He led
me back and forth among them, and I saw a great many bones on the

floor of the valley, bones that were very dry. He asked me, "Son of man, can these bones live?"

I said, "Sovereign Lord, you alone know."

Then he said to me, "Prophesy to these bones and say to them, 'Dry bones, hear the word of the Lord! This is what the Sovereign Lord says to these bones: I will make breath enter you, and you will come to life. I will attach tendons to you and make flesh come upon you and cover you with skin; I will put breath in you, and you will come to life. Then you will know that I am the Lord.'"

So I prophesied as I was commanded. And as I was prophesying, there was a noise, a rattling sound, and the bones came together, bone to bone. I looked, and tendons and flesh appeared on them and skin covered them, but there was no breath in them.

Then he said to me, "Prophesy to the breath; prophesy, son of man, and say to it, 'This is what the Sovereign Lord says: Come, breath, from the four winds and breathe into these slain, that they may live.'" So I prophesied as he commanded me, and breath entered them; they came to life and stood up on their feet—a vast army.

Then he said to me: "Son of man, these bones are the people of Israel. They say, 'Our bones are dried up and our hope is gone; we are cut off.' Therefore prophesy and say to them: 'This is what the Sovereign Lord says: My people, I am going to open your graves and bring you up from them; I will bring you back to the land of Israel. Then you, my people, will know that I am the Lord, when I open your graves and bring you up from them.

I will put my Spirit in you and you will live, and I will settle you in your own land. Then you will know that I the Lord have spoken, and I have done it, declares the Lord."[68]

The key difference between this text and the New Testament excerpt below is that this one focusses on the theme of nationalism whilst the other is attempting to prove the divinity of Yehoshua.

This small difference in direction does not detract from the fact that Yehoshua's words and actions often borrow from an older tradition.

In the time of Ezekiel (similarly to Yehoshua) the Jews were being oppressed by a foreign occupier and faced exile. In a similar context it is almost as if Yehoshua has hearkened back to Ezekiel's mission. In a time of hopelessness Yehoshua needed to retell Ezekiel's story.

This excerpt is from the Gospel according to John and seems very reminiscent of the emotive theme of hope and resurrection that was observed in the previous one.

"Now a man named Lazarus was sick. He was from Bethany, the village of Mary and her sister Martha. (This Mary, whose brother Lazarus now lay sick, was the same one who poured perfume on the Lord and wiped his feet with her hair.) So the sisters sent word to Jesus, "Lord, the one you love is sick."

When he heard this, Jesus said, "This sickness will not end in death. No, it is for G-d's glory so that G-d's Son may be glorified through it." Now Jesus loved Martha and her sister and Lazarus. So when he heard that Lazarus was sick, he stayed where he was two more days, and then he said to his disciples, "Let us go back to Judea."

"But Rabbi," they said, "a short while ago the Jews there tried to stone you, and yet you are going back?"

Jesus answered, "Are there not twelve hours of daylight? Anyone who walks in the daytime will not stumble, for they see by this world's light. It is when a person walks at night that they stumble, for they have no light."

After he had said this, he went on to tell them, "Our friend Lazarus has fallen asleep; but I am going there to wake him up."

His disciples replied, "Lord, if he sleeps, he will get better." Jesus had been speaking of his death, but his disciples thought he meant natural sleep.

So then he told them plainly, "Lazarus is dead, and for your sake I am glad I was not there, so that you may believe. But let us go to him."

Then Thomas (also known as Didymus) said to the rest of the disciples, "Let us also go, that we may die with him."

Jesus Comforts the Sisters of Lazarus

On his arrival, Jesus found that Lazarus had already been in the tomb for four days. Now Bethany was less than two miles from Jerusalem, and many Jews had come to Martha and Mary to comfort them in the loss of their brother. When Martha heard that Jesus was coming, she went out to meet him, but Mary stayed at home.

"Lord," Martha said to Jesus, "if you had been here, my brother would not *have died. But I know that even now G-d will give you whatever you ask."*

Jesus said to her, "Your brother will rise again."

Martha answered, "I know he will rise again in the resurrection at the last day."

Jesus said to her, "I am the resurrection and the life. The one who believes in me will live, even though they die; and whoever lives by believing in me will never die. Do you believe this?"
"Yes, Lord," she replied, "I believe that you are the Messiah, the Son of G-d, who is to come into the world."

After she had said this, she went back and called her sister Mary aside. "The Teacher is here," she said, "and is asking for you." When Mary heard this, she got up quickly and went to him. Now Jesus had not yet entered the village, but was still at the place where Martha had met him. When the Jews who had been with Mary in the house, comforting her, noticed how quickly she got up and went out, they followed her, supposing she was going to the tomb to mourn there.

When Mary reached the place where Jesus was and saw him, she fell at his feet and said, "Lord, if you had been here, my brother would not have died."

When Jesus saw her weeping, and the Jews who had come along with her also weeping, he was deeply moved in spirit and troubled. "Where have you laid him?" he asked.

"Come and see, Lord," they replied.

Jesus wept.

Then the Jews said, "See how he loved him!"

But some of them said, "Could not he who opened the eyes of the blind man have kept this man from dying?"

Jesus Raises Lazarus From the Dead

Jesus, once more deeply moved, came to the tomb. It was a cave with a stone laid across the entrance.

"Take away the stone," he said.

"But, Lord," said Martha, the sister of the dead man, "by this time there is a bad odor, for he has been there four days."

Then Jesus said, "Did I not tell you that if you believe, you will see the glory of G-d?"

So they took away the stone. Then Jesus looked up and said, "Father, I thank you that you have heard me. I knew that you always hear me, but I said this for the benefit of the people standing here, that they may believe that you sent me."

When he had said this, Jesus called in a loud voice, "Lazarus, come out!"

The dead man came out, his hands and feet wrapped with strips of linen, and a cloth around his face.

Jesus said to them, "Take off the grave clothes and let him go."[69]

The similarity of the themes of these passages is that both show the Lord resurrecting the dead (and in doing so breaking the laws of nature) for the sake of illustrating that there is always hope and that faith in G-d is stronger than death.

Yehoshua evidently borrowed this intensely Jewish view for himself because he lived and taught at a time when the story of the valley of dry bones would have had serious weight and emotional meaning for people (as it does even today).

Christian antisemitism ultimately makes no sense because of this. More often than not Jews are blamed and derided for not accepting the divinity of Yehoshua, yet the Christians evoke the status of Yehoshua as a Jew and attempt to connect him to the Old Testament as much as possible.

It is impossible to have it both ways. To reject Judaism is to reject Yehoshua and every last thing he stood for and died for.

An antisemite who has an enmity for the Jews must also have hatred for Christianity as the messiah antisemitic Christians claim to support was Jewish.

On the topic of borrowing from the Jewish tradition there is also great evidence of Yehoshua's Pharisaic leanings in the Gospel of Luke.

The Boy Jesus at the Temple

"Every year Jesus' parents went to Jerusalem for the Festival of the Passover. When he was twelve years old, they went up to the festival,

according to the custom. After the festival was over, while his parents were returning home, the boy Jesus stayed behind in Jerusalem, but they were unaware of it. Thinking he was in their company, they traveled on for a day. Then they began looking for him among their relatives and friends. When they did not find him, they went back to Jerusalem to look for him. After three days they found him in the temple courts, sitting among the teachers, listening to them and asking them questions. Everyone who heard him was amazed at his understanding and his answers. When his parents saw him, they were astonished. His mother said to him, "Son, why have you treated us like this? Your father and I have been anxiously searching for you."

"Why were you searching for me?" he asked. "Didn't you know I had to be in my Father's house?" But they did not understand what he was saying to them.

Then he went down to Nazareth with them and was obedient to them. But his mother treasured all these things in her heart. And Jesus grew in wisdom and stature, and in favor with G-d and man."

It is suggested in this passage that Yehoshua went to the temple and was known and respected by the Pharisees even at a young age. Most use this to show his divinity and the fact that he was said to be wiser than anyone else.

I see a far simpler and less supernatural theme in this passage. Here it is very possible that he could have met Rabbi Hillel or at least been acquainted with his teachings.

A Christian probably wouldn't want to admit that Yehoshua learned something from someone else, but in this case, it is probable that Yehoshua's ideas were shaped at the temple, and that this passage from Luke is a subtle implication of this.

There are also other parts of the New Testament which make differing claims. Matthew promotes the view that Yehoshua was actually from the Zealot party.

"Do not suppose that I have come to bring peace to the earth. I did not come to bring peace, but a sword. For I have come to turn a man against his father, a daughter against her mother, a daughter-in-law against her mother-in-law—a man's enemies will be the members of his own household."[70]

The violence of this imagery seems more to align with the Zealot position and in my view is an attempt to spur the Jews on in open revolt against the Romans and their Jewish allies.

When he says that he is there to turn people against their relatives it is a metaphor for a type of radicalism not too dissimilar to that of Judas of Gamala.

That is, Yehoshua is making an attempt to show that the preservation of Jewish identity may require the use of violence.

This is ultimately the main point of divergence between Yehoshua and the Pharisees, the Pharisees refused to fight back and saw the Zealots as extremists whilst Yehoshua accepted their point (that Rome needed to be removed even if that meant turning against those who refused to join in that struggle).

Apart from a contempt for Rome Yehoshua also endorsed the views of Davidic messianism and Jewish apocalypticism which the Zealots held.

In contrast to this Yehoshua also supported 'turning the other cheek' and 'loving your neighbour as yourself' which is far more connected to Hillel's philosophy.

In many ways Yehoshua was trying to mend a rift between two sides he saw deep problems with. The Zealots for him were too violent whilst the Pharisees were too accepting of the Romans.

This can feel contradictory and that is probably because he was trying to create balance in the face of endless division.

In adulthood Yehoshua was baptised in the River Jordan by John the Baptist and from then on went about his preaching.

II

A Theory Regarding John the Baptist

As I have already mentioned John the Baptist began preaching and cleansing people in the river Jordan in opposition to the incestuous and illegal nature of Antipas' marriage to Herodias.

The Baptist was later arrested and killed; his head was allegedly taken to Herodias' daughter Salome on a platter.

The Christian view is that he was the cousin of Yehoshua and that he Baptised him in the river Jordan.

The theory I would put forward is that John was a Jewish religious figure in his own right, and that when he met Yehoshua they formed an alliance of sorts.

Rather than being his cousin he was simply a man who largely shared Yehoshua's worldview and admired him. Together they crafted an image for their new movement and built it up with the masses.

In the Galilee the Baptist continued to preach for Yehoshua long after he had died which at least implies that he was involved in the political-religious issues of the time before Yehoshua's rise.

He didn't necessarily need Yehoshua which implies that he had a more general set of principles which existed independently of his friend.

John shared with Yehoshua a belief that the lechery and moral villainy of the Herodians would precede the coming of the messiah.

By Jewish standards a messiah was a human being who brought liberty to the Jewish people rather than the son of G-d.

Yehoshua never referred to himself as the son of G-d or as the messiah, instead he simply preached a healthy mix of Pharisaic religious morality and social justice with the plucky, Davidic radicalism of the Zealots.

In a lot of ways, the John-Yehoshua axis was the best of both traditions and the two worked together to their mutual benefit.

The idea that they were somehow related or that they were destined to be united forgets just how resourceful and intellectually in-synch they ended up being when they met.

A lot of Yehoshua's personal style and method of gathering supporters was arguably derived from what he learned from the more established John the Baptist.

John was a more localised version of Yehoshua, and the figure of 'Jesus' was probably an amalgamation of many different streams of thought at the time.

III

Yehoshua's Downfall

The fall of Yehoshua began with the rise of Pilate. In 30CE Pontius Pilate made Jerusalem the new Roman headquarters. To justify moving his troops to Jerusalem Pilate made the argument that they were only there to make winter quarters.

This argument was obviously a contrivance because the previous Roman stronghold of Caesarea was much warmer in winter than Jerusalem, moving the troops to the Capital was more likely a show of dominance and a way of avoiding uprisings.

He capitalised on his overwhelming control by having the Sanhedrin move its place of meeting from the temple complex to the Royal Stoa.

As this was a morally lax place being forced to meet in the marketplace was a humiliation for the Sanhedrin and diluted the religious sanctity of their work. As well as this Pilate now had total power over the body, non-Jews could enter the marketplace, so the Sanhedrin was no longer safe from bribery and threats.

If Pilate wanted to, he could send troops in and stop their meetings, he held a knife over their heads each time they made a decision, so they were forced to walk in lock step with what the Romans wanted.

This is the main reason I blame Rome for the death of Yehoshua, because after this point Rome called the shots in all affairs related to the Sanhedrin and it became nothing but a puppet of Roman power.

Beyond all of the small details that show Rome's responsibility this fact alone proves it. The Romans made all the real decisions, even if the Sanhedrin had decided in good faith to kill Yehoshua it was the Romans who did it.

When Yehoshua saw the temple (in 33CE) in its state of desecration he was furious as is recounted in the Gospel of Mark.

The Cleansing of the Temple

"On reaching Jerusalem, Jesus entered the temple courts and began driving out those who were buying and selling there. He overturned the tables of the money changers and the benches of those selling doves, and would not allow anyone to carry merchandise through the temple courts. And as he taught them, he said, "Is it not written: 'My house will be called a house of prayer for all nations'? But you have made it 'a den of robbers.'" The chief priests and the teachers of the law heard this and began looking for a way to kill him, for they feared him, because the whole crowd was amazed at his teaching. When evening came, Jesus and his disciples went out of the city."[1]

The flipping of the market stalls was an act of rebellion against a society and government which favoured money above people and piety. The corruption of the temple with money represented what many saw as the death of Judaism's soul.

The temple had been robbed of its status as a Holy place and for the reasons mentioned earlier regarding the foreign Jewry it had become a centre of commerce.

In Yehoshua's mind by having a marketplace in the temple the Jews were blaspheming and ignoring their faith.

It is understandable that the Jews created a marketplace in the temple considering the difficulties surrounding diaspora Jews coming for pilgrimage festivals, but it was more complicated than the temple itself and it was about a wider rejection of Jewish values for shallow Roman ones.

I would posit that this was part of a larger movement in Judaism that crossed multiple parties and ethnic groups. The belief in a religious restoration of Judaism through a radical political revolution was taken to its extremes by Yehoshua.

He believed that wealth was a sin, and that the poor should be exalted above all others. He saw a world order that repulsed him and yearned to return Israel to being a truly 'Holy land'.

I will refer to this as 'Jewish Redistributionism'. I refrain from using the words Communism or Socialism because Yehoshua's political views were not quite as refined or specific as the conditions of today, so using terms packed with preconceptions is not appropriate.

Communism developed as a result of the material conditions of the modern world, Yehoshua's conditions were very different, and he would probably have had a very different perception of what redistributionism means.

But the basic principles are the same. Yehoshua combined an intense, anti-materialist religiosity with a Socialistic belief in the economic rights of people.

His key principles are as follows and are distinguished from the principles of Socialism in important ways.

I- The poor must be preserved and dignified through a fair distribution of wealth

II- All people are equal in the eyes of G-d

III- Financial greed and economic inequality inherently go against the principles of the Jewish faith

Socialism is more specific to the relationship between workers and bosses and puts far more focus on Marx's notion of dialectical materialism which sets it apart from Yehoshua's ethos.

Yehoshua's belief in an afterlife paired with a lack of importance put into the material world goes fundamentally against the Marxist view that material conditions influence political changes and public opinion more than movements of thoughts and ideas.

The point of mentioning this is that it shows that Yehoshua was far more radical than a lot of his modern followers realise, and that ultimately economic equality was what he was fighting against.

To call yourself a Christian and condone poverty therefore is to forget the mistakes of the Judean authorities and to forget the principles which Yehoshua died to defend.

Yehoshua's belief in Jewish Redistributionism is often forgotten. I see him far more in this context than in a religious one, obviously this would be different for a Christian but as Joseph Sievers proved it is possible to use a shared contextual analysis to come to differing conclusions.

And this economic agenda and the symbolism of the temple becoming a marketplace is some of the most essential context we have.

When he did this, he caught the ire of the Romans and their puppets. They soon began the process which would ultimately kill him. When Antipas called for his death, the Pharisees warned him in advance as is recounted in the gospel according to Luke.

Jesus' Sorrow for Jerusalem

"At that time some Pharisees came to Jesus and said to him, "Leave this place and go somewhere else. Herod wants to kill you."

He replied, "Go tell that vixen, 'I will keep on driving out demons and healing people today and tomorrow, and on the third day I will reach my goal.' In any case, I must press on today and tomorrow and the next day— for surely no prophet can die outside Jerusalem!

"Jerusalem, Jerusalem, you who kill the prophets and stone those sent to you, how often I have longed to gather your children together, as a hen gathers her chicks under her wings, and you were not willing. Look, your house is left to you desolate. I tell you, you will not see me again until you say, 'Blessed is he who comes in the name of the Lord.'"[72]

Though in most translations the word Yehoshua uses to describe Antipas is 'fox' I choose to call him a vixen in line with the fact that the word in the original text is feminine.

The Pharisees warned Yehoshua which clearly shows that at the very least they didn't want him to die.

Luke is the only one who mentions this. I think this is because unlike the Jewish disciples Luke had no incentive or desire to suppress the Jewish roots of Yehoshua. The Christian Church wanted to rid itself of any associations with the Jewish faith and Saul of

Tarsus (who will be discussed later) was the primary architect of the blanket of revisionism which was thrown over Yehoshua.

Pilate arrested Yehoshua and sent him to the court of Antipas. It was easier to have someone else deal with it and incur the blame. But he was sent back. At this stage Pilate probably could have released him with a slap on the wrist, and frankly it would have been much easier to do.

This fact seems to contradict the passage in Matthew which claims that Pilate thought Yehoshua was innocent.

> *"When Pilate saw that he was getting nowhere, but that instead an uproar was starting, he took water and washed his hands in front of the crowd. "I am innocent of this man's blood," he said. "It is your responsibility!"*[73]

Pilate had to proactively have Yehoshua tried at great inconvenience in a situation where letting him go free probably would have been simpler. Claiming therefore that he was innocent of this crime seems remiss.

It is likely then that later Roman Christians wanted to portray a Roman official in a good light by removing references to his guilt and trying to vindicate his legacy.

More importantly Pilate was often known to intervene in the affairs of the Jews and tried to increase his power such as the example of the Sanhedrin, so it's almost out of character for him to suddenly consider a man who railed against Roman authority as 'innocent'.

It was far more in Pilate's character to use brutal repression and violence; this points to his complicity and guilt more than anything else.

Even if this weren't true, he still held the power, and there is only a slim difference between giving the order and doing the deed yourself. Guilt is guilt, no matter how many times you 'wash your hands' of it.

It is clear that Yehoshua was well-known and influential in his time. There is no smoke without a fire. There is no need to crucify a man who isn't important. Even to the Romans he was certainly a figure of some significance, albeit less than we attribute to Yehoshua today.

Cornelius Tacitus for instance refers to him in the Annals and agrees that he was the central figure for Christianity and that Pontius Pilate was responsible for his death.

> *"Nero fastened the guilt and inflicted the most exquisite tortures on a class hated for their abominations, called Christians by the populace. Christus, from whom the name had its origin, suffered the extreme penalty during the reign of Tiberius at the hands of one of our procurators, Pontius Pilatus, and a most mischievous superstition, thus checked for the moment, again broke out not only in Judæa, the first source of the evil, but even in Rome, where all things hideous and shameful from every part of the world find their centre and become popular."[74]*

The fact that Pilate is referred to as responsible for Yehoshua's death in a text written only decades after his death is also good evidence that Pilate was actually to blame. In the 120sCE Christianity was a minority religion and the Roman state actively persecuted Christians, there was therefore a certain pride in declaring Roman responsibility for Yehoshua's murder.

It was only later during the rise of Christianity as the main religion of the Roman empire that Constantine and the early Church fathers decided that they wanted to disassociate Rome with the death of Yehoshua.

The Romans did not want to hold on to their guilt and decided to instead project it onto the Jews.

Alternatively, Robert E. Van Voorst argued that Christian scribes altered the text of Tacitus to demonise the ancient Romans and emphasise the evil characterisation of Nero.[75]

In this sense it is possible that Tactius' lack of sympathy for the Christians is a product of the Christians themselves in an effort to be portrayed more as victims.

This still makes a good link to Roman Christian revisionism of their Christian-persecuting past because the early Church Fathers often wanted to portray themselves as victims of oppression rather than as the oppressors to extricate themselves from the guilt of their Roman past.

They wanted to avoid the inconvenient truth that they had killed Yehoshua by blaming others and shifting the blame onto caricatures which were easier to hate. By making Tacitus into a caricature, they made him far easier to fear and loathe, they could make themselves the martyrs of the story. In the past they had been martyrs but there was a point when they had control over most of the known world and it became much harder to make the case that they were still the victims.

St. Augustine of Hippo for instance was from a prominent Italian family who had settled in the Berber regions of North Africa (modern Algeria). He was born with the name Aurelius Augustinus. This Christian theologian had to spend his life living in a state and being from an ancestral line which was responsible for the death of Yehoshua.

Augustine was highly influential in the evolution of post-Constantinian Christianity. In a sense he was trying to marry the reality of Roman dominance with the unfortunate reality that they had killed Yehoshua.

The paradox of a Roman believing in Christianity had to be resolved, and the only way it could be fixed was by burying the truth and ignoring that which wouldn't fit in the hole they dug.

If you can't solve a problem, then at least you can pretend it isn't there. And that was exactly what Constantine the Great, and the Christian establishment chose to do.

Over time the Christian faith and the Romans became one in the same. Eventually the Catholic Church became an entirely Roman institution and even long after the Romans were extinguished in 476CE Roman symbols were preserved through the Church and completely merged with them.

The Greek-speaking Jew's religion adopted the use of Latin and had its chief seat of power in Rome. Even in death Yehoshua couldn't stop the Romans from pillaging all that he had and was.

The most powerless man in the world became a branding tool for the powerful. The man who fought the Roman establishment became a tool by which the same men of authority controlled the very people Yehoshua tried to free.

Now I will talk of the trial itself.

Biblical sources conflict on the exact events of the trial but they more or less agree on the basic events. Yehoshua was arrested after a final meal with his disciples, taken to the house of the High Priest and when he was being questioned, he was largely unresponsive.

"But Jesus remained silent and gave no answer.

Again the high priest asked him, "Are you the Messiah, the Son of the Blessed One?"

"I am," said Jesus. "And you will see the Son of Man sitting at the right hand of the Mighty One and coming on the clouds of heaven."

The high priest tore his clothes. "Why do we need any more witnesses?" he asked. "You have heard the blasphemy. What do you think?"

They all condemned him as worthy of death. Then some began to spit at him; they blindfolded him, struck him with their fists, and said, "Prophesy!" And the guards took him and beat him."[76]

Many cite this as proof that Yehoshua saw himself as the son of G-d, but I have two arguments which go against this. The first is that this was not written by Yehoshua himself and could easily have been altered later by his disciples to enhance his credentials and demonise the Sanhedrin.

The second argument is simply that he could have been using the term 'son of man' in a purely poetic way. Claiming to be a son of G-d does not necessarily imply that you are the sole son of G-d or that you're a divine being.

These characteristics were applied to him later by his servants and those who worshiped him.

Christianity is a religion made for Yehoshua, not by him. It is also important to remember that the Messiah was not considered divine by the Jews.

Cyrus the Great of Persia and Alexander the Great of Macedon had both been referred to as Messiah so assuming that he was using the word by its modern accepted definition is a bit of a stretch.

I am also not convinced that the questioning was as brutal as it is portrayed to be. This is because the Hillelist faction of the Pharisees voted to acquit him and even the Nasi Gamliel supported him.

If the dominant faction of the Sanhedrin supported him then at the very least, there would be some healthy debate in the chamber. The sympathetic voices aren't mentioned because the Christian sources knew that portraying the Jews in a bad light would promote the view that Christianity needed to cut itself off from its Jewish origins.

Much like the trial of Mariamne it is a strong possibility that the members of the Sanhedrin were threatened by the authorities to vote against the defendant. Only instead of Herod Pilate was the one doing the threatening.

Pilate had a record of using violence to get what he wanted. When he had previously put up the imperial regalia in Jerusalem, he offended the people so greatly that they swarmed his home. He then threatened them by having his men draw their swords, which did little to stop the Jews in their fervour.[77]

The implication of most narratives about the death of Yehoshua is that the Romans were less violent or otherwise less concerned than the Jews themselves, which when compared to Pilate's violent tendencies as governor doesn't seem to hold up.

The Zealots, the House of Shammai and the Sadducees voted to kill Yehoshua, but the Nasi Gamliel and the House of Hillel voted to free him.

He was then taken to the other side of the city and crucified. There is little point in recounting this event in detail, seeing as it is fairly well known and has become the central symbolic event of Christian worship.

Pilate offered the crowd a choice of which man they could release from execution. Christian sources imply that he had hoped they would release Yehoshua.

"Now it was the governor's custom at the festival to release a prisoner chosen by the crowd. At that time they had a well-known prisoner whose name was Jesus Barabbas. So when the crowd had gathered, Pilate asked them, "Which one do you want me to release to you: Jesus Barabbas, or Jesus who is called the Messiah?" For he knew it was out of self-interest that they had handed Jesus over to him.

While Pilate was sitting on the judge's seat, his wife sent him this message: "Don't have anything to do with that innocent man, for I have suffered a great deal today in a dream because of him."
But the chief priests and the elders persuaded the crowd to ask for Barabbas and to have Jesus executed.

"Which of the two do you want me to release to you?" asked the governor.

"Barabbas," they answered."[78]

My view is that Barabbas was a Zealot rebel, and that the crowd chose to release him instead of Yehoshua because Yehoshua was more moderate and less anti-Roman than his Zealot counterparts.

Yehoshua wasn't as extreme as a Zealot so in the political climate of ancient Judaea he probably would have seemed too soft.

In other words, they thought freeing Barabbas would do more for the Jewish liberation movement than Yehoshua would.

The fact that there seems to have been a slate of arrests made against anti-Roman rebels at this time seems to corroborate my view.

This is of course an inference, so it must be taken in a purely speculative way. After he was condemned, Yehoshua was flogged and locked in a cell before being taken to the place of his doom outside the walls of Jerusalem.

When he arrived at Golgotha Yehoshua was offered wine which he refused, and he was nailed to the cross and hauled up between two convicts.

Some have suggested that the convicts in question were other Jewish rebels, which would make sense considering the fact that Barabbas too had been arrested for a similar crime.[79]

By crucifying this assortment of rebels Rome was making an example of Yehoshua and the Zealots, who probably held enough views in common to be considered part of the same anti-Roman problem.

It is also important to emphasize that crucifixion was not a special form of execution, it was not reserved for particularly harsh or rare offences, and it was used quite frequently.

Although it holds symbolic importance today the Romans used crucifixion for a range of things. They even had an annual ceremony where they had their dogs crucified because they had failed to rouse Rome's defenders when the city was sacked by the Gauls in 390BCE.

This is not to say that it was anything short of a horrific way to die, just that it was far more common in Roman society than many would assume.

He was nailed to the Cross and died on it in 33CE. The Christian narrative continues after this but mine will not delve into notions of resurrection and superstition as these things are descriptions of events attributed to Yehoshua, not of who he was.

From the time Yehoshua died a culture of antisemitism developed regarding the crucifixion.

To offset their guilt the Romans blamed a small ethno-religious group in their empire, they blamed the Jews because the Jews were an easy target.

The canard that Yehoshua was killed by the Jews has had serious consequences, and many still believe it despite the evidence I have laid out because it gives them an easy excuse to blame anyone but themselves.

The truth of the matter is that Yehoshua was tried in a Roman-controlled court and crucified by the Roman authorities, to blame anyone else is simply an illustration of how delusional and unhistorical the conversation around Yehoshua's life has become.

The people Yehoshua advocated for, the people he fought to protect and free were the Jews, he was a Jew and every meaningful contribution he made to life, culture and philosophy is derived entirely from the Jewish tradition.

I do not blame Yehoshua for what his followers did with his legacy, but I do blame his Church. I will now discuss how his disciples ruinously altered his legacy for their personal advantage.

IV

A Tainted Legacy

After Yehoshua met his end his disciples continued his preaching, albeit with alterations.

These alterations would have undoubtedly shocked Yehoshua.

The Fulfillment of the Law

""Do not think that I have come to abolish the Law or the Prophets; I have not come to abolish them but to fulfill them."[80]

There it is. A direct statement from the man himself of his unwavering view that Jewish law was not to be changed by himself or his servants.

It was Peter, the very man who denied Yehoshua three times who started these changes. After assuming the leadership of the early Church Peter made the momentous decision to remove Kashrut from the law of the Christians.

In 38CE in the city of Jaffa Peter removed the requirement to observe Kosher eating, and never again would the Christians return to this law. The largely Jewish followers of the new Church kept the trappings of their identity, but as it spread and changed over time, they abandoned Kashrut in practice as well as in principle.

Peter's Vision

"About noon the following day as they were on their journey and approaching the city, Peter went up on the roof to pray. He became hungry and wanted something to eat, and while the meal was being prepared, he fell into a trance. He saw heaven opened and something like a large sheet being let down to earth by its four corners. It contained all kinds of four-footed animals, as well as reptiles and birds.

Then a voice told him, "Get up, Peter. Kill and eat."

"Surely not, Lord!" Peter replied. "I have never eaten anything impure or unclean."

The voice spoke to him a second time, "Do not call anything impure that G-d has made clean."[81]

Peter was a Jew and would have recognised the need to maintain Kosher eating rules, but this passage from Acts is often used as a justification for eating non-Kosher foods.

The Christian justification for this change boils down to two things. The first is that because Yehoshua died on the Cross, he created a new covenant with G-d. This means that Christians are no longer bound by Kashrut. The second argument is that no creature G-d created could truly be 'unclean' and not eating certain creatures implies that G-d's creation has dirty elements.

Irrespective of how you view the utility of Kashrut it is still the case that this abandonment of Jewish law went against what Yehoshua said in the book of Matthew, and it ultimately made Christianity drift so far from its roots that it lost its way altogether.

There was a man other than Peter who did far more for this anti-Jewish movement in the early Christian Church. Paul.

Among the Zealots in the Sanhedrin was Saul of Tarsus, who in his early days viciously derided and persecuted the Christians.

"Then Paul said: "I am a Jew, born in Tarsus of Cilicia, but brought up in this city. I studied under Gamaliel and was thoroughly trained in the law of our ancestors. I was just as zealous for G-d as any of you are today. I persecuted the followers of this Way to their death, arresting both men and women and throwing them into prison, as the high priest and all the Council can themselves testify. I even obtained letters from them to their associates in Damascus, and went there to bring these people as prisoners to Jerusalem to be punished."[82]

I suggest that Saul (Paul) was from the Zealot party because although he studied under Gamliel which implies that he sat in the Sanhedrin he was anti-Christian which would place him naturally with the Zealots.

I am sure that his later conversion to the Christian faith was valid and genuine, but it also goes to show just how changeable and opportunistic the apostle Paul was.

Paul was born a Jew, but he ended up doing more to distance Christianity from Judaism than anyone else. The primary reason for this was that the best audience for the early Church Fathers was the Greek one.

Because the Greeks had a very different cultural context an excessive focus on Jewish themes and rituals would have alienated the Greeks.

Greeks believed in materialism, mysticism, a very black-and-white afterlife and saw Jewish culture in a negative light. The Greeks wouldn't have understood the idea of a limited afterlife, nor would they have accepted circumcision due to their view that the male form was in some way sacred.

The Greeks also didn't share a belief in Jewish eschatology. They didn't understand the notion of the messiah coming to earth and triggering the apocalypse, Paul had to cater to these people in his Epistles (letters) by saying things that made more sense from a gentile's perspective. To do this he aggressively Hellenized the Christian faith to the point that it only really relied on its Jewish roots to maintain a sense of continuity and consistency.

The Jewish faith was well established and internally consistent in such a way that it was a useful foundation stone on which a new, more agile religion could be built. The chief proof of this is that Islam copied Judaism's notes in much the same ways as the Christians did.

The Hellenization of Yehoshua required three key changes which Paul went implementing.

I-Removal of Jewish rituals and imagery
II-Fetishization of death and the afterlife
III-The abandonment of Jewish eschatology

The new Christian Church couldn't reconcile Yehoshua's view that the apocalypse was coming imminently so they simply avoided the question and washed it away. As Hermann Reimarus posited, they pretended Yehoshua had always planned on delaying his return because they didn't want to go back to being fishermen.[83]

They now had a new religion which was versatile, could be applied to other nations and which had no expiration date of relevance. Most messianic claimants lost their credibility after they failed to start the messianic age and achieve the goals of the messiah, but with the alterations the disciples made to Yehoshua's views on Jewish eschatology they really did resurrect him, albeit as a zombified figure which they used for acts of self-advancement.

That is to say, the real meaning of Yehoshua's resurrection from death can be found in the fact that his words and likeness were used by his followers to continue his work.

The best metaphor I can come up with is that Yehoshua's figurative body was manipulated like weekend at Bernie's. His disciples picked up his corpse and pretended that it was alive to convince people that Christianity was the product of Yehoshua and that Christian teachings came from him rather than them being the ones deciding on the direction of the movement.

Not only did Paul kill Yehoshua, but he also ended up killing his legacy as well.

Eventually the efforts of Peter and Paul were successful enough for Judaism and Christianity to entirely split off from each other and even enter conflict.

The main reason they airbrushed Yehoshua after he died was because he believed in Jewish eschatology and therefore thought the apocalypse would come imminently after the messiah returned, the only way to make sense of this in the context of Yehoshua not bringing about the end times was to conveniently ignore it and simply say 'he'll come back again'.

This cheap escape from inconsistency seems to have largely taken away the importance of the issue, but I happen to think that it is a serious piece of evidence that Yehoshua was not the Jewish messiah. The religion that was created after Yehoshua died is so remote and alien from the Judaism he supported that it has in my opinion stopped speaking for Yehoshua.

The main difference between Christianity and Judaism is that when Judaism changed over time it did so with the preservation of a core ethos and worldview, Christianity changed far faster and was far more willing to conform to whatever position granted it more support.

Evangelism was what made the Christians as successful as they are, but it also condemned the Christian faith to an eternity of changeability. Eventually it changed so much that it lost the ideas it was really trying to put forward.

Through the fetishization of death Christianity has lost the vibrant love for life that Judaism embodies. Jews know the limits of life and the inevitability that everything G-d creates must come to an end. With this knowledge Jews live life as though it can only happen once.

As well as this Judaism seeks to healthily punish people in life rather than assuming it will be taken care of in death. Grief and wrath therefore are not unhealthily corrupted by the idea that the material world has no real meaning, but rather Jews remember that G-d is with them even in their worst moments.

Jews can experience tragedy and rise above it, rather than plugging their ears with 'eternal life' and 'heaven'.

This is the quintessential difference between Jewish and Christian eschatological views. Jews live in the real world. Yehoshua lived in the real world and wanted to flip it upside down with socio-economic radicalism.

This is not to say that optimism is a bad thing, or that Christians are naïve. Just that their perceptions of justice, the Law and death are utterly remote from their Jewish origins. The Christians take on a more Hellenistic, spiritual view of reality. This is another way in which Christianity takes the form of a sect, by building on a moral and religious framework set up by others.

As a matter of fact, I would argue that Jesus was the least Christian man who ever lived. If he were confronted with Right-Wing Republicans in America or 17th Century witch hunters in Salem, he would be mortified and repulsed.

If he walked into the Vatican and saw what became of his teachings Yehoshua would probably be just as angry as he was with the Romans in his own lifetime, he would rail against corruption and authority.

Making a Jewish Redistributionist rebel the central figure of a religion which aims to control the masses inherently leads all Christian arguments into the same vat of inconsistency and irrelevance. Ultimately, to believe in Christianity you have to view Yehoshua in such a severely warped way that you lose his character and nature entirely.

Some have been more successful in rehabilitating Christianity than others, but this fundamental problem is and remains the central reason that I reject Christianity. You can cover a cracked plate in gold, and it's still cracked.

In writing this I have aimed to reassess Yehoshua's legacy and at the very least bring to light the Jewish perspective on a Jewish man.

He may not have been the messiah, but he was worthy of much of his praise.

8

Chapter 8- The Origins
of Herod Agrippa

Marcus Julius Agrippa was born in 11BCE as the son of Prince
Aristobulus, making him an heir to both the Herodian and Hasmonean dynasties.

He was sent by his grandfather Herod the Great to live in Rome
and be educated there. Once his grandfather died (and since none
of his scheming aunts and uncles wanted him to return to Judaea)
he fell under the personal care first of Emperor Augustus and then
his successor Tiberius.

Before I can go in any further depth regarding Agrippa, I must
expound on the context of Roman imperial politics at this time.

The Roman monarchy was an equal to the Judean one in the
sense that it functioned as a revolving door of political intrigue and
assassinations which put the stability of the entire state at risk but
paradoxically only seemed to make it stronger.

Augustus was first married to Claudia, who he divorced soon
after the wedding due to political disputes with her mother Fulvia.

His second wife was Scribonia with whom he had a single daughter, Julia the elder. In fact, he found his first wife so disagreeable that he divorced her on the very same day their daughter was born.[84]

His third and final wife was Livia. Livia's father had fought against Augustus before his suicide, and Livia was already married with a young son (Tiberius) and was pregnant with a second (Drusus the Elder). There were two reasons that Augustus married this pregnant woman who had once been his enemy.

The first was that her pregnancy was proof that she was fertile, if she could have two children with her first husband, she was more likely to be able to give Augustus heirs.

The second and most important by far is that Augustus fell madly, hopelessly in love with her from the moment he saw her and never wavered in his unflinching adoration. Livia was a married woman with two young children from another man, he wasn't making any friends by marrying someone else's wife.

We are led to believe then that he chose Livia for the most uncynical of reasons, that being love of course. He always cherished her counsel and in all his decades of rule he only seemed to want Livia.

At their wedding her previous husband even gave her away. This seems to indicate a certain level of acceptance on his part, supporting the view that he was somehow persuaded into giving Livia to Augustus rather than it being a forced procedure.

"She was the daughter of Livius Drusus, who had been among those proscribed on the tablet and had committed suicide after the defeat in Macedonia, and the wife of Nero, whom she had accompanied in his flight, as has been related. And it seems that she was in the sixth month with child by him. At any rate, when Caesar was in doubt and enquired of the pontifices whether it was permissible to wed her while pregnant,

they answered that if there was any doubt whether conception had taken
place the marriage should be put off, but if this was admitted, there was
nothing to prevent its taking place immediately. Perhaps they really
found this among the ordinances of the forefathers, but certainly they
would have said so, even had they not found it. Her husband himself gave
the woman in marriage just as a father would; and the following incident
occurred at the marriage feast. One of the prattling boys, such as the
women keep about them for their amusement, naked as a rule, on seeing
Livia reclining in one place with Caesar, and Nero in another with a
man, went up to her and said:"What are you doing here, mistress? For
your husband," pointing him out, "is reclining over there." So much then,
for this. Later, when the woman was now living with Caesar, she gave
birth to Claudius Drusus Nero. Caesar both acknowledged him and sent
him to his real father, making his entry in his memoranda:"Caesar
returned to its father Nero the child borne by Livia, his wife." Nero died
not long afterward and left Caesar himself as guardian to the boy and to
Tiberius."[85]

Once Livia's first husband died her boys came under the guard-
ianship of the Emperor.

The first thing to note is that this was the Julio-Claudian dynasty,
through his marriage to Livia Augustus had linked the Julian family
to that of her first husband Tiberius Claudius Nero. People from
both sides of the family attained the imperial title and there was a
great deal of intermarriage between the Julians and the Claudians.

Tiberius therefore was only heir to Augustus because every
other option had already been exhausted.

In 23BCE Augustus had suffered a serious bout of illness and
almost died, indications seem to point to either his deputy Marcus

Agrippa (not to be confused with Herod Agrippa who was named after him) or his nephew Marcellus as slated to succeed him.[86]

Historians point to Agrippa because he was the only other person in the empire who shared the rank and authority of Augustus, but they also point to Marcellus because he was quickly married to Julia the Elder, Augustus' daughter which seems like an act which would increase his claim to power.

My theory is that Augustus probably wanted Marcellus because of his youth, and that in some ways he wanted the least capable of the two to succeed him in the hopes that it would enhance his image and legacy.

If the architect of his success overtook him then he would likely be erased by history, much like how history remembers Caesar before Pompey.

After this brush with the afterlife Augustus realised that Marcellus needed to be trained in the running of the government, so he was given greater responsibilities and more training.

In the end Marcellus caught a fever and died a number of years before his uncle.

When Agrippa died in 12BCE Augustus forced his stepson Tiberius to divorce his wife Vipsania Agrippina. He was happily married to this woman for 7 years and when he was coerced into leaving her and marrying Augustus' daughter Julia, he was heartbroken.

"At divorcing Agrippina he felt the deepest regret; and upon meeting her afterwards, he looked after her with eyes so passionately expressive of affection, that care was taken she should never again come in his sight."[87]

This unnatural divorce made Tiberius a bitter man and profoundly impacted his future life as Emperor of Rome. He never got over it and his later acts of lust seem to point towards an emotional hole that no excesses could ever seem to fill.

His younger brother Drusus the Elder was favoured by Augustus and given far more responsibility in public and political life.

For a long time, Augustus relied on his grandsons Gaius and Lucius as possible heirs. In 1BCE Augustus' daughter Julia (who was married to his stepson Tiberius) was accused of adultery and after days of gut-wrenching deliberations he was forced to send his beloved daughter Julia into banishment.

Her mother Scribonia volunteered herself to join Julia's banishment so that she would at least have one person with her.[88]

The adopted heirs Gaius and Lucius died within 2 years of each other (4CE and 2CE respectively) of mysterious illnesses. Many claim that the young princes were assassinated, and this is probably true. Considering Livia's penchant for having her political rivals killed it seems very feasible considering the short space of time in which they both died.

According to Suetonius this was Augustus' remark in response to the tragic events of his life. *"Would I were wifeless, or had childless died!"* He stoically continued his work but at the end of the day he was a family man and his family seemed to be falling apart at the seams.

Drusus was the next heir on Augustus' list, he was a capable soldier and popular with the army. He died in 9BCE just falling short of his thirties. His brother Tiberius had outlived Augustus' nephew, grandsons and his brother so he was the last one standing.

From 6BCE Tiberius became the heir in an official way and started sharing important offices of state with his stepfather. He wasn't the heir most people wanted, not least Augustus, but he was vaguely trusted and didn't seem to have any serious deficits of character or ability.

He was simply average; he was good enough. He was the sort of boring, anticlimactic choice that made no one feel happy but kept the peace.

To offset discontent with Tiberius he was formally adopted as the heir of Augustus in 4BCE on the condition that he in turn adopt his popular and charismatic nephew Germanicus as his heir. Germanicus was the son of Drusus the Elder (Tiberius's younger brother) and his immense popularity made many people want him as Augustus' successor.

Tiberius already had sons of his own, so this was a massive sacrifice to make, but he made it anyway.

This is the big reason that the first royal dynasty of Rome is called the Julio-Claudian dynasty, because the desired outcome of the succession was that the Julians and Claudians would share power and take turns claiming the crown.

It was expected that Tiberius would die and his nephew Germanicus (who was a descendant of the Julian clan through his great-grandmother Octavia who was sister to Augustus) would take the throne and return it to the line of Augustus and his descendants.

In the month for which Augustus was named he died in the city where his own father had met his end many years before. In 14CE Augustus died of an onset of illness. He was by this time an old man, but many sources claim that his wife Livia poisoned his figs.

Personally, I imagine this to be some scribbling of poetic license, and that his death was an entirely natural one. His last words were thus.

"Acta est fabula, plaudite"

Have I played the part well? Then applaud as I exit.

His daughter followed him into the afterlife not long after. This was possibly at the order of the new Emperor Tiberius, but it is also possible that her death was a natural one.[89]

Tiberius' reign got off to a poor start because in the simplest of terms he was trying to do what Augustus had done whilst also consistently failing to come anywhere near his skill or suave.

"Though he made no scruple to assume and exercise immediately the imperial authority, by giving orders that he should be attended by the guards, who were the security and badge of the supreme power; yet he affected, by a most impudent piece of acting, to refuse it for a long time; one while sharply reprehending his friends who entreated him to accept it, as little knowing what a monster the government was; another while keeping in suspense the Senate, when they implored him and threw themselves at his feet, by ambiguous answers, and a crafty kind of dissimulation; insomuch that some were out of patience, and one cried out, during the confusion, "Either let him accept it, or decline it at once;" and a second told him to his face, "Others are slow to perform what they promise, but you are slow to promise what you actually perform." At last, as if forced to it, and complaining of the miserable and burdensome service imposed upon him, he accepted the government; not, however, without giving hopes of his resigning it some time or other. The exact words he used were these: "Until the time shall come, when ye may think it reasonable to give some rest to my old age.""[90]

What Tiberius was trying to play off as charming and humble

actually came off as disrespectful and uncooperative. Augustus had been the reluctant leader in a time of crisis, Tiberius was taking on a job that had already been built in the image of Augustus.

Simple repetition of Augustus' methods wouldn't be any good and only seemed to make the Senate angry and the government dysfunctional.

One can imagine that Tiberius' feigned acts of humility felt like a cruel joke, or some kind of concerted attempt to keep everything in deadlock. He just seemed indifferent to the needs of others.

In private however it is said that he described the Senate as *"men fit to be slaves."*[91] Tiberius' glib rendering of charm didn't seem to work on the Senators, and no matter what he did it never would.

In the early days Livia used Tiberius as her puppet, but in the end, he was able to deprive her of any form of authority.

When Augustus died the care of Herod Agrippa and his welfare fell into Tiberius' lap. He had a great deal of affection for the boy, and he was also close to Tiberius' son Drusus the Younger.

Although it is also possible that his affection for Agrippa was less innocent in nature.
Tiberius liked young boys and was well-known for sexually abusing those who were unlucky enough to see themselves enter his court.

In his later life especially, his paedophilic acts became something of a commonality. There is no direct evidence that Herod Agrippa was subjected to this horror, but it is speculatively possible.

What we do know is that Tiberius' son Drusus was a close friend to Agrippa and would help him out of financial strains he got himself into.

There is a very fitting passage from Robert Graves' novel 'Claudius the G-d' that aptly describes who Herod Agrippa was.

"But a few men remain always true to a single extreme character: these

are the men who leave the strongest mark on history, and I should divide them into four classes. First there are the scoundrels with stony hearts, of whom Macro, the Guards Commander under Tiberius and Caligula, was an outstanding example. Next come the virtuous men with equally stony hearts, of whom Cato the Censor, my bugbear, was an outstanding example. The third class are the virtuous men with golden hearts, such as old Athenodorus and my poor murdered brother Germanicus. And last and most rarely found are the scoundrels with the golden hearts, and of these Herod Agrippa was the most perfect instance imaginable. It is the scoundrels with the golden hearts, these anti-Catos, who make the most valuable friends in time of need. You expect nothing from them. They are entirely without principle, as they themselves acknowledge, and only consider their own advantage. But go to them when in desperate trouble and say, 'For G-d's sake do so-and-so for me,' and they will almost certainly do it – not as a friendly favour but, they will say, because it fits in with their own crooked plans; and you are forbidden to thank them. These anti-Catos are gamblers and spendthrifts; but that is at least better than being misers. They also associate constantly with drunkards, assassins, crooked business men, and procurers; yet you seldom see them greatly the worse for liquor themselves, and if they arrange an assassination you may be sure that the victim will not be greatly mourned, and they defraud the rich defaulters rather than the innocent and needy, and they consort with no woman against her will.[92]

In other words, Agrippa embodies the phrase 'honour among thieves.' He was the swashbuckling antihero of his time and he got into more than a few adventures. But he did all this with a sense of decency, and when given the chance he conducted himself more highly than anyone before or after him.

The greatest King the Jews ever had just happened to be a suave and debonaire debtor. His tale was not a traditional 'rags to riches' story, it was far closer to a zig zag of riches, to rags, to riches, to rags and eventually to riches again.

Being raised in Rome with a Roman name gave this Jewish Prince connections within the Roman state which would not have otherwise been possible to create.

He grew up with all the major players in Roman politics from his generation. He was friends with Claudius, Drusus, Caligula and many others.

In 19CE Tiberius' popular nephew Germanicus was assassinated. His wife Agrippina the Elder also happened to be a granddaughter of Augustus which meant that their children were of the Julian dynasty on both sides.

They had a much better claim to the throne than Tiberius or his progeny so the death of Germanicus at the age of 33 was probably ordered by Tiberius.

The oldest sons of Germanicus met a brutal end when they were all sent to their deaths on false charges. The only children of Germanicus that remained alive were his youngest son Gaius (Caligula) and his three daughters.

Tiberius' son Drusus died in 23CE which put a spanner in the works for Tiberius. Drusus was also the primary benefactor of Agrippa. So, when his lavish lifestyle caught up with him Tiberius sent Agrippa away as to avoid his debts going to even greater heights.

Agrippa returned to his native land for the first time since he was a child and fell into an intense state of misery. His devoted wife Cypros was the only thing that kept him from suicide and destitution.

She sent letters to Herod Antipas and Agrippa's sister Herodias. These two hadn't seen each other in years and don't appear to have been close, but Herodias and her husband agreed to allow Agrippa to be the mayor of their new Capital Tiberias.

In this city Agrippa and his young family resided for a number of years. Agrippa was good at his job and kept the city bustling, he was also amicable with his sister and brother-in-law for most of the time.

It was only when Agrippa arrogantly asked for a raise in his wages that Antipas banished him from his Galilean holdings.

He fled to Damascus next under the protection of Lucius Pomponius Flaccus the governor of Syria. For a while he acted as a civil servant but was ensnared by a bribery scandal.

Once convicted he was forced to flee Syria in a flash. This sleazeball was unlikely aware that he was still to become the greatest King the Jews ever had.

Agrippa was cornered on his ship and through guile he was able to sail to Alexandria in the dead of the night,

When he arrived, Agrippa met Alexander the Alabarch, the chief representative of the Alexandrine Jewry. At first his charms were convincing, but Alexander was sceptical of Agrippa and of his ability to follow Jewish law.

"He then pretended that he would do as he bid him; but when night came on, he cut his cables, and went off, and sailed to Alexandria, where he desired Alexander the alabarch to lend him two hundred thousand drachmae; but he said he would not lend it to him, but would not refuse it to Cypros, as greatly astonished at her affection to her husband, and at the other instances of her virtue; so she undertook to repay it. Accordingly, Alexander paid them five talents at Alexandria, and promised to pay them the rest of that sum at Dicearchia [Puteoli]; and this he did out of the fear he was in that Agrippa would soon spend it. So this Cypros set

her husband free, and dismissed him to go on with his navigation to Italy,
while she and her children departed for Judea."[93]

Alexander was fair to Agrippa despite his deceptions and paid him what he needed. The only condition was that he raise his children as good Jews and have them educated in the Jewish way.

There is a passage from the fictional novel 'Claudius the G-d' that relays some version of the conversation shared between Agrippa and Alexander. I use it not to give the false impression that we know what was said, but to posit a theory driven by Agrippa's later actions.

"I am circumcised and so are my children, and I and my whole household
have always kept the Law revealed to your ancestor Moses as strictly as
our difficult position as Roman citizens and our imperfect consciences as
Edomites have allowed us.' 'There are no two ways about righteousness,'
said the Alabarch stiffly. 'Either the Law is kept, or it is broken.' 'Yet I
have read that the Lord once permitted Naaman, the Syrian proselyte, to
worship in the Temple of Rimmon by the side of the King, his master,'
said Herod. 'And Naaman proved a very good friend to the Jews, did he
not?' At last the Alabarch said to Herod: 'If I lend you this money will you
swear in the name of the Lord – to whom be Glory Everlasting – to keep
His Law as far as in you lies, and cherish His People, and never by sins of
commission or omission offend against His Majesty?'"

Herod Agrippa's love of his people and observance of the law at risk to his station and safety prove him to be a servant of the Jews. His good deeds began after he was saved from destitution by the Alabarch, so it is at least possible that he developed a more pious nature from this experience.

I don't believe that he ever broke this promise, even if it did take most of his adventurous life to fulfil.

Luckily for Agrippa Rome was in just enough of a state of chaos for him to make his comeback.

Anyone with any skill was dead. The Senatorial class had been decimated by Tiberius' treason trials which meant that there was a serious lack of leadership and a shortage of noblemen who could act as civil servants.

Being an Aedile by default made Agrippa an important asset. Tiberius decided to welcome the prince back to Rome so that he could act as an administrator. He was plucking desperately at straws by this time.

The state of Roman politics could best be summarized as follows. Tiberius had retired to an island of pleasures and wickedness called Capri, and from here he spent years hiding from the enemies he saw everywhere.

In his absence the Praetorian Prefect Sejanus ended up with the bulk of political authority in the empire. When Tiberius' only son died in 23CE (probably poisoned by Sejanus and Drusus' wife Livilla) Sejanus tried to have himself declared heir, and only saved himself by a small margin.

It had reached a stage where Sejanus was running the empire and feeding Tiberius small amounts of news by drip, so that he was in effect not having any meaningful say on how the state was run.

Eventually Tiberius figured out what was taking place and decided to have Sejanus killed. If he had been too direct Tiberius probably would have been deposed and executed, so he used a subtler method to lull Sejanus into a false sense of security.

He essentially arranged a Senate meeting to honour Sejanus with an award, and in the letter condemned him as a traitor. From here the Senate had Sejanus and his entire family executed and thrown down the Gemonian stairs.

This event is recounted by the Roman historian Cassius Dio.

"At the time of our narrative a great uproar took place in the city; for the populace slew anyone it saw of those who had possessed great influence with Sejanus and had committed acts of insolence to please him. The soldiers, too, angered because they had been suspected of friendliness for Sejanus and because the night-watch had been preferred to them for loyalty to the Emperor, proceeded to burn and plunder, despite the fact that all the officials were guarding the whole city in accordance with Tiberius' command. Moreover, not even the Senate remained quiet; but those of its members who had paid court to Sejanus were greatly disturbed by their fear of vengeance; and those who had accused or borne witness against others were filled with terror, because of the prevailing suspicion that their victims had been destroyed in the interest of Sejanus rather than of Tiberius. Very small, indeed, was the courageous element that remained free from these terrors and expected that Tiberius would become milder. For, as usually happens, they laid the responsibility for their previous misfortunes upon the man who had perished, and charged the Emperor with few or none of them; as for most of these things, they said he had either been ignorant of them or had been forced to do them against his will. Privately this was the attitude of the various groups; but publicly they voted, as if they had been freed from a tyranny, not to hold any mourning over the deceased and to have a statue of Liberty erected in the Forum; also a festival was to be held under the auspices of all the magistrates and priests, a thing that had never before happened; and the day on which Sejanus had died was to be celebrated by annual horse-races and wild-beast-hunts under the direction of the members of the four priesthoods and of the Sodales Augustales, another thing that had never

before been done. Thus, to celebrate the overthrow of the man whom they
had led to his destruction by the excessive and novel honours bestowed
upon him, they voted observances that were unknown even in honour of
the g-ds. So clearly, indeed, did they comprehend that it was chiefly these
honours that had bereft him of his senses, that they at once expressly
forbade the granting of excessive honours to anybody and likewise the
taking of oaths in the name of anyone besides the Emperor. Nevertheless,
though they passed such votes, as if under some divine inspiration, they
began shortly afterward to fawn upon Macro and Laco. They granted
them large sums of money, and also gave Laco the rank of an ex-quaestor
and Macro that of an ex-praetor; they furthermore allowed them to
witness the games in their company and to wear the purple-bordered toga
at the votive festivals. The two men, however, did not accept these
honours, for the example still so fresh in their minds served as a deter-
rent. Nor did Tiberius take any of the many honours that were voted
him, chief among which was the proposal that he should begin to be
termed Father of his Country now, at any rate, and also one that his
birthday should be marked by ten horse-races and a banquet of the
Senators. On the contrary, he gave notice anew that no one should intro-
duce any such motion. These were the events that were taking place in the
city.
Tiberius for a time had been in great fear that Sejanus would occupy the
city and sail against him, and so he had got ships in readiness in order to
escape if anything of the sort came to pass; he had also commanded
Macro, as some report, to bring Drusus before the Senate and people, in
the event of any uprising, and declare him Emperor. When, now, he
learned that Sejanus was dead, he rejoiced, as was natural, but he would
not receive the embassy that was sent to congratulate him, though many

members of the Senate and many of the knights and the populace had been sent out, as before. Indeed, he even rebuffed the consul Regulus, who had always been devoted to his interests and had come in response to the Emperor's own command, in order to ensure the safety of his journey to the city.

Thus perished Sejanus, after attaining to greater power than any of those who held this position either before or after him, with the exception of Plautianus. Moreover, his relatives, his associates, and all the rest who had paid court to him and had proposed the granting of honours to him were brought to trial. The majority of them were convicted for the acts that had previously made them the objects of envy; and their fellow-citizens condemned them for the measures which they themselves had previously voted. Many men who had been tried on various charges and acquitted were again accused and now convicted, on the ground that they had been saved before as a favour to the man now fallen. Accordingly, if no other complaint could be brought against a person, the very fact that he had been a friend of Sejanus sufficed to bring punishment upon him — as if, forsooth, Tiberius himself had not been fond of him and thereby caused others to display such zeal in his behalf. Among those who gave information of this sort were the very men who had been foremost in paying court to Sejanus; for, inasmuch as they had accurate knowledge of those who were in the same position as themselves, they had no difficulty either in seeking them out or in securing their conviction. So these men, expecting to save themselves by this procedure and to obtain money and honours besides, were accusing others or bearing witness against them; but, as it turned out, they realized none of their hopes. For, as they were liable themselves to the same charges on which they were prosecuting the others, they perished also, partly for this very reason and partly as betrayers of their friends. Of those against whom charges were brought, many were present to hear their accusation and make their defence, and some expressed their minds very freely in so doing; but the majority made away with themselves before their conviction. They did this chiefly to avoid suffering insult and outrage. For all who incurred any such charge, Senators as well as knights, and women as well as men, were crowded together in the prison, and upon being condemned either paid the penalty there or were hurled down from the Capitol by the tribunes or even by the consuls, after which the bodies of all of them were cast into the Forum and later thrown into the river. But their object was partly that their children might inherit their property, since very few estates of such as voluntarily died before their trial were confiscated, Tiberius in this way inviting men to become their own murderers, so that he might avoid the reputation of having killed them — just as if it were not far more dreadful to compel a man to die by his own hand than to deliver him to the executioner. Most of the estates of those who failed to die in the manner were confiscated, only a little or even nothing at all being given to their accusers; for now Tiberius was inclined to be far more strict in the matter of money. For this reason he increased to one per cent. a certain tax which had been only one-half of one per cent. and was accepting every inheritance that was left to him; and for that matter, nearly everybody left him something, even those who made away with themselves, as they had also done to Sejanus while he was alive."[94]

Rome fell into chaos because almost everyone with any type of power at that point was close to Sejanus, so in the spree of murders that followed many of the most powerful politicians in Rome ended up dead.

It was in this state of chaos where job vacancies in the Roman state were almost total that Agrippa was able to get back into Tiberius' good graces.

While he was on the island of Capri Tiberius was also grooming Gaius (Caligula) and Gemellus. Gemellus was his young grandson and was not quite old enough to rule, whilst Caligula being the son of Germanicus was popular but also a direct threat to the Emperor.

These possible heirs were both viable options. In a practical sense Gaius was much more popular and capable, but Gemellus was Tiberius' own grandson.

The only certainty in the succession was that Tiberius would lose. If Gemellus got the throne he would probably not be very good at it, and some other Sejanus would just control the government from behind the curtain.

Caligula meanwhile was too good if anything. He was the perfect choice, which meant firstly that the people would like him more than Tiberius, tainting his legacy. And secondly it meant that he would probably end up killing Gemellus to eliminate the threat.

Giving Caligula the throne would condemn his grandson. If he gave his grandson, the throne he was condemning his country.

He refused to make any clear decision on which candidate he preferred and in doing so forced them to compete for his affection and respect.

In the end Tiberius made the choice of not choosing. He gave them joint control of the empire; he basically just decided to flip a coin and hope for the best. Little did he know that this was the worst thing he could have done for Rome.

Agrippa was given the important job of educating Gemellus as his main tutor. On being allowed to return he befriended Caligula. The friendship was politically advantageous, but the pair also seemed to genuinely get on well. There is plenty of evidence later during Caligula's rule that backs this up.

Agrippa loved Caligula so much in fact that one day he wished Tiberius dead in a private conversation, that Caligula may take his place. He was overheard by a freedman who reported him to Tiberius.

For this offence Agrippa was locked in prison and sentenced to die. Fearing his death Agrippa was disheartened, that is until he saw a strange omen of what was to come.

In his cell Agrippa caught sight of an owl during the daytime. His cellmate informed him that this was not just an owl, but an omen that Agrippa would be a great King. But he was warned as well that when the owl returned it would be an omen of his destruction.

With this hope Agrippa awaited the news of his release.
Tiberius named his grandson Gemellus and Caligula the joint heirs to the throne in 35CE.

During the months and years that followed Caligula made important allies including the Praetorian Prefect Macro, who spoke highly of him to the Emperor.

In 37CE Tiberius died. Some say Caligula suffocated him, others that he simply died in his sleep. Being 78 years old the latter was probably the case. The main reason that I dispute the notion of assassination is that it seems like Caligula could have done it earlier.

The succession had been in place for 2 years already by the time Tiberius met his end, so I seriously question why Caligula only chose to kill Tiberius 2 years on. The motivation to kill Tiberius cannot be doubted.

He had murdered Caligula's mother and brothers, and probably been involved in the death of his father as well. He had terrorised Caligula for years, kept him as a hostage on an island sex colony and presumably did a great number of depraved things to the young man.

Caligula was probably unimaginably traumatised and desensi-tised to violence.

The hatred Caligula felt was probably palpable, but he was a smart man, he kept it in and knew when to strike. We will never know if he killed old Tiberius, but that doesn't matter.

The Emperor was dead after 23 years and a great deal was about to change. Caligula was swept in with a stream of popular support. Tiberius had been an absentee leader for many years and Rome had suffered under dire, draconian administration as a result.

The Roman people wanted two things. Firstly, a return to a Julian Emperor and secondly an Emperor who was actually in Rome governing.

This bar was pretty low, and Caligula met the expectations of his people perfectly. This was the same boy who had been dressed in a soldier's attire as a toddler and paraded around the army camp by his father.

This was the same boy who had been spared by Tiberius. He was a son of the man everyone in Rome loved.

The best modern equivalent I can think of is Martin Sheen and his son Charlie. Martin Sheen is a beloved and respected actor; his son Charlie rode his fame and went on to become something of a problematic figure.

Caligula was the Charlie Sheen of ancient Rome; he was ex-pected to be a star but ended up disappointing just about everyone involved.

They say you should never meet your heroes. Well, the same applies to having them rule over you. Like most child celebrities Caligula was spoilt, glib and lacking in empathy.

He was a traumatised young man who was given the most important job imaginable. He grew up knowing he was only alive because of the magnanimity of a tyrant. Anyone he was close to had faced persecution and death. This man needed a therapist, not an empire.

Due to the immense notoriety of Caligula, I consider it appropriate to first speak of his life, and then in a subsequent chapter of how he influenced the life of Herod Agrippa. An attempt at combining their tales into one chapter would do an injustice to both accounts.

9

Chapter 9- Mad Emperor Gaius

Gaius Julius Caesar was born in 12CE. This Gaius Julius Caesar was named in honour of the original Gaius Julius Caesar and to avoid confusion will be referred to as Gaius, or by his nickname Caligula.

Caligula grew up on campaign, his father Germanicus was a prominent general and had won many victories for the empire.

The nickname Caligula came from the fact that he wore Caligae (Soldiers' boots) as a child and was paraded around the army camp by his father.

Gaius hated the nickname Caligula; it was demeaning and had been thrust on him as a child on campaign. 'Little Boots' isn't exactly a moniker that symbolises authority or respectability.

"Caligula; having been born in the camp and brought up as the child of the legions, he had been wont to be called by this name, nor was there any

by which he was better known to the troops, but by this time he held
"Caligula" to be a reproach and a dishonour."[95]

Seneca the Younger used this example to show the importance of having a good temper which implies that the sources available to him spoke of Gaius as hating his nickname enough that it made him furiously angry.

What can be known without a doubt is that no one called him by it, he was Gaius and no one with any love of his life would have dared to refer to him by it.

Germanicus died in 19CE at Antioch under mysterious circumstances. The rocky childhood Caligula faced after his father's death is recounted by Suetonius.

"It was to the jokes of the soldiers in the camp that he owed the name of
Caligula, he having been brought up among them in the dress of a
common soldier. How much his education amongst them recommended
him to their favour and affection, was sufficiently apparent in the mutiny
upon the death of Augustus, when the mere sight of him appeased their
fury, though it had risen to a great height. For they persisted in it, until
they observed that he was sent away to a neighbouring city, to secure him
against all danger. Then, at last, they began to relent, and, stopping the
chariot in which he was conveyed, earnestly deprecated the odium to
which such a proceeding would expose them.

He likewise attended his father in his expedition to Syria. After his
return, he lived first with his mother, and, when she was banished, with
his great-grandmother, Livia Augusta, in praise of whom, after her
decease, though then only a boy, he pronounced a funeral oration in the
Rostra. He was then transferred to the family of his grandmother,
Antonia, and afterwards, in the twentieth year of his age, being called by

Tiberius to Capri, he in one and the same day assumed the manly habit, and shaved his beard, but without receiving any of the honours which had been paid to his brothers on a similar occasion. While he remained in that island, many insidious artifices were practised, to extort from him complaints against Tiberius, but by his circumspection he avoided falling into the snare. He affected to take no more notice of the ill-treatment of his relations, than if nothing had befallen them. With regard to his own sufferings, he seemed utterly insensible of them, and behaved with such obsequiousness to his grandfather and all about him, that it was justly said of him, "There never was a better servant, nor a worse master."[96]

The young Caligula was thrown from relative to relative and never got to feel safe, all of his relatives were sent away or killed by Tiberius and he lived with a knife hanging over his head each and every day, this must have seriously put a strain on his mind that may well have influenced his later depravity.

Eventually when Tiberius' own heir Drusus died, he took Caligula into his personal care for six years.

After six years on a perverted sex island Caligula was finally Emperor. Rather than directly honouring Tiberius' will Caligula took on sole rule of the empire but made the young Gemellus his heir to avoid conflict and honour the Claudian element of the Julio-Claudian dynasty.

Caligula was very young, only becoming Emperor at the age of 24. Making Gemellus his heir wasn't exactly a promise of imperium, it was highly likely that Caligula would live and rule for many decades, so it was in many ways a distant and meaningless promise.

His chief ally was the Praetorian Prefect Macro. Macro was something of a Sejanus in his own right, although he didn't exercise nearly as much direct power as his predecessor.

The immediate popularity Caligula had cannot be overstated. He was utterly and entirely loved by the Roman people; they had been without a direct ruler for over a decade, and this was the first Emperor since Augustus who was of the Julian line.

People sacrificed 160,000 or more animals in the first three months of Caligula's reign to mark the joy they felt and to honour their new leader.[97]

"Caligula himself inflamed this devotion, by practising all the arts of popularity. After he had delivered, with floods of tears, a speech in praise of Tiberius, and buried him with the utmost pomp, he immediately hastened over to Pandataria and the Pontian islands, to bring thence the ashes of his mother and brother; and, to testify the great regard he had for their memory, he performed the voyage in a very tempestuous season. He approached their remains with profound veneration, and deposited them in the urns with his own hands. Having brought them in grand solemnity to Ostia, with an ensign flying in the stern of the galley, and thence up the Tiber to Rome, they were borne by persons of the first distinction in the equestrian order, on two biers, into the mausoleum, at noon-day. He appointed yearly offerings to be solemnly and publicly celebrated to their memory, besides Circensian games to that of his mother, and a chariot with her image to be included in the procession. The month of September he called Germanicus, in honour of his father.

By a single decree of the Senate, he heaped upon his grandmother, Antonia, all the honours which had been ever conferred on the Empress Livia. His uncle, Claudius, who till then continued in the equestrian order, he took for his colleague in the consulship. He adopted his brother, Tiberius, on the day he took upon him the manly habit, and conferred upon him the title of "Prince of the Youths." As for his sisters, he ordered

these words to be added to the oaths of allegiance to himself: "Nor will I
hold myself or my own children more dear than I do Caius and his
sisters:" and commanded all resolutions proposed by the consuls in the
Senate to be prefaced thus: "May what we are going to do, prove fortunate
and happy to Caius Caesar and his sisters." With the like popularity he
restored all those who had been condemned and banished, and granted an
act of indemnity against all impeachments and past offences. To relieve
the informers and witnesses against his mother and brothers from all
apprehension, he brought the records of their trials into the forum, and
there burnt them, calling loudly on the g-ds to witness that he had not
read or handled them. A memorial which was offered him relative to his
own security, he would not receive, declaring, "that he had done nothing
to make any one his enemy:" and said, at the same time, "he had no ears
for informers."[98]

In his first days Caligula freed the banished, removed the elements of Tiberius' police state and gave amnesty to all those who
had condemned his relatives to death.

Rather than make even more enemies Caligula chose to make
friends, he chose to be merciful in a way that suited him and
enhanced his reputation. He did of course keep copies of all the
burnt papers, he was not stupid enough to get rid of all the evidence
of the misdeeds of the Senate.

But the message was clear, the public display was of a new start
and a new Emperor. People were optimistic, they saw a golden age
heading in their direction. They were sorely mistaken.

The old austere style of Tiberius was gone, Caligula was a much
more libertine spender and made sure to use the money Tiberius
had saved up.

Much like Herod the Great Caligula was a builder, and much like Herod his personal depravity ended up largely drowning this out. He spent exorbitant amounts on infrastructure including waterways and roads.

Among the banished people he allowed to return were his beloved sisters Drusilla, Agrippina and Livilla.

In the latter part of his first year as Emperor Caligula fell into a deathly illness. Though his ailment is something of a mystery we know that it involved a severe fever and that when he recovered, he began behaving in eccentric ways and had bouts of unquenchable paranoia.

It is likely that he suffered some form of meningitis which damaged his brain enough to give him these delusional streams of thought.

We will never know definitively but this explanation is the simplest one available to us.

People were deeply upset by Caligula's misfortune. So beloved was he that many men prayed for his recovery, and some even offered up their lives in place of his own.

When he woke up the Emperor was very different. The golden man so many had admired was now brutal and changeable.

Macro was in a deep hole of his own design when the Emperor arose. He had befriended Gemellus in case the Emperor succumbed to his ailment, so he was in effect guilty of conspiracy against Caligula and so was Gemellus by extension.

At first, he played around with Macro, even 'promoting' him to the Prefecture of Egypt.

Being promoted to governor of Egypt was a bit like being made Emperor of Malta, it was a big title for a little job.

It was the polite way of banishing someone from Rome, it was where you sent someone you didn't want in close proximity to you. Later Emperors often employed Caligula's strategy of simply sending his problems to Egypt.

Before he could even get to his placement in Egypt Macro was beheaded in a public display and Gemellus (who by now was Caligula's adopted son as well as his cousin) was forced to kill himself.

In Rome suicide was considered an honourable escape and if someone was unwilling to do it of their own accord they were held down and forced to stab themselves. As much of an oxymoron as 'forced suicide' is it did function as a more diplomatic alternative to just having someone killed.

It also diminished the personal responsibility of Caligula because in a literal sense he hadn't killed Gemellus, he had just forced him to commit suicide.

By early 38CE Caligula began picking off his enemies like flies. Ironically, he started acting more and more like Tiberius, throwing himself into depravity to escape from an unsustainable paranoid fear of everyone around him.

Perhaps if Caligula had not outdone him Tiberius would be remembered as 'the mad Emperor' instead, but history has a funny way of remembering the depraved ones over the merely deplorable ones.

He would sleep with the wives of Senators and turned his palace into an altar of lust and indignity. He was all-powerful and he knew it.

As well as this it is said that Caligula had those who had offered up their lives for his own killed, so that the G-ds would not be displeased.

Caligula declared himself a living deity and began signing his documents as such. The term Divi was commonly applied to dead people of note as an honorific title, it loosely translated to 'G-d-like', whilst a Deus was a living G-d.

Caligula was the first Emperor to refer to himself as a Deus while he was still alive, and his delusions of grandeur became unmanageable.

He even slept with his three sisters under the belief that he was a deity on the same level as Jupiter, and that he should emulate Jupiter by mating with his sisters.

Among them was Agrippina, who was the ambitious one of the three. She wanted power and to advance herself by producing an heir with Caligula.

But the one Caligula loved and cherished was Drusilla. He didn't just sleep with her to produce an heir or to inflate his own grandiosity, he did it because he saw her as his wife in all but name.

The scandalous nature of Caligula's love life cannot be overstated. People perceived what he was doing as utterly sinful and immoral. When news broke of Drusilla being pregnant the public began to hate the Emperor, incest was in ancient Rome regarded as evil.

You were not merely judged for it; you were destroyed by it. Drusilla was the one Caligula endlessly trusted, so it was fitting that she was the one who became pregnant in 38CE.

She was already married to another man, but Caligula didn't care. He made Drusilla the head of his household and gave her all the powers, titles and privileges an Emperor would traditionally afford to his spouse.

The poor girl suffered complications from her pregnancy and fell ill. Caligula saw his own illness as the method through which he had been transformed into a G-d, so he probably assumed that she would do the same.

But it would not turn out this way, Drusilla died with Caligula by her side (he never left it for a moment). Their baby also perished. He is said to have refused to even let her body be taken away, under the false hope that she was somehow going to come back to him.

He had nobody to turn to when he had to bury the woman he loved, most of them were already dead.

One of the only people who didn't suffer under Caligula's reprisals was in fact his uncle Claudius. Claudius was the moderately disabled younger brother of Germanicus, he was often derided and scolded by the rest of his family because of his lame leg and proneness to stuttering even though he was fairly intelligent.

Unlike the rest Claudius was not very threatening, at least not in Caligula's mind.

Claudius became the chief administrator of the empire when Caligula was in his state of mourning, he gained levels of authority no one ever thought he would gain and actually did a remarkably good job despite his inexperience.

The Emperor's displays of grief were absurd, costly and most of all intense. He saw her as a G-ddess and wanted every single Roman to honour her memory.

Before the Senators Caligula adorned the apparel of a widower and demanded that they make her a G-ddess. This was not a mere ceremony, she was in fact declared to have been a version of the G-ddess Venus, and she was given the new name of Panthea.

The other measures Caligula took are listed by Suetonius.

"He lived in the habit of incest with all his sisters; and at table, when much company was present, he placed each of them in turns below him, whilst his wife reclined above him. It is believed, that he deflowered one of them, Drusilla, before he had assumed the robe of manhood; and was even caught in her embraces by his grandmother Antonia, with whom they were educated together. When she was afterwards married to Cassius Longinus, a man of consular rank, he took her from him, and kept her constantly as if she were his lawful wife. In a fit of sickness, he

by his will appointed her heiress both of his estate and the empire. After
her death, he ordered a public mourning for her; during which it was
capital for any person to laugh, use the bath, or sup with his parents,
wife, or children. Being inconsolable under his affliction, he went hastily,
and in the night-time, from the City; going through Campania to
Syracuse, and then suddenly returned without shaving his beard, or
trimming his hair. Nor did he ever afterwards, in matters of the greatest
importance, not even in the assemblies of the people or before the soldiers,
swear any otherwise, than "By the divinity of Drusilla." The rest of his
sisters he did not treat with so much fondness or regard; but frequently
prostituted them to his catamites. He therefore the more readily
condemned them in the case of Aemilius Lepidus, as guilty of adultery,
and privy to that conspiracy against him. Nor did he only divulge their
own hand-writing relative to the affair, which he procured by base and
lewd means, but likewise consecrated to Mars the Avenger three swords
which had been prepared to stab him, with an inscription, setting forth
the occasion of their consecration."[99]

No matter how many frivolous titles he threw at her grave, or
how many tears he shed there was no way to bring her back. One
can imagine that the most powerful man in the world felt like all
his power was for nothing.

Oaths now had to be sworn to her, people had to mourn her. For
all his madness no one can say that Caligula was without a heart.

His other sisters along with Drusilla's husband Marcus Lepidus
were found to be plotting against Caligula, and for this his sisters
were banished, and Lepidus was executed.

By 39CE Caligula was far less popular than before and even his
most ardent supporters had figured out that he wasn't what they
had hoped him to be.

He was disliked and viewed more as a depraved successor to Tiberius than as a saintly realization of Germanicus' potential. Suetonius recounts the key instances of his insanity.

"Whether in the marriage of his wives, in repudiating them, or retaining them, he acted with greater infamy, it is difficult to say. Being at the wedding of Caius Piso with Livia Orestilla, he ordered the bride to be carried to his own house, but within a few days divorced her, and two years after banished her; because it was thought, that upon her divorce she returned to the embraces of her former husband. Some say, that being invited to the wedding-supper, he sent a messenger to Piso, who sat opposite to him, in these words: "Do not be too fond with my wife," and that he immediately carried her off. Next day he published a proclamation, importing, "That he had got a wife as Romulus and Augustus had done." Lollia Paulina, who was married to a man of consular rank in command of an army, he suddenly called from the province where she was with her husband, upon mention being made that her grandmother was formerly very beautiful, and married her; but he soon afterwards parted with her, interdicting her from having ever afterwards any commerce with man. He loved with a most passionate and constant affection Caesonia, who was neither handsome nor young; and was besides the mother of three daughters by another man; but a wanton of unbounded lasciviousness. Her he would frequently exhibit to the soldiers, dressed in a military cloak, with shield and helmet, and riding by his side. To his friends he even showed her naked. After she had a child, he honoured her with the title of wife; in one and the same day, declaring himself her husband, and father of the child of which she was delivered. He named it Julia Drusilla, and carrying it round the temples of all the g-ddesses, laid it on the lap of Minerva; to whom he recommended the

care of bringing up and instructing her. He considered her as his own
child for no better reason than her savage temper, which was such even in
her infancy, that she would attack with her nails the face and eyes of the
children at play with her."[100]

Some of this is probably exaggerated but it sets the general tone
of Caligula's later reign.

Caesonia was his new wife, and she satisfied his desires in every
regard, his depravities were accepted by her. She was a considerably
older woman than him and of no notable birth, but the fact that
she had multiple children proved her fertility, and the fact that they
never had any children of their own probably proves that he lacked
fertility.

The thing that ultimately pushed Caligula over the edge was his
brutality to the Senators. To pay for his exorbitant building projects
(in tribute to himself) he started having them executed on false
treason charges.

He also began forcing them to run for many miles at his whim
and made them serve him at dinner like slaves. He had people put
to death for trivial things and began to take pleasure in watching
them die. People were branded, scourged, burned alive, forced to
fight wild beasts, quite literally cut to pieces and met a litany of
other cruel ends.

"He generally prolonged the sufferings of his victims by causing them to
be inflicted by slight and frequently repeated strokes; this being his well-
known and constant order: "Strike so that he may feel himself die."
Having punished one person for another, by mistaking his name, he said,
"he deserved it quite as much.""[101]

Any pretences at reason or justice melted away with each swing of the sword.

Life simply wasn't worth living under Caligula. He humiliated all those around him and made their existence unendurable. In the end people feared Caligula's reign more than they feared his wrath, so they started plotting his downfall.

There is an argument to be made that at least some of what Caligula said can be attributed to a form of dark humour.

"And at a sumptuous entertainment, he fell suddenly into a violent fit of laughter, and upon the consuls, who reclined next to him, respectfully asking him the occasion, "Nothing," replied he, "but that, upon a single nod of mine, you might both have your throats cut.""[102]

The fact that he considered this sort of thing funny points to his mental instability, but it also points to a sardonic element of his madness. In a lot of ways, he saw the farcical nature of his rule and knew exactly where he was going.

He approached life with a measure of absurdist levity, he knew it was all for nothing, so he chose not to care about anything.

Or at least when he did care he did so without any restrictions. The best example of his is his wife Caesonia, who was very dear to him.

"As often as he kissed the neck of his wife or mistress, he would say, "So beautiful a throat must be cut whenever I please;" and now and then he would threaten to put his dear Caesonia to the torture, that he might discover why he loved her so passionately."[103]

He had found his soulmate, someone who at best was pretending to be as mad as him, or at worst actually was.

Many years before Caligula had heard a prophecy from the sooth-sayer Thrasyllus, who told him he had as much chance of becoming Emperor as he did of riding a horse across the Bay of Baiae.

This was considered impossible so Caligula in an act of pettiness, defiance and sarcasm decided to make it happen.

He built an elaborate pontoon bridge across the bay of Baiae and crossed it on his horse. This endeavour cost a lot of money and was probably seen in a negative light by observers.

This display leads me to the view that some of his other outland-ish acts were meant more as symbolic displays rather than literal manifestations of insanity. When he was claimed to have made his horse Incitatus a Roman Consul many assumed that he had done this because he was insane.

I choose to regard it as a joke, more of a threat made with the implication that a horse would do a better job than any of the men serving as Senators.

Caligula used humour to deride and mock people, his humour was then reimagined in a more literal way and some of the impact of the jokes was lost to time. It is also possible that Incitatus' planned consulship was either an outright lie or a literal gesture.

We will never know, trying to psychoanalyse a dead man is not always a fruitful endeavour, although it remains a fascinating one.

For a long time, it was thought that this event was a fable, until in 1930CE the remains of the boats were found in Lake Nemi. Though much of the find was destroyed during the allied invasion of Italy it does at least prove that one of the more outlandish stories about Caligula was actually true.

So fond of money was Caligula that is it claimed that he even rolled around in it when the people gave him tributary gifts.

Caligula is said to have killed the King of Mauritania in 40CE and took his holdings as two Roman provinces. The fact that he did this but also gave Agrippa a Kingdom implies that Agrippa was given his high position as a token of love rather than as a politically expedient decision.

In military affairs Caligula was not his father. He was not wise or capable, and more importantly he didn't have anyone to fight. In terms of foreign policy most other nations bore Caligula good will.

The only untouched area Rome could now expand into was Britannia. No one, not his father or even Julius Caesar had been able to go across the English Channel and take Britain for the empire.

It was considered an impossible task and the issues involved with sending ships designed for short Mediterranean voyages to a remote island were not small.

But Caligula was divine in his own eyes, so he went about trying to do the impossible anyway.

"Soon after this, there being no hostilities, he ordered a few Germans of his guard to be carried over and placed in concealment on the other side of the Rhine, and word to be brought him after dinner, that an enemy was advancing with great impetuosity. This being accordingly done, he immediately threw himself, with his friends, and a party of the pretorian knights, into the adjoining wood, where lopping branches from the trees, and forming trophies of them, he returned by torch-light, upbraiding those who did not follow him, with timorousness and cowardice; but he presented the companions, and sharers of his victory with crowns of a new form, and under a new name, having the sun, moon, and stars represented on them, and which he called Exploratoriae. Again, some hostages were by his order taken from the school, and privately sent off; upon notice of which he immediately rose from table, pursued them with the cavalry, as if they had run away, and coming up with them, brought them back in fetters; proceeding to an extravagant pitch of ostentation likewise in this military comedy. Upon his again sitting down to table, it

being reported to him that the troops were all reassembled, he ordered them to sit down as they were, in their armour, animating them in the words of that well-known verse of Virgil:

Durate, et vosmet rebus servate secundis.—Aen. 1.

Bear up, and save yourselves for better days.

In the mean time, he reprimanded the Senate and people of Rome in a very severe proclamation, "For revelling and frequenting the diversions of the circus and theatre, and enjoying themselves at their villas, whilst their Emperor was fighting, and exposing himself to the greatest dangers."

At last, as if resolved to make war in earnest, he drew up his army upon the shore of the ocean, with his balistae and other engines of war, and while no one could imagine what he intended to do, on a sudden commanded them to gather up the sea shells, and fill their helmets, and the folds of their dress with them, calling them "the spoils of the ocean due to the Capitol and the Palatium." As a monument of his success, he raised a lofty tower, upon which, as at Pharos, he ordered lights to be burnt in the night-time, for the direction of ships at sea; and then promising the soldiers a donative of a hundred denarii a man, as if he had surpassed the most eminent examples of generosity, "Go your ways," said he, "and be merry: go, ye are rich."

In making preparations for his triumph, besides the prisoners and deserters from the barbarian armies, he picked out the men of greatest stature in all Gaul, such as he said were fittest to grace a triumph, with some of

the chiefs, and reserved them to appear in the procession; obliging them
not only to dye their hair yellow, and let it grow long, but to learn the
German language, and assume the names commonly used in that country.
He ordered likewise the gallies in which he had entered the ocean, to be
conveyed to Rome a great part of the way by land, and wrote to his
comptrollers in the city, "to make proper preparations for a triumph
against his arrival, at as small expense as possible; but on a scale such as
had never been seen before, since they had full power over the property of
every one."[104]

In summary, the Emperor had attempted to invade Britain, but due to logistical issues and issues of morale he had been forced instead to put Gauls in chains and carry them in a triumph to brush off his disastrous waste of a campaign as a victory.

It is difficult to say whether he really did believe that he was fighting Neptune, one could argue that he used this as a symbolic gesture and that it was actually a prudent crisis management strategy. Such a carefully contrived plan does not seem like the product of a purely insane mind, but rather of a politically agile one.

It could also be said that he was so delusional that he thought he could whip the sea and defeat Poseidon. I choose to imagine that both factors were at play, that on a shallow level he was insane but in practice used this to his advantage.

The impossible task of conquering the Britons would be achieved, just not by Caligula. In many ways the failure in Britain came into direct conflict with Caligula's self-imagined greatness.

"Styling himself Jupiter Latiaris, he attached to his service as priests his
wife Caesonia, Claudius, and other persons who were wealthy, receiving
ten million sesterces from each of them in return for this honour. He also

consecrated himself to his own service and appointed his horse a fellow-priest; and dainty and expensive birds were sacrificed to him daily. He had a contrivance by which he gave answering peals when it thundered and sent return flashes when it lightened. Likewise, whenever a bolt fell, he would in turn hurl a javelin at a rock, repeating each time the words of Homer, "Either lift me or I will thee."[105]

He was comparing himself to Jupiter and believed that he was responsible for the weather. He also began demanding that provincial subjects of the empire should worship him and gave them 'gifts' of statues dedicated to himself.

This particularly angered the Jews which will be discussed in the next chapter. Anger was shared among all in Rome though, Caligula's belief that he was divine had reached a point of such severity that he had taken to dressing as Venus and Jupiter, he began punishing people severely for minor offences so that he could take their money.

He was also cruel to his uncle Claudius. He gave him many honourable positions in government. Though this seems like a positive thing it must be remembered that being in high positions and orders required a lot of money, and the payments Claudius was forced to make for his positions amounted to vastly more money than he had.

By making Claudius his most powerful civil servant he also plunged him into debt. Some have theorised that Claudius was involved in Caligula's death but considering the fact that he was found hiding behind a curtain by the guards afterwards it seems like he was more of an innocent bystander.

It is however highly likely that he knew about the plots and turned a blind eye precisely because of all the debts he had been forced to rack up.

In 41CE the Roman aristocracy had enough. They plotted to kill Caligula and in January of that year they made their attempt.

Caligula was in attendance of a performance (ironically in honour of Augustus) and his guards decided to strike out against him. Suetonius recounts what took place on January 24th 41CE.

"On the ninth of the calends of February [24th January], and about the seventh hour of the day, after hesitating whether he should rise to dinner, as his stomach was disordered by what he had eaten the day before, at last, by the advice of his friends, he came forth. In the vaulted passage through which he had to pass, were some boys of noble extraction, who had been brought from Asia to act upon the stage, waiting for him in a private corridor, and he stopped to see and speak to them; and had not the leader of the party said that he was suffering from cold, he would have gone back, and made them act immediately. Respecting what followed, two different accounts are given. Some say, that, whilst he was speaking to the boys, Chaerea came behind him, and gave him a heavy blow on the neck with his sword, first crying out, "Take this:" that then a tribune, by name Cornelius Sabinus, another of the conspirators, ran him through the breast. Others say, that the crowd being kept at a distance by some centurions who were in the plot, Sabinus came, according to custom, for the word, and that Caius gave him "Jupiter," upon which Chaerea cried out, "Be it so!" and then, on his looking round, clove one of his jaws with a blow. As he lay on the ground, crying out that he was still alive, the rest dispatched him with thirty wounds. For the word agreed upon among them all was, "Strike again." Some likewise ran their swords through his privy parts. Upon the first bustle, the litter bearers came running in with their poles to his assistance, and, immediately afterwards, his German body guards, who killed some of the assassins, and

also some Senators who had no concern in the affair.
He lived twenty-nine years, and reigned three years, ten months, and
eight days. His body was carried privately into the Lamian Gardens,
where it was half burnt upon a pile hastily raised, and then had some
earth carelessly thrown over it. It was afterwards disinterred by his
sisters, on their return from banishment, burnt to ashes, and buried.
Before this was done, it is well known that the keepers of the gardens
were greatly disturbed by apparitions; and that not a night passed with-
out some terrible alarm or other in the house where he was slain, until it
was destroyed by fire. His wife Caesonia was killed with him, being
stabbed by a centurion; and his daughter had her brains knocked out
against a wall."[106]

So it was that Emperor Gaius Julius Caesar was stabbed by the conspirators until he died. His loyal guardsmen were furious and decided to launch a campaign of retribution throughout the city, which mainly involved viciously murdering some conspirators and a great many more perfectly innocent people.

Most of the conspirators survived and tried to survive the reign of terror that took place after the assassination.

Cassius Chaerea led these men, he was the first (but by no means the last) Praetorian Prefect to take part in his Emperor's murder. He set the precedent that when the Praetorians were discontented, they could simply stick a sword through their leader and replace him with

someone who was more pliable and willing to pay them off.
In Caligula's case he had abused his guards and treated them with contempt, his insanity and unreasonable conduct tipped them over the edge.

The most memorable thing Caligula ever said was, *"I wish the Roman people had but one neck."*[107]

And that statement largely summarises his rule. He thought everyone was out to get him to such a severe extent that in the end they actually were. His reactions to unfounded fears of conspiracy created the conspiracies that finished him off.

The fact that Claudius was able to spend a decent amount of money to bribe people into supporting him ultimately shows that Caligula's excesses were probably overexaggerated, that even if he had squandered a great deal of money, he had done so to a lesser extent than is claimed.

It doesn't matter in the end, he still died, and with him his wife Caesonia and their daughter Julia Drusilla.

It was fairly obvious that anyone related to Caligula had to die, once a drop of blood was spilled an entire bucket had to be filled. Anyone close to the Emperor was put to death.

Claudius expected to die in just the same way, but when the guards found him instead of putting their swords in him, they bowed.

They hoisted the 50-year-old man up and declared him Emperor. His family would have been in serious danger if he had refused so he accepted their acclamation and succeeded Caligula in 41CE.

Claudius the fool, Claudius the lame, Claudius the stutterer. The man everyone had underestimated and mocked at every turn was the same one who ended up taking the throne.

The same man who had been spared from death only because his nephew preferred laughing at him to watching him die, the same man who had been abused by his relatives all his life.

The same man who avoided assassination merely because he was not considered worth the trouble. This man had won either by pretending to be a fool, or by actually being one.

Everyone else had underestimated him, and now he was the Emperor of Rome.

It is possible that Claudius was involved in the killing of his nephew, and it is just as possible that he had no clue what was going on.

That didn't matter either in the end, he had got the crown that he didn't want by doing nothing at all.

And he could do nothing about it. But he could do something to honour his long-time friend Herod Agrippa who had been instrumental in him getting the throne.

When Claudius was still in a profound state of confusion and extremely desperate for allies it was Agrippa who rallied people and built up a measure of legitimacy. He invested in Claudius when no one else would, this ended up paying off for him.

10

Chapter 10- The Redemption of Judea by Herod Agrippa I

With an understanding of Caligula, a narrative of King Agrippa's relationship with him can be recounted correctly.

Agrippa was delivered from execution by Tiberius' death. Caligula became the new Emperor of Rome and Agrippa gained much more authority.

Caligula was also able to stop a war between the Jews and the Nabateans in its tracks. This had a serious impact on Antipas and probably saved the Jews from further ravaging conflict.

Agrippa was soon made King of the realms his uncle Herod Philip had held. He now outranked all of his relatives who were merely tetrarchs.

Antipas and Herodias began to fear Agrippa's influence on the new Emperor. They assumed that he was out to get them, and that he would use his position to take their lands for himself.

This was a self-fulfilling prophecy as their schemes towards this end ultimately gave Agrippa all that he needed to oust them from their position.

"But Herodias, Agrippa's sister, who now lived as wife to that Herod who was tetrarch of Galilee and Peres, took this authority of her brother in an envious manner, particularly when she saw that he had a greater dignity bestowed on him than her husband had; since, when he ran away, it was because he was not able to pay his debts; and now he was come back, he was in a way of dignity, and of great good fortune. She was therefore grieved and much displeased at so great a mutation of his affairs; and chiefly when she saw him marching among the multitude with the usual ensigns of royal authority, she was not able to conceal how miserable she was, by reason of the envy she had towards him; but she excited her husband, and desired him that he would sail to Rome, to court honors equal to his; for she said that she could not bear to live any longer, while Agrippa, the son of that Aristobulus who was condemned to die by his father, one that came to her husband in such extreme poverty, that the necessaries of life were forced to be entirely supplied him day by day; and when he fled away from his creditors by sea, he now returned a king; while he was himself the son of a king, and while the near relation he bare to royal authority called upon him to gain the like dignity, he sat still, and was contented with a privater life. "But then, Herod, although thou wast formerly not concerned to be in a lower condition than thy father from whom thou wast derived had been, yet do thou now seek after the dignity which thy kinsman hath attained to; and do not thou bear this contempt, that a man who admired thy riches should be in greater honor than thyself, nor suffer his poverty to show itself able to purchase greater things than our abundance; nor do thou esteem it other than a shameful

thing to be inferior to one who, the other day, lived upon thy charity. But let us go to Rome, and let us spare no pains nor expenses, either of silver or gold, since they cannot be kept for any better use than for the obtaining of a kingdom."[108]

Sources seem to indicate that Herodias was more active in the scheming than her husband, and that he often went along with her for the sake of appeasement. In some ways the trope of the 'scheming wife' comes from a sexist culture that saw women as treacherous but considering Herodias' position and parentage the notion of her being at least a bit of a deceptive character is somewhat justified.

The fact that Agrippa was appointed King when the empire simply could have annexed the region strongly implies that Caligula had a genuine closeness with Agrippa, a closeness that led him to give up a swathe of land.

When Agrippa was in his new Kingdom Antipas decided to sail to Rome and turn the Emperor against his friend. On hearing this Agrippa set sail as well, he sent gifts to the Emperor and made haste to arrive first.

Fortunately, Agrippa arrived before his uncle and raised charges of wicked conspiracy against Antipas. He claimed that his uncle had conspired against Tiberius and was now conspiring against Caligula.

Agrippa claimed that Antipas had 70,000 suits of armour in his possession. When Antipas admitted to this it was seen as proof of his guilt (he did not have these suits of armour for any malevolent reason, but he could not prove it). Antipas had his money and land taken, these were gifted to Agrippa, and his uncle was banished to France.

Herodias was spared by her brother, he interceded on her behalf to free her of punishment and even to keep her money. When she was informed of the offer Herodias rejected Caligula's mercy for the sake of her husband.

"Thou, indeed, O Emperor! actest after a magnificent manner, and as becomes thyself in what thou offerest me; but the kindness which I have for my husband hinders me from partaking of the favor of thy gift; for it is not just that I, who have been made a partner in his prosperity, should forsake him in his misfortunes."[109]

Even when Antipas was condemned to a life of misery and obscurity his wife stood by him.

It is my honest belief that Agrippa only resorted to this move because Antipas was making moves against him, I do not think Agrippa was willingly cruel or petty and that had he been left alone he would never have raised the charges.

The main reason for this is that he interceded on behalf of Herodias by asking Caligula to let her keep her money and continue living in Judea. If he had done it out of contempt, then I doubt he would have been so kind to his sister in the end.

Agrippa was now the King of Galilee, Perea and Batanea. He was the first true King of the Jews in almost half a century. As the King of the Jews Agrippa derived a new level of authority in the region, he was the enforcer for Caligula in the eastern regions and was arguably his most trusted deputy in the middle east.

He was able to delicately preserve the interests of his people without getting his head cut off.

As the Emperor lost his mind Agrippa's was sharper than ever. He didn't complain or bat an eye when Caligula declared himself to be divine. Caligula did this in the most absurd and theatrical ways imaginable, it earned him the distrust of most people who believed in the Roman religion, but it outright terrified and incensed anyone who believed in a monotheistic religion like Judaism.

To be ruled by a man who saw himself as a living G-d created a religious schism so severe that it threatened the stability of Judaea as a Roman province. The Jews began to become riotous as a result of the Emperor's moral depravity and idolatry.

Agrippa was sent to Alexandria to check on Aulus Avilius Flaccus, who was the Prefect of Egypt at this time. The Jews had rioted in Alexandria and so too had the goyim (non-Jews) of the city countered these riots.

The issue arose when Caligula gifted statues of himself to all the houses of worship in the empire. The Jews regarded idols as sinful and rejected the statues. They raucously refused to let Rome push their religion on them.

The non-Jews of the city were also upset because they perceived the refusal of the Jews to take on the Roman religion as a sign of disloyalty.

Alexandria had a sizeable Jewish population at this time and tensions between them and the Greeks got worse when the Jews refused to behave 'like everyone else'.

It became so bad that Agrippa was sent as the emissary of the Jews to make peace. The mere fact that he was regarded as King of the Jews proves his popularity and legitimacy. If he could speak for the Jewish people then it can be inferred that they felt reasonably comfortable with having him as their representative.

The riots got worse when the King of the Jews came because he was seen as a foreign leader, the notion that Alexandrine Jews were more loyal to a foreign state than the one in which they resided created endless ethnic tensions.

They were seen as a foreign race that needed to be sent back to where they came from or killed.

If one were to be cynical about it then it could be argued that Caligula knew exactly what he was doing by sending Agrippa in, and that the riots had been generated on purpose to consolidate Roman control of the east.

If the Greeks and Jews were fighting each other they would be much easier to suppress. It also gave Caligula a viable excuse to have Flaccus killed, which he had been wanting to do for some time anyway.

Perhaps then what is often regarded as a sign of Caligula's madness was actually a sign of his ingenuity and political savvy.

Caligula was however deeply incensed by the notion that the Jews would reject his divine status. He wanted to exterminate them and place his statue forcibly in the Holy Temple in Jerusalem.

When he was told of this Herod Agrippa did something so bold that it will be remembered forever. He marched in front of the Emperor and did something no one else ever could, he told him no.

He is said to have done it in a very polite and sly way. Josephus recounts what Caligula said to his friend Agrippa at a feast.

"I knew before now how great a respect thou hast had for me, and how great kindness thou hast shown me, though with those hazards to thyself, which thou underwentest under Tiberius on that account; nor hast thou omitted any thing to show thy good-will towards us, even beyond thy ability; whence it would be a base thing for me to be conquered by thy affection. I am therefore desirous to make thee amends for every thing in which I have been formerly deficient; for all that I have bestowed on thee, that may be called my gifts, is but little. Everything that may contribute to thy happiness shall be at thy service, and that cheerfully, and so far as my ability will reach."[110]

Agrippa was clever and used this chance to avoid the ruin of his faith and his people.

"Since thou, O my lord! declarest such is thy readiness to grant, that I am worthy of thy gifts, I will ask nothing relating to my own felicity; for what thou hast already bestowed on me has made me excel therein; but I desire somewhat which may make thee glorious for piety, and render the Divinity assistant to thy designs, and may be for an honor to me among those that inquire about it, as showing that I never once fail of obtaining what I desire of thee; for my petition is this, that thou wilt no longer think of the dedication of that statue which thou hast ordered to be set up in the Jewish temple by Petronius."[111]

Caligula was apparently caught off guard by this, and to avoid being accused of being a liar he did as Agrippa wished. If anyone else had done this or if Agrippa had done it in a less elegant way, he probably would have been killed.

Caligula is alleged to have killed many people for relatively small infractions. Caligula also relented on putting his statues up in synagogues, this only ended up making the ethnic tensions worse, however.

The Greeks of Alexandria felt that the Jews were being given special treatment and that they were in some way exerting control on the government. This has obvious antisemitic parallels with modernity as well.

Even though the Jews had gained a small victory they were now subjected to endless racially motivated pogroms in the foreign cities they occupied, and even in the cities in Judaea where enough of the population were non-Jews.

It is said that Caligula changed his mind and tried to have the temple desecrated, but because his lackies in the east didn't want to trigger a racial conflict they delayed doing it for quite some time.

They delayed it so long in fact that Caligula died before it had the chance to be done. For obvious reasons anyone with a proper understanding of the Roman east would not have wanted to desecrate the Holiest location in Judaism.

When Caligula was assassinated in 41CE Agrippa was a prominent supporter of Claudius as his successor. When Claudius attained the purple, he rewarded Agrippa for his help in rallying supporters.

Claudius made Agrippa King of all of Judea in 41CE, including cities which hadn't even been in Herod's old Kingdom. Judaea was under Jewish rule again and Agrippa was the most legitimate claimant left.

He was a grandson of Herod, but he was also a grandson of Mariamne, and by extension he had Hasmonean heritage.

Agrippa was at this time a Roman more than a Jew, but during his reign he grew to be more of a Jew than a Roman. Despite this he was a Maccabee, a Hasmonean, a Herodian, and with all of these branches on his family tree he was the all-encompassing King of the Jews.

Claudius even released an edict in support of the Jews living in other parts of the empire to please his friend Agrippa.

"Tiberius Claudius Cæsar Augustus Germanicus, high priest, tribune of the people, chosen consul the second time, ordains thus: Upon the petition of king Agrippa and king Herod, who are persons very dear to me, that I would grant the same rights and privileges should be preserved to the Jews which are in all the Roman empire, which I have granted to those of Alexandria, I very willingly comply therewith; and this grant I

make not only for the sake of the petitioners, but as judging those Jews for
whom I have been petitioned worthy of such a favor, on account of their
fidelity and friendship to the Romans. I think it also very just that no
Grecian city should be deprived of such rights and privileges, since they
were preserved to them under the great Augustus. It will therefore be fit to
permit the Jews, who are in all the world under us, to keep their ancient
customs without being hindered so to do. And I do charge them also to use
this my kindness to them with moderation, and not to show a contempt of
the superstitious observances of other nations, but to keep their own laws
only. And I will that this decree of mine be engraven on tables by the
magistrates of the cities, and colonies, and municipal places, both those
within Italy and those without it, both kings and governors, by the means
of the ambassadors, and to have them exposed to the public for full thirty
days, in such a place whence it may plainly be read from the ground."[112]

This ensured the safety of the Jews (to a limited degree) in the
empire for a time. It certainly bought Agrippa a great deal of public
support from his subjects who saw him as their liberator and a true
brother.

This was not some hateful foreigner; this was the true King who
the Jews had been waiting for.

The chief evidence that this was done out of love rather than
political utility is that Claudius generally preferred a policy of making eastern territories into provinces, he made a stark and obvious
exception for his friend Agrippa by giving him the biggest and most
powerful Kingdom in the Roman east.

Although Claudius had put Agrippa in his position, Agrippa did
not rule for him, he ruled for the Jews.

Agrippa built many useful buildings across the Kingdom, rather
than making monuments to his vanity.

Like the old Herod this new Herod chose to build waterways and theatres and other symbols of modernity.

He also went entirely against the interests of Rome by building a defensive wall around Jerusalem. Claudius forced him to stop the construction of this wall but what it illustrates is that Agrippa was not going to be subservient to Rome.

From 41CE until 45CE Herod was the undisputed ruler of a free Jewish state. The most notable incident of his reign occurred in the Jewish temple during the Holy festival of Sukkot.

He began to read from the book of Deuteronomy, and when he reached Book 17, verse 15.

"You may not put a foreigner over you, for he is not your brother."

Agrippa was touched by this line; it represented all his insecurities and the legacy of his grandfather. He sobbed in front of the crowd because he felt foreign, he loved his people but somewhere inside himself he feared that they didn't love him back.

When he read from Deuteronomy the people heard his Hebrew and it was better than they had imagined. He also refused to sit on the luxuriant litter they built for him, he stood tall and spoke the words of the Torah.

Rabbi Gamliel, the Nasi of this time was deeply moved by Agrippa's tears, knowing that they came from his earnest soul.

He embraced Agrippa and remarked simply. *"You are our brother."*

And with that Agrippa cemented the love his people bore for him. They applauded and never forgot his righteousness and piety.

No King of the Jews had ever been so loved, and none would ever be so loved again. In 45CE Agrippa was sadly met with doom. At the peak of his power and at the peak of Jewish prosperity Herod saw a horrid sight. He saw the owl.

Just as had been foretold the owl came back during the daytime, an announcement of his imminent death.

The tragic end of Agrippa is recounted by Flavius Josephus.

"Now when Agrippa had reigned three years over all Judea he came to the city Caesarea, which was formerly called Strato's Tower; and there he exhibited spectacles in honor of Caesar, for whose well-being he'd been informed that a certain festival was being celebrated. At this festival a great number were gathered together of the principal persons of dignity of his province. On the second day of the spectacles he put on a garment made wholly of silver, of a truly wonderful texture, and came into the theater early in the morning. There the silver of his garment, being illuminated by the fresh reflection of the sun's rays, shone out in a wonderful manner, and was so resplendent as to spread awe over those that looked intently upon him. Presently his flatterers cried out, one from one place, and another from another, (though not for his good) that he was a g-d; and they added, "Be thou merciful to us; for although we have hitherto reverenced thee only as a man, yet shall we henceforth own thee as superior to mortal nature." Upon this the king neither rebuked them nor rejected their impious flattery. But he shortly afterward looked up and saw an owl sitting on a certain rope over his head, and immediately understood that this bird was the messenger of ill tidings, just as it had once been the messenger of good tidings to him; and fell into the deepest sorrow. A severe pain arose in his belly, striking with a most violent intensity. He therefore looked upon his friends, and said, "I, whom you call a g-d, am commanded presently to depart this life; while Providence thus reproves the lying words you just now said to me; and I, who was by you called immortal, am immediately to be hurried away by death. But I

*am bound to accept what Providence allots, as it pleases G-d; for we have
by no means lived ill, but in a splendid and happy manner." When he had
said this, his pain became violent. Accordingly he was carried into the
palace, and the rumor went abroad everywhere that he would certainly
die soon. The multitude sat in sackcloth, men, women and children, after
the law of their country, and besought G-d for the king's recovery. All
places were also full of mourning and lamentation. Now the king rested
in a high chamber, and as he saw them below lying prostrate on the
ground he could not keep himself from weeping. And when he had been
quite worn out by the pain in his belly for five days, he departed this life,
being in the fifty-fourth year of his age and in the seventh year of his
reign. He ruled four years under Caius Caesar, three of them were over
Philip's tetrarchy only, and on the fourth that of Herod was added to it;
and he reigned, besides those, three years under Claudius Caesar, during
which time he had Judea added to his lands, as well as Samaria and
Cesarea."[113]*

Agrippa seems to have suffered from the same genetic disease
which impacted his grandfather, or at least something similar. His
symptoms seemed to avoid the same genital gangrene which probably means Herod the Great had a longer illness which produced
more severely gangrenous flesh.

Some think Agrippa was killed by Claudius for his attempts to
make Judea a more independent nation, but this seems to contradict the way Claudius treated Agrippa and the favours he poured
on him.

One does not often install someone as a King only to kill him
covertly, it feels fanciful as well considering Agrippa's immense
popularity with his subjects.

In his reign Agrippa had restored a worthy man (Simon, son of Herod Boethus) as the High Priest, he had the government restored to order and put Judaism at the forefront of all his many works.

He died a man more beloved than any other and left his country happy and pious. Claudius annexed Judaea into the Roman empire as a province. Every scrap of Jewish land was now for the first time a province of the Roman empire.

What followed on from Agrippa's golden age was an epoch of Roman repression that eventually led to the first (but not the last) attempt at genocide against the Jews.

Agrippa was the greatest King of the Jews, but he was not the last. That honour is reserved for a man who made honour into a farce.

11

Chapter 11- How the Julio-Claudians Met Their End

The latter portion of the Julio-Claudian dynasty's rule coincided with the events of Herod Agrippa II's fall, which makes it essential to discuss this context prior to discussing events in Judaea.

Claudius was born in 10BCE to Drusus the Elder (Son of Livia and her first husband) and Antonia the Younger (a daughter of Mark Anthony).

His father died only a year after his birth, so he was left to be raised by his mother who loathed him. Antonia would belittle and attack Claudius, despite the fact that he was the most dutiful of her children.

She (and his other relatives) loathed him because he was physically hampered by a series of bodily deformities. The extent of his mobility issues has been recounted by Cassius Dio.

"In mental ability he was by no means inferior, as his faculties had been in constant training (in fact, he had actually written some historical treatises); but he was sickly in body, so that his head and hands shook slightly. Because of this his voice was also faltering, and he did not himself read all the measures that he introduced before the Senate, but would give them to the quaestor to read, though at first, at least, he was generally present. Whatever he did read himself, he usually delivered sitting down. Furthermore, he was the first of the Romans to use a covered chair, and it is due to his example that to-day not only the Emperors but we ex-consuls as well are carried in chairs; of course, even before his time Augustus, Tiberius, and some others had been carried in litters such as women still affect even at the present day. It was not these infirmities, however, that caused the deterioration of Claudius so much as it was the freedmen and the women with whom he associated; for he, more conspicuously than any of his peers, was ruled by slaves and by women. From a child he had been reared a constant prey to illness and great terror, and for that reason had feigned a stupidity greater than was really the case (a fact that he himself admitted in the Senate); and he had lived for a long time with his grandmother Livia and for another long period with his mother Antonia and with the freedmen, and moreover he had had many amours with him. Hence he had acquired none of the qualities befitting a freeman, but, though ruler of all the Romans and their subjects, had become himself a slave. They would take advantage of him particularly when he was inclined to drink or to sexual intercourse, since he applied himself to both these vices insatiably and when so employed was exceedingly easy to master. Moreover, he was afflicted by cowardice, which often so overpowered him that he could not reason out

anything as he ought. They seized upon this failing of his, too, to accomplish many of their purposes; for by frightening him they could use him fully for their own ends, and could at the same time inspire the rest with great terror. To give but a single example, once, when a large number of persons were invited to dinner on the same day by Claudius and by these associates, the guests neglected Claudius on one pretence or another, and flocked around the others."[114]

So now this partially disabled man who was in his fifties and who had only survived because no one remembered to kill him was the Emperor of the Roman empire. He had beaten all the odds and he would keep beating them for the rest of his reign.

Although some of these lines are overdramatic and resembled polemics more than history, they do illustrate something that was eminently true – that the women in his life did have an intense amount of control over his administration.

These women were often of a higher rank than him and fiercely intelligent by any measure, Agrippina the Younger for instance was the wiliest and most cunning of Claudius' wives.

In his early life Claudius had been a historian and wrote a history of the civil wars which had racked the Roman state in the time before his birth. This history was suppressed by the Julio-Claudians and generated lasting anger at Claudius, he had evidently been too critical of

Augustus or of other prominent members of his own family. Either way the fact that he was what amounted to the ancient equivalent of a suppressed journalist shows how much he seemed to value truth and honesty.

People still seemed to underestimate him, this mistake ended up costing a few of them their lives and was the primary reason Claudius was able to rise to the top.

Suetonius also recounts the degree to which people underestimated Claudius in his early and middle years.

"Claudius was born at Lyons, in the consulship of Julius Antonius, and
Fabius Africanus, upon the first of August, the very day upon which an
altar was first dedicated there to Augustus. He was named Tiberius
Claudius Drusus, but soon afterwards, upon the adoption of his elder
brother into the Julian family, he assumed the cognomen of Germanicus.
He was left an infant by his father, and during almost the whole of his
minority, and for some time after he attained the age of manhood, was
afflicted with a variety of obstinate disorders, insomuch that his mind
and body being greatly impaired, he was, even after his arrival at years
of maturity, never thought sufficiently qualified for any public or private
employment. He was, therefore, during a long time, and even after the
expiration of his minority, under the direction of a pedagogue, who, he
complains in a certain memoir, "was a barbarous wretch, and formerly
superintendent of the mule-drivers, who was selected for his governor, on
purpose to correct him severely on every trifling occasion." On account of
this crazy constitution of body and mind, at the spectacle of gladiators,
which he gave the people, jointly with his brother, in honour of his
father's memory, he presided, muffled up in a pallium—a new fashion.
When he assumed the manly habit, he was carried in a litter, at mid-
night, to the Capitol, without the usual ceremony."[115]

Although it is clear to us today that the people who mocked and insulted Claudius were cruel and morally defective, this general trend of viewing Claudius with contempt because of his physical defects does explain the abusiveness of his mother's treatment.

Antonia was dead by the time Claudius achieved the purple; she had killed herself after Caligula killed Gemellus in cold blood. Both Gemellus and Caligula were her grandsons so it was an act of viciousness she simply couldn't live with.

During Caligula's reign Claudius had been something resembling a jester. He was used, abused, put into debt and mocked. People mocked him to please the Emperor, and the Emperor put all of his burdens and difficult offices on his uncle (in the expectation that he would fail at them).

In actuality Claudius did rather well in the circumstances afforded to him, and often was able to save himself from execution because he feigned ignorance. In 41CE when Caligula was stabbed to death Claudius was the last adult male of his line.

He was quite literally the only option anyone had. Even so he was a very good Emperor by most accounts and succeeded in far more than Gaius had.

He took the titles and honours thrust upon him with reluctance, he was only Emperor by chance and often put duty before any level of ego or self-indulgence.

Claudius carefully reformed the government and reversed the unjust tax policies of his nephew; he also brought his nieces Livilla and Agrippina back from their ignominious exile.

Rather than directly and explicitly deriding his nephew's rule Claudius simply decided to show people that he was different. He burned the treason papers which Caligula had used to execute the Senators, and he removed the extravagant statues of Gaius which had been placed all over the empire.

Claudius deified his grandmother Livia and honoured his mother despite all the wrongs she had done him.

Claudius refused to be vain and refused many honours the Senate bestowed on him. So too did he refuse the statues and ornaments they voted for him to have.

He saw statues as folly and wanted to be honoured by the good works of the Roman people.

In fact, Claudius didn't even let his family have excessive honours.

"He celebrated the marriage of his daughter and the birth-day of a grandson with great privacy, at home."[116]

The standard at this time was that the Senate passed laws requiring the celebration of birthdays and weddings of members of the royal family. To relegate his family to a lower status by rejecting these festivities indicates a measure of humility and good sense that separates Claudius from most other Roman Emperors.

Refusing these honours would be the equivalent of the Duke and Duchess of Cambridge getting married at Buckingham Palace without any cameras or any news coverage. It went against precedent and seemed to be indicative of Claudius' desire for a less prominent life.

In 43CE Claudius succeeded in conquering Britain for the empire, this feat had not been achieved by Julius Caesar, Germanicus, Caligula or Augustus. It was something many had assumed was impossible, but with appropriate preparations and good organisation Claudius made a success of it.

He refused to accept the title of Britannicus but allowed it to be given to his young son who is commonly known by that moniker today.

Valeria Messalina was the boy's mother and Claudius' third wife. She was and is a subject of great controversy and scandal.

Messalina is said to have been a serial adulterer, her sexual exploits have become semi-mythical. She was finally slain in 48CE when she allegedly married another man in public.

"Messalina, as if it were not enough for her to play the adulteress and harlot, — for in addition to her shameless behaviour in general she at times sat as a prostitute in the palace himself and compelled the other women of the highest rank to do the same, — now conceived a desire to have many husbands, that is, men really bearing that title. And she would have been married by a legal contract to all those who enjoyed her favours, had she not been detected and destroyed in her very first attempt. For a time, indeed, all the imperial freedmen had been hand in glove with her and would do nothing except in agreement with her; but when she falsely accused Polybius and caused his death, even while she was maintaining improper relations with him, they no longer trusted her; and thus, having lost their good-will, she perished. It came about on this wise. She caused Gaius Silius, son of the Silius slain by Tiberius, to be registered as her husband, celebrated the marriage in costly fashion, bestowed a royal residence upon him, in which she had already brought together the most valuable of Claudius' heirlooms; and finally she appointed him consul. Now all these doings, though for some time they had been either heard about or witnessed by everybody else, continued to escape the notice of Claudius. But finally, when he went down to Ostia to inspect the grain supply and she was left behind in Rome on the pretext of being ill, she got up a banquet of no little renown and carried on a most licentious revel. Then Narcissus, having got Claudius by himself, informed him through his concubines of all that was taking place. And by frightening him with the idea that Messalina was going to kill him and set up Silius as ruler in his stead, he persuaded him to arrest and torture a number of persons. While this was going on, the Emperor himself hastened back to the city; and immediately upon his arrival he put to death Mnester together with

many others, and then slew Messalina herself after she had retreated into
the gardens of Asiaticus, which more than anything else were the cause of
her ruin."[117]

This wife was replaced with Agrippina the Younger, Claudius'
niece. Agrippina was ambitious and through machinations was able
to convince Claudius to appoint her son by a minor nobleman as
the heir apparent.

Nero was adopted as Claudius' son and set to inherit the empire.
This was a repeat of precedent in many ways. The Claudians had
the throne in the form of Claudius, and the Julians would get it back
again in the form of Nero.

Agrippina would have a great deal of influence throughout the
remainder of Claudius' reign and this trend did not change later
when her son ruled.

Claudius ruled for 13 years and died in 54CE. It is highly likely
that Claudius was killed by his wife Agrippina via poison. His death
is recounted by Suetonius.

"Soon afterwards he made his will, and had it signed by all the magis-
trates as witnesses. But he was prevented from proceeding further by
Agrippina, accused by her own guilty conscience, as well as by informers,
of a variety of crimes. It is agreed that he was taken off by poison; but
where, and by whom administered, remains in uncertainty. Some authors
say that it was given him as he was feasting with the priests in the
Capitol, by the eunuch Halotus, his taster. Others say by Agrippina, at his
own table, in mushrooms, a dish of which he was very fond. The accounts
of what followed likewise differ. Some relate that he instantly became
speechless, was racked with pain through the night, and died about day-
break; others, that at first he fell into a sound sleep, and afterwards, his

food rising, he threw up the whole; but had another dose given him; whether in water-gruel, under pretence of refreshment after his exhaustion, or in a clyster, as if designed to relieve his bowels, is likewise uncertain."[118]

Regardless of how it happened Claudius ate something that killed him, his 13 years on the throne were over and now Nero, who was only 16 came to inhabit Rome's throne.

Cassius Dio's account of Claudius' death was far more dramatic compared to Suetonius'.

"In such a manner did Claudius meet his end. It seemed as if this event had been indicated by the comet, which was seen for a very long time, by the shower of blood, by the thunder-bolt that fell upon the standards of the Praetorians, by the opening of its own accord of the temple of Jupiter Victor, by the swarming of bees in the camp, and by the fact that one incumbent of each political office died. The Emperor received the state burial and all the other honours that had been accorded to Augustus. Agrippina and Nero pretended to grieve for the man whom they had killed, and elevated to heaven him whom they had carried out on a litter from the banquet. On this point Lucius Junius Gallius, the brother of Seneca, was the author of a very witty remark. Seneca himself had composed a work that he called "Pumpkinification" — a word formed on the analogy of "deification"; and his brother is credited with saying a great deal in one short sentence. Inasmuch as the public executioners were accustomed to drag the bodies of those executed in the prison to the Forum with large hooks, and from there hauled them to the river, he remarked that Claudius had been raised to heaven with a hook.

Nero, too, has left us a remark not unworthy of record. He declared mushrooms to be the food of the g-ds, since Claudius by means of the mushroom had become a g-d."[19]

In this account more credence is given to the supernatural, but it does illustrate Agrippina's part in the death and the fact that Nero at the very least derived benefit from the death, even if he had been too young to have a serious part in the plot.

Claudius had achieved a great deal, and in many ways his successor was set for success.

Claudius had done all the work, endured all the risks, and he had left Rome in a better state than before.

All Nero had to do was avoid angering too many people and consolidate Claudius' achievements.

The only thing that stopped Nero from initially doing these things was the influence of his mother, who acted as the ruler of Rome in all but name.

Agrippina ran the empire with the help of Seneca the Younger and Sextus Afranius Burrus.

Burrus was the Praetorian Prefect and Seneca was a high-ranking Senator and intellectual of the day.

Nero was tutored by Seneca and also married Claudius' daughter Claudia Octavia to ensure his legitimacy as Emperor.

Claudius' son was in his lower teens so whilst he couldn't run the empire, many people favoured him as the heir above Nero because he was the biological son of Claudius and because he was younger which made him more pliable.

The opening speech Nero made to the Senate was applauded, this was largely because Seneca wrote it for him.

Relations with the Senate consistently got worse as time went on, Seneca's influence could not repair a relationship that was always in terminal decline.

The new Emperor is alleged to have done all manner of despicable and excessive things.

According to Cassius Dio, when Nero wanted to give 10,000,000 sesterces to a friend of his Agrippina brought the sum out in front of Nero to illustrate how much money it was.

Instead, Nero doubled it saying, *"I did not realize that I had given him so little."*

The result of this was increases in tax according to Dio. This seems like a fabrication considering how much the general public liked Nero, it does not seem realistic that he would raise taxes on them and still keep their favour. This (along with a lot of the other accusations) are probably fabrications of the aristocratic Roman historians.

History to the Romans was far less about telling the truth in an objective way than it was about promoting the worldview of the person who wrote it. If you wrote a history that was too critical or too supportive of someone the Senate liked or disliked then you would simply be killed or suppressed, much like how Claudius' history of Rome's civil wars was suppressed.

Often a historian was paid by someone of authority to write a history favouring whoever the person of authority wanted, or to condemn the memory of someone they disliked.

In the case of histories around this period however it was largely Senators themselves that wrote them. For obvious reasons this makes their accounts dubious, especially in consideration of Emperors who had a poor relationship with the Senators.

Nero evidently did something to make them angry, because multiple Senatorial sources have painted him as something between Hannibal Lecter and the antichrist.

These claims are obviously made up to some degree, but there's no smoke without a fire. To overexaggerate something there still has to be a nugget of truth in it. We can infer that even if Nero wasn't as bad as we have been led to believe, he was still bad enough to turn the entire Senate against him.

The Emperor spent his early years exploring his creative interests in music and the arts, he indulged in his baser urges and chose to spend the time he had on women, wine and everything in-between.

Seneca and Burrus didn't seem to mind this, it played to their advantage if anything.

Agrippina meanwhile found it threatening, she felt that Nero's sexual encounters would allow other women to have influence over him.

As he strayed more and more from his wife Agrippina began plotting behind the scenes. She even supported Britannicus as the rightful heir to the throne in the hopes of reminding Nero that she was the one who made him Emperor (and that by extension she could unmake him if she chose to do so).

Instead of making him submit this just emboldened him, he had Britannicus killed by poisoning in 55CE.

In 57CE a crisis emerged when Tiridates was made the King of Armenia. Armenia had traditionally been a Roman client Kingdom and appointing Tiridates I (the Parthian King's brother) to that throne was seen as an act of war.

Nero captured the Armenian capital Artaxata, but the whole conflict ended in a peace deal where Tiridates I would remain King but would accept his crown from Nero. This rather unsatisfactory peace deal probably had a negative impact on Nero's reputation, especially considering the military successes of his predecessor Claudius.

Some compare Nero to Caligula, and whilst they ended their reigns in the same gory fashion,

I would not say it is an apt comparison. It is easy to put them in the same category, but in the end their styles and levels of competence were wildly different.

Caligula squandered the goodness of his reign after only 4 years, Nero on the other hand ruled Rome for more than a decade and did so with consistently wide public support.

These figures are similar in the sense that they both indulged in a measure of familial ruthlessness, but this sort of analysis ignores the pressures they were under and just how ruthless the other members of their family were.

Augustus killed many relatives of his, he banished a great number more too. Although Augustus was among the least murderous Emperors, he did not attain his high office innocently. He purged, killed and maimed his way into power and every Emperor used such methods to keep their throne.

Tiberius meanwhile killed a great number of Senators and relatives to cement his rule. This fact often seems to get overlooked when Nero and Caligula are described as the 'mad Emperors.'

Tiberius was a pervert and a potential paedophile, he indulged himself on a secluded sex island and tortured his successor Caligula for 6 years. To me this at least resembles what Nero and Caligula are accused of.

The primary conclusion of this point is that I would argue for fairness in how we view the Julio-Claudians. If we are going to characterize Caligula and Nero as 'mad' then at the very least Tiberius should be lumped in with them and recognized as one of the worst Emperors Rome had in the early stages of the empire.

In some ways I think the primary reason that Tiberius is viewed more favourably than Caligula or Nero is that the Emperors of the Roman empire that came after the Julio-Claudians were (for the most part) so much worse that Tiberius' capabilities were inflated because relatively speaking he wasn't quite as bad as the rest.

Tiberius, Caligula and Nero all shared a commonality, when it came down to it, they were willing to kill whoever they needed to.

In 59CE the relationship between Agrippina and her son declined so severely that he decided to get rid of her.

Initially he tried to rig her boat to sink, but when she swam safely to shore, he cut the elaborate pretences and sent Anicetus his freedman to cut Agrippina down.

When the men came in with their swords Agrippina knew why they had been sent, as well as who sent them and remarked only this, *"Strike here, Anicetus, strike here, for this bore Nero."*

With that she was stabbed to death, and in honour of her request they stabbed her in the belly.

In all fairness she had killed Claudius and tried to kill Caligula, she had a penchant for murdering Emperors which made her a direct and credible threat to him. Now that she was alienated from a position of power it was a reasonable fear for Nero that she would try to kill him.

In many ways this act of matricide was pre-emptive self-defence rather than some poetically malicious act of violence. There was little Nero could do but stop the threat, even if in doing so he committed a great and heinous crime that no one would soon forget.

The Emperor was also known for his popularity with the people because he performed in public as an actor, poet and musician. He was highly acclaimed for his artistry, and it ultimately endeared him to the general public, who saw him as both down-to-earth and fiercely talented.

The Senate saw this as a farce meanwhile and disliked Nero's public appeal, they saw it as threatening and this back-and-forth of implicit distaste ultimately generated a great deal of violence from the Emperor. He began putting people to death on arbitrary charges and eventually even Seneca began to fear him.

Seneca spoke to Nero before some of his crimes could take place. He said these fitting words, that rang truer than perhaps any others.

"No matter how many you may slay, you cannot kill your successor."[120]

These words apparently got under Nero's skin. And who can blame him? Seneca had a way with words and from how the historical sources portrayed it he often said things with sarcastic overtones and even snide remarks.

A year after the death of his mother Nero faced another serious challenge. The warrior Queen of the Iceni tribe Boudica mounted a successful rebellion against the Romans in Britain.

Her husband Prasutagus King of the Iceni left his Kingdom jointly to the Romans and his daughters. The Romans ended up raping Boudica's daughters and having the woman herself flogged.

In a righteous flurry of outrage, she declared herself Queen and went to war with Rome.

The Roman governor Paulinus tried to rescue the displaced people of the cities of Camulodunum and Londinium (these and many more were levelled by Boudica), he fled north and faced Boudica's vastly larger armies.

Despite being soundly surrounded Paulinus was able to defeat the Britons and Boudica was forced to poison herself in 61CE.

Paulinus' campaign of retribution was so severe in fact that Nero had to move him to another posting.

Soon after this episode Nero did the most publicly damaging thing imaginable, he tried to get rid of his wife.

Divorces weren't inherently frowned upon by Roman society, but in the case of Nero's he was divorcing a woman of very noble birth and treated her so poorly that people largely felt sympathy for her.

Claudia Octavia was eventually subjected to a humiliating divorce and sent to the same island which had housed Agrippina the Elder (Caligula's mother) and Livilla (Caligula's sister).

Poor Octavia did not have to endure this torment for long because in 62CE Nero sent his men to kill her. They tied her up and cut her arms to make it look like a suicide, but when this didn't work, they threw her into a room so full of steam that she suffocated in it.

Her severed head was taken to the new Empress as a gift. This cruel act cannot be forgiven, but it does somewhat mirror the way other Emperors treated wives they no longer wanted to be with.

In 64CE one of the most memorable events of Nero's reign occurred. The Great Fire of Rome.

The fire began near the circus maximus and ended up burning for 7 days. It reignited and burned for 3 more.

The fire was immense and consumed a large portion of Rome, it affected the rich and the poor alike. It totally decimated the city and left many people homeless, parts of the city were completely lost.

To some it made Nero even more popular because of the timeless desire to have a strong leader during a crisis, and in others it created a burning hatred for the Emperor who had let his city burn while he was away in Antium (a city south of Rome where Nero is said to have been when the fire broke out).

Some sources claim that Nero fiddled while Rome burned or that he burned the city himself so that the flames could act as a backdrop for his theatrical parody of the siege of Troy, but he was most likely away on a foreign trip and even if he wasn't this version of events is frankly silly.

Some even blame him for the fire entirely, as he used it as an excuse to build monuments to himself later.

This seems like some form of propaganda at best and is likely an outright lie. Rome was vulnerable to fires and frankly it is surprising that it didn't occur earlier, the tightly packed wooden buildings that covered Rome's streets better resembled kindling than any sort of safe architecture.

In previous years Augustus had to limit the number of floors new buildings could have and fire safety became a serious issue for the Roman government.

Advanced city planning didn't stop Rome from being a matchbox. If one baker let a fire start or one person's lamp broke it had the potential of burning the entire city down. Nero just happened to be the unfortunate soul who inherited this precariously dense city at the wrong time.

And in fairness to Nero, he let the homeless and displaced live around his palaces and provided the greatest of reliefs for them that he could. Nero provided all of this at his own expense even though he could have cut corners or could have gotten the Senate to pay for it.

To pay for all of this and the reconstruction of the city Nero devalued the coinage. Even though this had disastrous impacts on Rome in the long term it was done with the best of intentions and there weren't any other options left.

Around this time Nero had a baby with his second wife Poppaea. The new Empress was a noblewoman called Poppaea Sabina. She was of high birth but was also already married to a certain Otho.

Otho was forced to divorce her so that Nero could take her for himself. He seemed to genuinely love his new wife, and for a time her distractions seemed to placate him.

This marriage was probably due to Poppaea having become pregnant already by Nero. In 63CE they had a baby girl, but she died in infancy.

They ended up becoming fiercely argumentative and in 65CE he killed his wife in a fit of rage. Both Suetonius and Cassius Dio gave accounts of this event.

"He married Poppaea twelve days after the divorce of Octavia,, and entertained a great affection for her; but, nevertheless, killed her with a kick which he gave her when she was big with child, and in bad health, only because she found fault with him for returning late from driving his chariot."[121]

This short account by Suetonius gives greater detail to the death itself and less to what happened thereafter, the account of Cassius Dio does the opposite.

"Sabina also perished at this time through an act of Nero's; either accidentally or intentionally he had leaped upon her with his feet while she was pregnant. The extremes of luxury indulged in by this Sabina I will indicate in the briefest terms. She caused gilded shoes to be put on the mules that drew her and caused five hundred asses that had recently foaled to be milked daily that she might bathe in their milk. For she bestowed the greatest pains on the beauty and brilliancy of her person, and this is why, when she noticed in a mirror one day that her appearance was not comely, she prayed that she might die before she passed her prime. Nero missed her so greatly after her death that on learning of a woman who resembled her he at first sent for her and kept her; but later he caused a boy of the freedmen, whom he used to call Sporus, to be castrated, since he, too, resembled Sabina, and he used him in every way like a wife. In due time, though already "married" to Pythagoras, a freedman, he formally "married" Sporus, and assigned the boy a regular dowry according to contract; and the Romans as well as others publicly celebrated their wedding."[122]

Nero's marriage to Sporus was considered a scandalous affair, but not for the reasons most would expect. The way he had killed his wife was the main point of contention, because Nero was taking the active role sexually, he was not considered to be unmasculine nor was he going against the norms of Roman society.

This account by Dio seems to put greater emphasis on Nero's sexual depravity and derides him for having a homosexual relationship more than for the fact that he murdered his wife.

Dio is often cited by Christians because of their obvious negative views of Nero, so it is important to take his accounts with a handful of salt.

The Christians faced intense persecution from the Neronian government because he blamed them for the great fire. It is recorded that he used the Christians as human candles at his parties, and that they were burned alive, fed to wild beasts and also crucified.

According to Eusebius the Apostles Peter and Paul met their ends at Nero's hand too.

"Thus publicly announcing himself as the first among G-d's chief enemies, he was led on to the slaughter of the apostles. It is, therefore, recorded that Paul was beheaded in Rome itself, and that Peter likewise was crucified under Nero. This account of Peter and Paul is substantiated by the fact that their names are preserved in the cemeteries of that place even to the present day."[123]

The Christian writer Tertullian is the first person to have explicitly referred to Nero as a persecutor of the Christians. His lost work 'Apologeticum' is quoted by Eusebius in his 'Church History.'

"Examine your records. There you will find that Nero was the first that persecuted this doctrine."[124]

Nero is even regarded by some as the Antichrist because the Hebrew numerical transliteration of his name comes to 666.

This sort of biased view has no place in a historical analysis beyond simply acting as an indicator of what people thought about what really happened.

Contempt for Nero from the Christians and the Senators implies that he made moves which antagonised these groups. Nothing in history can ever be considered concrete but this form of inference is an essential guide that can be just as useful as a direct statement of fact.

In the same year as Poppaea's death the first major conspiracy against Nero came about.

Gaius Calpurnius Piso rallied Senatorial support to have Nero killed and take his place as Emperor.

The plot gained a great deal of support and could have been a success, but unfortunately for the conspirators it ended up getting leaked to the Emperor.

A slave girl by the name of Epicharis divulged a part of the plan to Volusius Proculus, a man of the navy who bemoaned his lack of favours from the Emperor. What the girl didn't bet on was that Proculus was loyal to Nero and reported the conspiracy immediately.

Many high-ranking officials were implicated including Seneca. The old man was told to kill himself, this was a far less humiliating end than he would have been given had he been executed for treason.

"It would be no small task to speak of all the others that perished, but the fate of Seneca calls for a few words. It was his wish to end the life of his wife Paulina at the same time with his own, for he declared that he had

taught her both to despise death and to desire to leave the world in company with him. So he opened her veins as well as his own. But as he died hard, his end was hastened by the soldiers; and she was still alive when he passed away, and thus survived. He did not lay hands upon himself, however, until he had revised the book which he was writing and had deposited his other books with some friends, fearing that they would otherwise fall into Nero's hands and be destroyed. Thus died Seneca, notwithstanding that he had on the pretext of illness abandoned the society of the Emperor and had bestowed upon him his entire property, ostensibly to help to pay for the buildings he was constructing. His brothers, too, perished after him."[125]

It was in this way that Seneca died, he bled too slowly to die so he was suffocated in a steaming bath. Nero had killed the only person left who had known him as a boy (Burrus died in 62CE), he was truly alone.

There was no one left to whisper in his ear, no one left to steady his course. Now the only thing governing him was himself, his reign would see a marked decline from this point on.

So too was the poet Lucan put to death in the same way. Many wise and just men opened their wrists in 65CE.

Nero was not just known for his string of Senatorial killings, but also for his desire of prowess in the arts and sport.

Nero competed in the Olympics and according to Cassius Dio he 'won' many of the contests.

"At the Olympic games he fell from the chariot he was driving and came very near being crushed to death; yet he was crowned victor. In acknowledgement of this favour he gave to the Hellanodikai the million sesterces which Galba later demanded back from them."[126]

The Hellanodikai were the judges at the games. It seems from this that Nero bribed his way into acclamation and victory, which is probably true.

Whether or not this actually happened it does illustrate the image Nero wanted to create for himself, and his general narcissism.

What ultimately caused Nero's downfall wasn't his barbarity, or his sexual depravity, or his lavish spending. It was the thing that ultimately makes or breaks all leaders in the end. Tax.

Vindex, the governor of Gallia Lugdunensis declared his open opposition to Nero's rule in 68CE and declared his support for Servius Sulpicius Galba, a prominent Roman nobleman positioned in Spain.

Nero's miscalculation was to put Galba to death. Galba had professed his loyalty and opposed the notion that he should be Emperor, but Nero put him to death anyway.

Once he had been sentenced to death Galba had nothing to lose. If he was going to be executed, he might as well make moves for the throne. What had been a fledgling movement became a full-scale rebellion because Nero arrogantly forgot that Galba would be forced to mount a rebellion in this situation.

A far more prudent move would have been to have Galba killed quietly, or to deceive him into a false sense of security. Simply condemning him gave him no other option but to march on Rome.

Even at this stage Galba probably could have been stopped, but Nero failed to move decisively.

Galba's revolt created a domino effect, he emboldened the Senate to plot against Nero and in the end Nero's enemies overpowered him politically.

The Senate declared him a public enemy and his guardsmen abandoned him in the night. It was over, Nero decided to flee the country from a port in Ostia, but even the sailors now denied him.

The Senate had won, Nero resigned himself to a tragic and isolated death.

The Roman elites disliked him, but the troops and the common people loved him. For decades after his death people came out as 'Nero reborn' and tried to claim that the Emperor people adored had come back to life.

Before the advent of modern technology, it was fairly easy to just pretend that you were somebody else. Without cameras or voice recording devices there was no way to verify what the Emperor looked like or what he sounded like.

Most news reached the provinces and rural areas over a long period of time and much like a game of Chinese whispers the information could easily be manipulated or lost. If you came up to a poor farmer in Gaul and told them the Emperor had come back, they would probably be inclined to believe you.

And even if they did not there would be no way to disprove the claims that you made.

There are many historical examples of pretenders, such as Lambert Simnel and Perkin Warbeck who pretended to be Yorkist successors to the English throne.

Both Simnel and Warbeck were imposters trained as boys to pretend to be nobles in the hopes of deposing Henry VII. Neither of them succeeded but they caused enough trouble to be worth talking about.

People of this sort would simply claim they were a person of note and try to gain popular support.

Often these attempts failed because the people in power could kill or imprison the imposters fairly easily, but they also generated a lot of upheaval.

The pretenders of Nero ended up becoming a long-standing issue for his successors.

Nero inherited the whole world, and the madness of his bloodline. The madness overtook all of his positive qualities in the end.

He fled to a villa in the countryside, knowing that there was no way out, no escape, no respite of any sort.

"All who surrounded him now pressing him to save himself from the indignities which were ready to befall him, he ordered a pit to be sunk before his eyes, of the size of his body, and the bottom to be covered with pieces of marble put together, if any could be found about the house; and water and wood, to be got ready for immediate use about his corpse; weeping at every thing that was done, and frequently saying, "What an artist is now about to perish!" Meanwhile, letters being brought in by a servant belonging to Phaon, he snatched them out of his hand, and there read, "That he had been declared an enemy by the Senate, and that search was making for him, that he might be punished according to the ancient custom of the Romans." He then inquired what kind of punishment that was; and being told, that the practice was to strip the criminal naked, and scourge him to death, while his neck was fastened within a forked stake, he was so terrified that he took up two daggers which he had brought with him, and after feeling the points of both, put them up again, saying, "The fatal hour is not yet come." One while, he begged of Sporus to begin to wail and lament; another while, he entreated that one of them would set him an example by killing himself; and then again, he condemned his own want of resolution in these words: "I yet live to my shame and disgrace: this is not becoming for Nero: it is not becoming. Thou oughtest in such circumstances to have a good heart: Come, then: courage, man!" The horsemen who had received orders to bring him away alive, were now approaching the house. As soon as he heard them coming, he uttered with a trembling voice the following verse,

Hippon m'okupodon amphi ktupos ouata ballei;

The noise of swift-heel'd steeds assails my ears;

he drove a dagger into his throat, being assisted in the act by Epaphrodi-
tus, his secretary. A centurion bursting in just as he was half-dead, and
applying his cloak to the wound, pretending that he was come to his
assistance, he made no other reply but this, "'Tis too late;" and "Is this
your loyalty?" Immediately after pronouncing these words, he expired,
with his eyes fixed and starting out of his head, to the terror of all who
beheld him. He had requested of his attendants, as the most essential
favour, that they would let no one have his head, but that by all means his
body might be burnt entire. And this, Icelus, Galba's freedman, granted.
He had but a little before been discharged from the prison into which he
had been thrown, when the disturbances first broke out."[127]

Nero paced around his villa, consumed by a sense of doom and repeating a phase, *"What an artist dies in me."*

Sporus was by his side, as were his freedmen. Nero eventually built up the courage to kill himself, with the help of his faithful freedmen. He stabbed himself in the throat just before the men who had been sent for him arrived.

The men tried in vain to save Nero, perhaps to bring him for his execution, or perhaps out of loyalty.

As Nero choked on his own blood, he looked up at the soldiers who had been sent to collect him. He spoke his final words to them, *"Too late, this is fidelity."*

In their attempt to arrest Nero and have him clubbed to death before the masses the Senate failed. Nero died before justice could be done, he died on his terms (just as he had lived).

There is no excusing some of the things he allegedly did, but his legacy should still be re-examined with the evidence we have today.

The words Lady Caroline Lamb used to describe Lord Byron also fittingly describe Nero. He was *"mad, bad and dangerous to know."* This fact seems to have outlived all the others.

Nero died a renegade, a rebel and a rockstar. If he had been born today Nero would probably have been some sort of celebrity. Perhaps he would be driven by a vague sense of narcissism, but still loved, nonetheless.

It was in this way that the Julio-Claudian dynasty came to an end, in a blaze of gruesome glory.

12

Chapter 12- The Destruction of Judea by Herod Agrippa II

In 44CE Herod Agrippa was dead. His successor Herod Agrippa II (his son) was only 17 years old so Claudius, seeing the possible consequences of a teenager ruling Judea chose instead to send Cuspius Fadus to rule the province.

This may have been done out of genuine concern for the fate of Judea under a boy-King, but it was probably also simply a convenient excuse for Claudius to cement his control of the east.

Strategically speaking, Rome was far better off annexing and controlling Judea than having it as a separate Kingdom. Had Agrippa I for instance built his wall around Jerusalem it would have given him much more power and would have made it much more difficult for the Romans to keep order there.

Independence increased the odds of rebellions and decreased the ability of the Roman state to do anything about it.

But it must also be said that attempts at repression and control were met with an equal and opposite reaction. The rebellions and strings of Messianic claimants returned; the banditry of the Zealots came back more intensely than ever.

Fadus used brutal repression to deal with the issue of religious unrest. For instance, when Theudas claimed to be the Messiah and asked his followers to cross the river Jordan with him they were butchered before they could get there.[128]

Theudas himself was taken by the Romans and beheaded. Although this small insurrection was short lived it does illustrate just how unpopular the Romans were among the Jews and how much the Roman approach to controlling the Jews ended up backfiring.

Fadus only remained in office for two years but none of his successors would shy away from using these tactics.

A conflict between the Samaritans and the Galileans broke out which ended up generating contempt for the Romans (because they had refused to do anything to quell the discontent).

Agrippa II was at Rome at this time and implored Claudius to support the Jews over the Samaritans. Though he was not so attached to them as his father had been he still did his utmost for their preservation in this matter.

Unlike most Roman provinces Judaea was allowed to keep the Great Sanhedrin and this body was allowed to set tax rates as it saw fit.

As mentioned previously the Roman and Jewish tax systems were very different. The Sanhedrin's power over taxation generated the belief among the Romans that the Jews were keeping money for themselves and not paying their fair share.

Herod Agrippa I's brother Herod of Chalcis was also allowed to keep dominion over the temple and its treasury.

Nominally Herod Agrippa II was given control of Judaea as its King, but in practice he spent little time there and let the Romans do as they pleased. He valued his status as a minor Roman noble above his Jewish heritage.

Antisemitic canards took root in Roman culture that made the treatment of Jews harsher than it had ever been in the Roman world.

Cities like Tiberias, Alexandria and Caesarea became hotbeds of antisemitism from the Greek populations there.

In Caesarea especially problems began to arise because of the presence of a merchant house opposite a synagogue.

The Greek merchants wanted the Jews to leave their Synagogue because they saw it as demeaning to trade next to Jews, and the Jews wanted the merchants to stop trading outside their place of worship.

A back and forth ensued which saw the Greeks attempt to expand their building enough to cover the Synagogue's entrance, but this failed. The Greeks ended up sacrificing birds (augury) on the steps of the Synagogue, which was considered an act of religious desecration.

The Jews desperately pleaded with Gessius Florus (who was governor from 64-66CE), they even offered him a large sum of money but all he ended up doing was keeping the money and fleeing the city with his riches.

King Agrippa II was not there to help them because he was rarely in Judaea and spent the majority of his time in Berytus (modern Beirut).

Agrippa II was not like his father, he was a Hellenist and a Roman citizen, and valued his Roman credentials above his Jewish ones.

Josephus also seems to imply that Agrippa II and his sister Berenice shared an incestuous relationship,[129] a view that many historians corroborate.

This is because Agrippa II never married, and Berenice's marriages did not last very long. This could have been because of their relationship but nothing is definitive. The Roman satirist Juvenal even wrote a satire claiming that the pair were lovers.

Satire VI:136-160 The Rich and Beautiful

'"Then why does Caesennia's husband swear she's the perfect wife?'
She brought him ten thousand in gold, enough to call her chaste.

He's not been hit by Venus's arrows, or scorched by her torch:
It's the money he's aflame with, her dowry launched the darts.

Her freedom's bought. She can flirt, wave her love-letters in his
Face: she's a single woman still: a rich man marries for greed.

'Why then does Sertorius burn with love, for Bibula, his wife?
If you want the truth, it's the face he fell for, and not the bride.

The moment she's a wrinkle or two, her skin's dry and flabby,
Her teeth become discoloured, her eyes like beads in her head,
'Pack your bags' she'll hear his freedman cry, 'Away with you.
Nothing but a nuisance now, always blowing your nose. Be off,
Make it snappy. There's a dry nose coming to take your place.'

Meanwhile she's hot, she reigns, demanding of her husband
Canusian sheep and shepherds, demanding Falernian vines –
Such tiny requests! – his house-slaves, those in the prison gangs,
Whatever her neighbour has, her house lacks, must be bought.
Then from the Campus where the booths hide Jason in winter,

His Argonauts too, concealed, behind their whitened canvas,
She'll bear away crystal vases, huge, the largest pieces of agate,
And some legendary diamond made the more precious by once
Gracing Berenice's finger, a gift to his incestuous sister from
Barbarous Herod Agrippa, a present for her, in far-off Judaea,
Where barefoot kings observe their day of rest on the Sabbath,
And their tradition grants merciful indulgence to elderly pigs."

Juvenal's Satires are the closest thing the Romans had to gossip. Vulgar and rude poems were often a form of entertainment and a tool used to smear political figures. If the rumours of incest were this prominent then it is fair to say that they were probably true.

It is fair to say that this poem has an antisemitic tone, but rather than the incest being an anti-Jewish falsehood it seems more like a statement of truth used to mock Jews in general.

The Pharisees deplored the King for his impiety and sexual deviance, but the Sadducees remained the conservative and pro-Roman faction in the Sanhedrin.

It was in these delicate, tense conditions that the first Jewish-Roman war started. A war seemed almost impossible considering the fact that the Jews didn't even have an army.

But there was one woman who unknowingly gave the Jews the soldiers they needed to fight back.

Helena of Adiabene was a virtuous woman from the east who had converted to Judaism. Her virtue is recounted in the Talmud.

מַעֲשֶׂה בְּהֵילְנִי הַמַּלְכָּה שֶׁהָלַךְ בְּנָהּ לְמִלְחָמָה וְאָמְרָה אִם יָבוֹא
בְּנִי מִן הַמִּלְחָמָה בְּשָׁלוֹם אֱהֵא נְזִירָה שֶׁבַע שָׁנִים וּבָא בְּנָהּ מִן
הַמִּלְחָמָה וְהָיְתָה נְזִירָה שֶׁבַע שָׁנִים וּבְסוֹף שֶׁבַע שָׁנִים עָלְתָה לָאָרֶץ
וְהוֹרוּהָ בֵּית הִלֵּל שֶׁתְּהֵא נְזִירָה עוֹד שֶׁבַע שָׁנִים אֲחֵרוֹת וּבְסוֹף שֶׁבַע

שָׁנִים נִטְמֵאת וְנִמְצֵאת נְזִירָה עֶשְׂרִים וְאַחַת שָׁנָה אָמַר רַבִּי יְהוּדָה
לֹא הָיְתָה נְזִירָה אֶלָּא אַרְבַּע עֶשְׂרֵה שָׁנָה:

"The mishna cites a related story: An incident occurred with regard to Queen Helene, whose son had gone to war, and she said: If my son will return from war safely, I will be a nazirite for seven years. And her son returned safely from the war, and she was a nazirite for seven years. And at the end of seven years, she ascended to Eretz Yisrael, and Beit Hillel instructed her, in accordance with their opinion, that she should be a nazirite for an additional seven years. And at the end of those seven years she became ritually impure, and was therefore required to observe yet another seven years of naziriteship, as ritual impurity negates the tally of a nazirite. And she was found to be a nazirite for twenty-one years. Rabbi Yehuda said: She was a nazirite for only fourteen years and not twenty-one."[130]

A Nazirite took a vow from the book of Numbers which prevented them from cutting their hair, drinking wine or coming into contact with dead bodies. It was an intense and semi-ascetic vow. It also had a negative impact on health, considering people of antiquity often mixed water into wine to make it safer to drink.

The Nazirites were in some ways a less intense equivalent to the Essenes. The Essenes were of course an ascetic minority in Judaism which regarded it as sinful to relieve yourself on Shabbat, and as a result of living in such severe conditions the Essenes often died young.

The Nazirites probably also had issues of the same sort, albeit in a much less severe way. Regardless of how long Helena observed her vow it does show that she was sincere in her Jewish beliefs.

When she was old, she moved to Jerusalem and left her unit of guards in the city after she passed.

Apart from relieving the Jews of a famine during the reign of Agrippa I Helena of Adiabene also left the Jews the only army units they were formally allowed to have.[131]

The guards acted as the main military force the Jews had at their disposal after the Romans had banned them from having an army of their own. These soldiers would be instrumental in the Jewish struggle for freedom.

In 66CE anger at the poor management of Judaea by Florus had reached a peak, Agrippa II happened to be in Jerusalem at the time.

Despite this he did nothing to stop Florus plundering the temple of all its wealth. He entered the temple and took 17 talents, a large sum in today's money.

But the Jews did not take this laying down.

"Some also of the seditious cried out upon Florus, and cast the greatest reproaches upon him, and carried a basket about, and begged some spills of money for him, as for one that was destitute of possessions, and in a miserable condition."[132]

Yes, the Jews mockingly passed a collection basked around for 'poor Florus'. They chose to laugh at him and mock his shameful conduct rather than use violence or simply let him in unimpeded.

Florus on the other hand murdered some of the protesters and left a Roman garrison in Jerusalem. The Jews ended up just barricading the Romans in their own forts.

Soon the High Priest even stopped sacrificing animals twice a day in the name of the Roman Emperor. Agrippa II left in disgrace and tried to stop a conflict breaking out.

But everyone knew at this stage which side he was really on, and the Jews would not forgive him for it.

The Jews managed to take over Jerusalem because of the low number of troops who garrisoned it, but the Syrian governor Gaius Cestius Gallus marched towards the Jews in the hopes of crushing them.

He vastly outnumbered their newly formed army and the small ceremonial troupe left by Helena of Adiabene.

At Beit Horon Gallus suffered a crushing defeat at the hands of the Jews (led by Simon bar Giora), they had employed the same tactics as their Maccabean ancestors and saw great success in this.

After this massacre Gallus tried to siege Jerusalem from the eastern side but failed because his dead comrades were looted by the Jews for their arms, meaning that the Jews now had access to the same equipment as the Romans.

Gallus was forced to flee back north, and his wounds later killed him.

Simon bar Giora was denied advancement because he was not aristocratic. This was probably a saving grace for him considering the later purge of the aristocracy by the Idumeans.

A massive wave of anti-Jewish sentiment hit the cities of the empire once news of this battle spread, Jews were killed en masse in Romanized cities.

Agrippa II was forced to flee Jerusalem with his family and Judea formed a republican government. Ananus ben Ananus the High Priest of the time and Joseph Ben-Gurion formed the government.

Ben-Gurion was the secular head of state and acted in a similar capacity to a President. The head of the Sanhedrin was the great-grandson of Hillel, Simeon ben Gamliel.

With Simeon ben Gamliel as Prime Minister, Ananus as High Priest and Ben-Gurion as President Judea was essentially the closest thing to a modern republic that part of the world had ever seen, but with an obvious religious element in the running of state affairs.

Most of the cities of Judea willingly defected to the new government and rejected Agrippa II (and his true masters, the Romans).

Nero sent Vespasian to quell the Jews. Vespasian was a decorated general and war veteran, sending him sent a serious message, but it was also a message Rome needed to send.

If the Jews could assert their freedom others would follow, making an example of the Jews was essential for avoiding other similar revolts in the future.

Joseph ben Mattathias was sent to prepare the defence of the northern portions of Judea as the region's chief general and administrator.

Joseph was a well-off man and was a top-end Yeshiva graduate, he had some political opposition but as far as appointments go this was not a terrible choice.

You cannot buy competence, and Joseph certainly had that in abundance. He was also fluent in Latin and aware of Roman customs which made him better able to calculate their potential moves.

The only problem with Joseph was that his countrymen in the north intensely distrusted their southern counterparts and they often refused to comply with his instructions.

John of Gischala, a former bandit leader ended up causing Joseph more initial inconvenience than even the Romans.

"However, John's want of money had hitherto restrained him in his ambition after command, and in his attempts to advance himself. But when he saw that Josephus was highly pleased with the activity of his temper, he persuaded him, in the first place, to intrust him with the repairing of the walls of his native city, [Gischala,] in which work he got

a great deal of money from the rich citizens. He after that contrived a very shrewd trick, and pretending that the Jews who dwelt in Syria were obliged to make use of oil that was made by others than those of their own nation, he desired leave of Josephus to send oil to their borders; so he bought four amphorae with such Tyrian money as was of the value of four Attic drachmae, and sold every half-amphora at the same price. And as Galilee was very fruitful in oil, and was peculiarly so at that time, by sending away great quantities, and having the sole privilege so to do, he gathered an immense sum of money together, which money he immediately used to the disadvantage of him who gave him that privilege; and, as he supposed, that if he could once overthrow Josephus, he should himself obtain the government of Galilee; so he gave orders to the robbers that were under his command to be more zealous in their thievish expeditions, that by the rise of many that desired innovations in the country, he might either catch their general in his snares, as he came to the country's assistance, and then kill him; or if he should overlook the robbers, he might accuse him for his negligence to the people of the country. He also spread abroad a report far and near that Josephus was delivering up the administration of affairs to the Romans; and many such plots did he lay, in order to ruin him."[133]

In simpler terms, John of Gischala was given money to build defensive walls for his own city and embezzled it, then he gained a monopoly over oil imports under false pretences only to raise the prices very high for personal profit.

In the end their quarrels stopped, but Joseph had to share power with John, they entered a sort of stalemate and ended up having to focus more on the defence of the north than on their mutual contempt.

Vespasian's forces came in full and captured more land, it was at Yodfat that Joseph made his final stand.

This was a key city, and its fall would have meant a cataclysmic defeat for the Jews. Without a supply of water inside the walls, the city was far easier to siege than most.

The Roman strategy was to wait the Jews out. Joseph used this to his advantage, he gambled on the idea that if he had people wash their clothes in the sight of the Romans that they would assume the Jews had plenty of water.

This waste of water made Vespasian believe that the Jews had more water than they did, which prevented him from just waiting them out.

This forced the Romans to go on an unnecessary offensive against the walls which ultimately cost them men and resources and the whole thing was a great distraction to the war effort.

The Romans had the numbers so none of this ended up mattering, and the prominent Jews of the city had to hide in caves under the city. They resolved to commit a form of mutual suicide which involved each person killing another until only one remained.

"His death was occasioned by the following treachery; for there was one of those that were fled into the caverns, which were a great number, who desired that this Antonius would reach him his right hand for his security, and would assure him that he would preserve him, and give him his assistance in getting up out of the cavern; accordingly, he incautiously reached him his right hand, when the other man prevented him, and stabbed him under his loins with a spear, and killed him immediately."[134]

Suicide was considered a grave sin so mutual assisted suicide felt like an effective way to avoid damnation. Joseph was the last man left standing, so he surrendered to the Romans instead of dying by suicide in the cave.

The commander of the Jewish garrison at Yodfat left the cave and handed himself to the Romans. The fall of Yodfat came in 67CE and marked the defeat of the Jews in the northern portion of their nation.

When Joseph was taken as a prisoner he was locked in a cell for a while, and when he had adequately gathered his thoughts, he asked to see Vespasian.

Vespasian spoke with Joseph and the captive caught his attention with a prophetic message.

"Since it pleaseth thee, who hast created the Jewish nation, to depress the same, and since all their good fortune is gone over to the Romans, and since thou hast made choice of this soul of mine to foretell what is to come to pass hereafter, I willingly give them my hands, and am content to live. And I protest openly that I do not go over to the Romans as a deserter of the Jews, but as a minister from thee."[135]

This was essentially an appeal to Vespasian's vanity and belief in the supernatural. The Romans had a fairly rudimentary knowledge of Jewish religious views and customs, in many ways the G-d of the Jews was seen as mysterious and enigmatic by the Romans. Joseph claimed that Vespasian was destined to become the Emperor of Rome.

When Joseph tried to claim that he was a messenger of the G-d of Israel it must have come as a shock and perhaps even instilled a little bit of fear in Vespasian.

To Vespasian this was unbelievable, he was an old man and had no royal blood in him at all, in fact he was the son of a mule breeder and had risen through the ranks of the Roman army.

His relatively lowly position was gained entirely on merit so the notion of Vespasian becoming Emperor was almost too absurd to imagine.

But power is a cruel mistress, and it corrupts everyone eventually. Vespasian was intrigued and he couldn't get Joseph's words out of his head.

In Rome social mobility came in extremes. Over the course of the empire's history the army gained authority over choosing new Emperors until the Senate lost its relevance altogether.

Therefore, in the case of the army as long as you had successes on the battlefield you could easily go from being of a lowly class to becoming the Emperor.

But at this point the Senate still controlled the appointment of Emperors, in a lot of ways Vespasian was a trendsetter who set the precedent that the man with the biggest army and the most notoriety in battle could take the throne.

It is also important to remember that no one outside of the Julio-Claudian dynasty had ever been Emperor before. Someone from a different family let alone a poor one wouldn't have dreamed of gaining such an office.

The prophecy came before any of these later events so it would have still been met with scepticism at best.

Vespasian left Joseph alive because of what he had said. He couldn't send him to anyone else for fear that he would recite his prophecy to others which would then earn the ire of Nero.

He couldn't kill him on the spot either, he was intensely superstitious and saw it as a slight to the Lord of the Jews. The best and frankly the only option Vespasian had available was to keep Joseph captive until such a time as his prophecy could be proven true or false.

This was likely Joseph's plan; he had a gift for finding clever ways to escape death. The fact that he was almost definitely wrong kept Joseph alive because of Vespasian's curiosity, the fact that he ended up being exactly right caused Vespasian to lavish Joseph with gifts and even to adopt him as a client to the Flavian house.

Joseph ben Mattathias, the Jewish general became Flavius Josephus, a loyalist to the Romans.

Vespasian's war against the Jews didn't stop, it accelerated, and the means of warfare became more and more diabolical.

The only thing more destructive than a war of conquest is a war of attrition.

With the defeat in Galilee the Galilean soldiers fled south, they were cut off from the coast when Vespasian took Jaffa so only the southern portion of Judea remained in Jewish hands.

So too was John of Gischala defeated in his hometown. He made one last defence of the settlement, but the Romans were too strong.

The campaign in Galilee was completely lost when John fled the city with his remaining men.

He had convinced the Romans to stop their siege during Shabbat and used this chance to make his daring escape.

All the soldiers from the north and the coast fled to Jerusalem, this created some obvious conflict considering the fairly limited resources available to the city compared to what it needed to sustain all the people within the walls.

There was also a lot of tension because of mutual distrust. The southerners and northerners were somewhat culturally different and viewed each other negatively.

It was almost the reverse of the north-south divide in the USA. The north was an intensely religious, agricultural region whilst the south was full of the elite, focussed mainly on trade and was less intensely religious.

The Galileans distrusted the southerners because they saw them as condescending and elitist whilst the Jerusalemites saw the Galileans as primitive and poor, the Galilee was where a lot of new religious movements had sprung up and was also the primary area the waves of banditry had taken place in.

An uneasy coexistence had to be established. They ultimately had a bigger enemy to deal with than each other.

This fact was lost on some people from both sides, which created tensions in the city. Having an army of extremist pro-Zealot soldiers in the city caused a lot of political unrest as well, especially considering the confused state of the new government.

Much like Israeli politics today this government was an ideologically diverse coalition of different groups.

The main issues of conflict were the issue of the monarchy and the question of how peace should be achieved.

The House of Shammai and the Sadducees wanted the monarchy restored. The Essenes were neutral, and the Zealots wanted the Davidic line restored to power.

The House of Hillel were the only ones who wanted a republican style of government. The issue of peace was even more divisive. The Houses of Hillel and Shammai both agreed along with the Zealots that they wanted a fully independent Jewish state, the Essenes and the Sadducees meanwhile wanted a peace agreement with Nero rather than a full-scale revolt.

The government simply didn't have a direction, and opportunists realised that they could exploit the chaos.

John of Gischala was asked to calm the Zealots down, as he was trusted among them. Instead of calming them he ordered them to take over the temple by force and deposed the High Priest Ananus ben Ananus.

"And now the multitude were going to rise against them already; for Ananus, the ancientest of the high priests, persuaded them to it. He was a very prudent man, and had perhaps saved the city if he could but have

escaped the hands of those that plotted against him. These men made the
temple of G-d a strong hold for them, and a place whither they might
resort, in order to avoid the troubles they feared from the people; the
sanctuary was now become a refuge, and a shop of tyranny. They also
mixed jesting among the miseries they introduced, which was more
intolerable than what they did; for in order to try what surprise the
people would be under, and how far their own power extended, they
undertook to dispose of the high priesthood by casting lots for it, whereas,
as we have said already, it was to descend by succession in a family. The
pretense they made for this strange attempt was an ancient practice, while
they said that of old it was determined by lot; but in truth, it was no
better than a dissolution of an undeniable law, and a cunning contrivance
to seize upon the government, derived from those that presumed to
appoint governors as they themselves pleased.

Hereupon they sent for one of the pontifical tribes, which is called
Eniachim, and cast lots which of it should be the high priest. By fortune
the lot so fell as to demonstrate their iniquity after the plainest manner,
for it fell upon one whose name was Phannias, the son of Samuel, of the
village Aphtha. He was a man not only unworthy of the high priesthood,
but that did not well know what the high priesthood was, such a mere
rustic was he! yet did they hail this man, without his own consent, out of
the country, as if they were acting a play upon the stage, and adorned
him with a counterfeit tree; they also put upon him the sacred garments,
and upon every occasion instructed him what he was to do. This horrid
piece of wickedness was sport and pastime with them, but occasioned the
other priests, who at a distance saw their law made a jest of, to shed tears,
and sorely lament the dissolution of such a sacred dignity."[136]

Phannias ben Samuel had no Rabbinical education for his office and was unqualified by most standards.

The casting of lots was not the traditional method of appointment but the Zealot forces claimed that it was.

The members of the provisional government were killed in a ruse contrived by the Zealots.

They falsely claimed to the Idumean forces entering the city that the provisional government was defecting to Rome's side and so these men slaughtered them.

When they found out that they had been lied to they left in shame, having made their repentances known.

"But by this time the Idumeans repented of their coming, and were displeased at what had been done; and when they were assembled together by one of the zealots, who had come privately to them, he declared to them what a number of wicked pranks they had themselves done in conjunction with those that invited them, and gave a particular account of what mischiefs had been done against their metropolis. He said that they had taken arms, as though the high priests were betraying their metropolis to the Romans, but had found no indication of any such treachery; but that they had succored those that had pretended to believe such a thing, while they did themselves the works of war and tyranny, after an insolent manner. It had been indeed their business to have hindered them from such their proceedings at the first, but seeing they had once been partners with them in shedding the blood of their own countrymen, it was high time to put a stop to such crimes, and not continue to afford any more assistance to such as are subverting the laws of their forefathers; for that if any had taken it ill that the gates had been shut against them, and they

had not been permitted to come into the city, yet that those who had excluded them have been punished, and Ananus is dead, and that almost all those people had been destroyed in one night's time. That one may perceive many of themselves now repenting for what they had done, and might see the horrid barbarity of those that had invited them, and that they had no regard to such as had saved them; that they were so impudent as to perpetrate the vilest things, under the eyes of those that had supported them, and that their wicked actions would be laid to the charge of the Idumeans, and would be so laid to their charge till somebody obstructs their proceedings, or separates himself from the same wicked action; that they therefore ought to retire home, since the imputation of treason appears to be a Calumny, and that there was no expectation of the coming of the Romans at this time, and that the government of the city was secured by such walls as cannot easily be thrown down; and, by avoiding any further fellowship with these bad men, to make some excuse for themselves, as to what they had been so far deluded, as to have been partners with them hitherto."[137]

Ananus ben Ananus and Joseph Ben-Gurion were dead and so was any hope of a stable and unified government.

This would have been a perfect time to attack the city, but Vespasian chose not to. This was when Simon bar Giora came into the picture. He had won the battle of Beit Horon and was one of the only officials from the old government that survived the Idumeans, this was probably because of Joseph Ben-Gurion's refusal to promote him because he was not of an aristocratic origin.

Simon managed to raise his own army and retook the city of Jaffa. He did this in direct opposition to the Zealot led government in Jerusalem and was able to build up a strong naval defence.[138]

He managed to use these ships to blockade the eastern portion of the empire which he hoped would create a grain shortage in the city of Rome.

The grain dole meant that any blockade impacting Egypt would essentially cause the city of Rome itself to run out of food.

Simon's wife was eventually taken by the Zealots and after a back-and-forth of threats the two sides became reconciled.

The situation in Rome had deteriorated arguably even more than the one in Jerusalem. The next chapter will recount the events that caused Rome to be in such a deplorable state of affairs and the one after will resume the First Jewish-Roman war.

13

Chapter 13- The Year of 4 Emperors

After Nero's death Galba arrived at Rome with his men to claim the empire for himself. Galba was the first Emperor ever to not come from the Julio-Claudian dynasty. He had no biological or marital relation to any previous Emperor, so he destroyed an almost 100-year precedent.

Galba was known for his strictness and cruelty. He put to death the wives and children of the Roman officials who refused to support his campaign as he marched from Spain to Rome.[139]

This man was in his seventies and had a reputation for extreme punishments stretching as far back as Caligula's reign.

Galba's greatest mistake was not his harshness but his refusal to give a donative to the soldiers.

Due to this the soldiers soon defected to the side of Otho. Otho had expected to be appointed as Galba's successor, but this honour was given to Lucius Calpurnius Piso Frugi Licinianus instead. This man was a very high-end nobleman, but Otho felt cheated.

Because of this, and the mutiny of a commander in Germany called Vitellius Otho rallied the Praetorian guard and had Galba slain.

Otho was declared Emperor and reinstated Nero's legacy. The purge of Neronian officials was reversed and Otho even married Nero's 'wife' Sporus.

Otho did this in spite of the fact that Nero had banished him from Rome and forcibly married his wife Poppaea. It is hard to find a personal reason for Otho to favour Nero, this points to the fact that there was utility in doing it because Nero was popular with most people.

Aulus Vitellius was also declared Emperor and Otho offered to share the empire with him if he laid down his arms, but Vitellius did not listen.

Paulinus (the same man who had fought Boudica) now commanded Otho's soldiers and lost to Vitellius' vastly larger army at the battle of Bedriacum in 69CE.

With no cards left to play Otho decided to take the easy way out. He killed himself in a form of ritual suicide to spare the Romans more war, paving the way for Vitellius to take control of the empire.

Otho had only reigned for a few months, his reign was even shorter than Galba's 8 months.

"He then gave orders that no violence should be offered to any one; and keeping his chamber-door open until late at night, he allowed all who pleased the liberty to come and see him. At last, after quenching his thirst with a draught of cold water, he took up two poniards, and having examined the points of both, put one of them under his pillow, and shutting his chamber-door, slept very soundly, until, awaking about break of

day, he stabbed himself under the left pap. Some persons bursting into the room upon his first groan, he at one time covered, and at another exposed his wound to the view of the bystanders, and thus life soon ebbed away. His funeral was hastily performed, according to his own order, in the thirty-eighth year of his age, and ninety-fifth day of his reign.

The person and appearance of Otho no way corresponded to the great spirit he displayed on this occasion; for he is said to have been of low stature, splay-footed, and bandy-legged. He was, however, effeminately nice in the care of his person: the hair on his body he plucked out by the roots; and because he was somewhat bald, he wore a kind of peruke, so exactly fitted to his head, that nobody could have known it for such. He used to shave every day, and rub his face with soaked bread; the use of which he began when the down first appeared upon his chin, to prevent his having any beard. It is said likewise that he celebrated publicly the sacred rites of Isis, clad in a linen garment, such as is used by the worshippers of that g-ddess. These circumstances, I imagine, caused the world to wonder the more that his death was so little in character with his life. Many of the soldiers who were present, kissing and bedewing with their tears his hands and feet as he lay dead, and celebrating him as "a most gallant man, and an incomparable Emperor," immediately put an end to their own lives upon the spot, not far from his funeral pile.

Many of those likewise who were at a distance, upon hearing the news of his death, in the anguish of their hearts, began fighting amongst themselves, until they dispatched one another. To conclude: the generality of mankind, though they hated him whilst living, yet highly extolled him after his death; insomuch that it was the common talk and opinion, "that

Galba had been driven to destruction by his rival, not so much for the sake of reigning himself, as of restoring Rome to its ancient liberty.""[140]

For his suicide Otho was viewed highly in death by the Roman public. Vitellius meanwhile was intensely disliked. He was self-indulgent in a time of want, jovial in a time of despair, incompetent in a time where competence was needed.

He tried to have Sporus publicly assaulted in a re-enactment of the rape of Proserpina, but instead Sporus committed suicide to avoid such a fate.

"He was chiefly addicted to the vices of luxury and cruelty. He always made three meals a day, sometimes four: breakfast, dinner, and supper, and a drunken revel after all. This load of victuals he could well enough bear, from a custom to which he had enured himself, of frequently vomiting. For these several meals he would make different appointments at the houses of his friends on the same day. None ever entertained him at less expense than four hundred thousand sesterces. The most famous was a set entertainment given him by his brother, at which, it is said, there were served up no less than two thousand choice fishes, and seven thousand birds. Yet even this supper he himself outdid, at a feast which he gave upon the first use of a dish which had been made for him, and which, for its extraordinary size, he called "The Shield of Minerva." In this dish there were tossed up together the livers of char-fish, the brains of pheasants and peacocks, with the tongues of flamingos, and the entrails of lampreys, which had been brought in ships of war as far as from the Carpathian Sea, and the Spanish Straits. He was not only a man of an insatiable appetite, but would gratify it likewise at unseasonable times, and with any garbage that came in his way; so that, at a sacrifice, he

would snatch from the fire flesh and cakes, and eat them upon the spot.
When he travelled, he did the same at the inns upon the road, whether the
meat was fresh dressed and hot, or what had been left the day before, and
was half-eaten."[141]

These acts were not appropriate to the gravity of Rome's dire situation in the eyes of the people, so Vitellius was quickly loathed.

In the east Vespasian was declared Emperor by his legions and the troops managed to defeat Vitellius' armies.

Vespasian's son Domitian and his brother Flavius were in the city of Rome at the time, which made their position extremely precarious.

Titus was 12 years older than Domitian, so the young son of Vespasian was left to be raised by his uncle in the city of Rome, as a result he had a much better grasp on domestic policy and economics than his father or brother who were largely gifted at war.

When the Flavian armies reached Rome Vitellius tried to use Flavius as an intermediary to negotiate a surrender, but the soldiers refused to comply with such a cowardly act and hunted Flavius and Domitian down.

Domitian was able to escape just in time, but the men butchered his uncle Flavius in cold blood.

Little did Domitian know when he was abandoning his uncle to be killed that he would become one of the greatest Emperor's Rome ever had.

"The enemy now pressing forward both by sea and land, on one hand
he opposed against them his brother with a fleet, the new levies, and a
body of gladiators, and in another quarter the troops and generals who
were engaged at Bedriacum. But being beaten or betrayed in every

direction, he agreed with Flavius Sabinus, Vespasian's brother, to abdi-
cate, on condition of having his life spared, and a hundred millions of
sesterces granted him; and he immediately, upon the palace-steps, publicly
declared to a large body of soldiers there assembled, "that he resigned the
government, which he had accepted reluctantly;" but they all remonstrat-
ing against it, he deferred the conclusion of the treaty. Next day, early in
the morning, he came down to the Forum in a very mean habit, and with
many tears repeated the declaration from a writing which he held in his
hand; but the soldiers and people again interposing, and encouraging him
not to give way, but to rely on their zealous support, he recovered his
courage, and forced Sabinus, with the rest of the Flavian party, who now
thought themselves secure, to retreat into the Capitol, where he destroyed
them all by setting fire to the temple of Jupiter, whilst he beheld the
contest and the fire from Tiberius's house, where he was feasting. Not
long after, repenting of what he had done, and throwing the blame of it
upon others, he called a meeting, and swore "that nothing was dearer to
him than the public peace;" which oath he also obliged the rest to take.
Then drawing a dagger from his side, he presented it first to the consul,
and, upon his refusing it, to the magistrates, and then to every one of the
Senators; but none of them being willing to accept it, he went away, as if
he meant to lay it up in the temple of Concord; but some crying out to
him, "You are Concord," he came back again, and said that he would not
only keep his weapon, but for the future use the cognomen of Concord."[142]

Vitellius was horrified at what had been done to Flavius, his only
hope of escape was dead on the floor, there was nowhere to run to,
he had no means of negotiation. He was going to die.

Ironically the people who condemned him were his own men, who in their eagerness to keep their authority refused Vitellius' resignation.

Eventually the Flavian forces overpowered Vitellius, and he was executed in the forum for all to see. His lifeless body was cast into the river Tiber and Vespasian came to claim the throne for himself.

Vespasian was in the perfect position to do this. He was outrageously popular, had no connections to any of the failed Emperors that came before him, and he also had a devoted and loyal following in the form of his legions.

The war largely came to a halt in 69CE because Vespasian wanted to let the chaos boil to a breaking point. He knew that he couldn't do anything anyway because the chain of command in the government had been totally destroyed 4 times over.

Despite this cynically deliberate strategic error Vespasian was still the most experienced, popular and capable person left who could take power.

His son Titus was now his Caesar (heir), and the Flavian dynasty was established.

14

Chapter 14- The Fall of Jerusalem

Simon bar Giora surrounded Jerusalem as his wife was kept as a captive there. The Zealots had his wife, but Giora had the soldiers necessary to kill the Zealots so both sides chose to come together.

The Zealots didn't have to submit to bar Giora's authority and continued to control the temple complex, but bar Giora was now the head of state.

He held the Commander-in-Chief role in a similar way to Joseph Ben-Gurion, but he obviously had a lot less authority now that the war had started turning in favour of the Romans.

Now the Jewish armies were united, and Joseph was adopted by Vespasian for the correctness of his prediction, he was given the name Flavius Josephus.

The Jewish defenders ended up burning most of their food supplies during an internal conflict of the Zealots, which John of Gischala ultimately won.

*"And now there were three treacherous factions in the city, the one parted
from the other. Eleazar and his party, that kept the sacred first-fruits,
came against John in their cups. Those that were with John plundered the
populace, and went out with zeal against Simon. This Simon had his
supply of provisions from the city, in opposition to the seditious. When,
therefore, John was assaulted on both sides, he made his men turn about,
throwing his darts upon those citizens that came up against him, from the
cloisters he had in his possession, while he opposed those that attacked
him from the temple by his engines of war. And if at any time he was
freed from those that were above him, which happened frequently, from
their being drunk and tired, he sallied out with a great number upon
Simon and his party; and this he did always in such parts of the city as he
could come at, till he set on fire those houses that were full of corn, and of
all other provisions. The same thing was done by Simon, when, upon the
other's retreat, he attacked the city also; as if they had, on purpose, done it
to serve the Romans, by destroying what the city had laid up against the
siege, and by thus cutting off the nerves of their own power. Accordingly,
it so came to pass, that all the places that were about the temple were
burnt down, and were become an intermediate desert space, ready for
fighting on both sides of it; and that almost all that corn was burnt, which
would have been sufficient for a siege of many years. So they were taken
by the means of the famine, which it was impossible they should have
been, unless they had thus prepared the way for it by this procedure."*[143]

Now the Jews were trapped in a state of distrust and with no
food. The Romans didn't even have time to destroy the Jews before
they destroyed themselves.

The siege was long, and the fighting was intense. Despite their disadvantages in numbers and supplies the Jews were in a familiar place, they used the geography to their advantage and successfully repelled the Romans.

The Romans attacked the north-western portion of the city and managed to break through the wall that had been put up by Herod Agrippa I. The advance was slow, and the Roman casualties were high.

In the end Titus sent Josephus to speak to the Jews in the hopes that he could convince them to surrender to the Romans. According to Josephus himself he gave a long and elaborate speech to rally the Jews to his side.

"So Josephus went round about the wall, and tried to find a place that was out of the reach of their darts, and yet within their hearing, and besought them, in many words, to spare themselves, to spare their country and their temple, and not to be more obdurate in these cases than foreigners themselves; for that the Romans, who had no relation to those things, had a reverence for their sacred rites and places, although they belonged to their enemies, and had till now kept their hands off from meddling with them; while such as were brought up under them, and, if they be preserved, will be the only people that will reap the benefit of them, hurry on to have them destroyed. That certainly they have seen their strongest walls demolished, and that the wall still remaining was weaker than those that were already taken. That they must know the Roman power was invincible, and that they had been used to serve them; for, that in case it be allowed a right thing to fight for liberty, that ought to have been done at first; but for them that have once fallen under the power of the Romans, and have now submitted to them for so many long years, to

*pretend to shake off that yoke afterward, was the work of such as had a
mind to die miserably, not of such as were lovers of liberty. Besides, men
may well enough grudge at the dishonor of owning ignoble masters over
them, but ought not to do so to those who have all things under their
command; for what part of the world is there that hath escaped the
Romans, unless it be such as are of no use for violent heat, or for violent
cold? And evident it is that fortune is on all hands gone over to them; and
that G-d, when he had gone round the nations with this dominion, is now
settled in Italy. That, moreover, it is a strong and fixed law, even among
brute beasts, as well as among men, to yield to those that are too strong
for them; and to suffer those to have the dominion who are too hard for
the rest in war; for which reason it was that their forefathers, who were
far superior to them, both in their souls and bodies, and other advantages,
did yet submit to the Romans, which they would not have suffered, had
they not known that G-d was with them. As for themselves, what can they
depend on in this their opposition, when the greatest part of their city is
already taken? and when those that are within it are under greater
miseries than if they were taken, although their walls be still standing?
For that the Romans are not unacquainted with that famine which is in
the city, whereby the people are already consumed, and the fighting men
will in a little time be so too; for although the Romans should leave off the
siege, and not fall upon the city with their swords in their hands, yet was
there an insuperable war that beset them within, and was augmented
every hour, unless they were able to wage war with famine, and fight
against it, or could alone conquer their natural appetites. He added this
further, how right a thing it was to change their conduct before their
calamities were become incurable, and to have recourse to such advice as
might preserve them, while opportunity was offered them for so doing;*

for that the Romans would not be mindful of their past actions to their
disadvantage, unless they persevered in their insolent behavior to the end;
because they were naturally mild in their conquests, and preferred what
was profitable, before what their passions dictated to them; which profit
of theirs lay not in leaving the city empty of inhabitants, nor the country
a desert; on which account Caesar did now offer them his right hand for
their security. Whereas, if he took the city by force, he would not save
any of them, and this especially, if they rejected his offers in these their
utmost distresses; for the walls that were already taken could not but
assure them that the third wall would quickly be taken also. And though
their fortifications should prove too strong for the Romans to break
through them, yet would the famine fight for the Romans against them.
While Josephus was making this exhortation to the Jews, many of them
jested upon him from the wall, and many reproached him; nay, some
threw their darts at him: but when he could not himself persuade them by
such open good advice, he betook himself to the histories belonging to
their own nation, and cried out aloud, "O miserable creatures! are you so
unmindful of those that used to assist you, that you will fight by your
weapons and by your hands against the Romans? When did we ever
conquer any other nation by such means? and when was it that G-d, who
is the Creator of the Jewish people, did not avenge them when they had
been injured? Will not you turn again, and look back, and consider
whence it is that you fight with such violence, and how great a Supporter
you have profanely abused? Will not you recall to mind the prodigious
things done for your forefathers and this holy place, and how great
enemies of yours were by him subdued under you? I even tremble myself
in declaring the works of G-d before your ears, that are unworthy to hear
them; however, hearken to me, that you may be informed how you fight

not only against the Romans, but against G-d himself. In old times there was one Necao, king of Egypt, who was also called Pharaoh; he came with a prodigious army of soldiers, and seized queen Sarah, the mother of our nation. What did Abraham our progenitor then do? Did he defend himself from this injurious person by war, although he had three hundred and eighteen captains under him, and an immense army under each of them? Indeed he deemed them to be no number at all without G-d's assistance, and only spread out his hands towards this holy place, which you have now polluted, and reckoned upon him as upon his invincible supporter, instead of his own army. Was not our queen sent back, without any defilement, to her husband, the very next evening?—while the king of Egypt fled away, adoring this place which you have defiled by shedding thereon the blood of your own countrymen; and he also trembled at those visions which he saw in the night season, and bestowed both silver and gold on the Hebrews, as on a people beloved by G-d. Shall I say nothing, or shall I mention the removal of our fathers into Egypt, who, when they were used tyrannically, and were fallen under the power of foreign kings for four hundred years together, and might have defended themselves by war and by fighting, did yet do nothing but commit themselves to G-d! Who is there that does not know that Egypt was overrun with all sorts of wild beasts, and consumed by all sorts of distempers? how their land did not bring forth its fruit? how the Nile failed of water? how the ten plagues of Egypt followed one upon another? and how by those means our fathers were sent away under a guard, without any bloodshed, and without running any dangers, because G-d conducted them as his peculiar servants? Moreover, did not Palestine groan under the ravage the Assyrians made, when they carried away our sacred ark? as did their idol Dagon, and as also did that entire nation of those that carried it away,

how they were smitten with a loathsome distemper in the secret parts of
their bodies, when their very bowels came down together with what they
had eaten, till those hands that stole it away were obliged to bring it back
again, and that with the sound of cymbals and timbrels, and other
oblations, in order to appease the anger of G-d for their violation of his
holy ark. It was G-d who then became our General, and accomplished
these great things for our fathers, and this because they did not meddle
with war and fighting, but committed it to him to judge about their
affairs. When Sennacherib, king of Assyria, brought along with him all
Asia, and encompassed this city round with his army, did he fall by the
hands of men? were not those hands lifted up to G-d in prayers, without
meddling with their arms, when an angel of G-d destroyed that prodi-
gious army in one night? when the Assyrian king, as he rose the next
day, found a hundred fourscore and five thousand dead bodies, and when
he, with the remainder of his army, fled away from the Hebrews, though
they were unarmed, and did not pursue them. You are also acquainted
with the slavery we were under at Babylon, where the people were
captives for seventy years; yet were they not delivered into freedom again
before G-d made Cyrus his gracious instrument in bringing it about;
accordingly they were set free by him, and did again restore the worship
of their Deliverer at his temple. And, to speak in general, we can produce
no example wherein our fathers got any success by war, or failed of
success when without war they committed themselves to G-d. When they
staid at home, they conquered, as pleased their Judge; but when they went
out to fight, they were always disappointed: for example, when the king
of Babylon besieged this very city, and our king Zedekiah fought against
him, contrary to what predictions were made to him by Jeremiah the
prophet, he was at once taken prisoner, and saw the city and the temple

demolished. Yet how much greater was the moderation of that king, than
is that of your present governors, and that of the people then under him,
than is that of you at this time! for when Jeremiah cried out aloud, how
very angry G-d was at them, because of their transgressions, and told
them they should be taken prisoners, unless they would surrender up
their city, neither did the king nor the people put him to death; but for
you, [to pass over what you have done within the city, which I am not able
to describe as your wickedness deserves,] you abuse me, and throw darts
at me, who only exhort you to save yourselves, as being provoked when
you are put in mind of your sins, and cannot bear the very mention of
those crimes which you every day perpetrate. For another example, when
Antiochus, who was called Epiphanes, lay before this city, and had been
guilty of many indignities against G-d, and our forefathers met him in
arms, they then were slain in the battle, this city was plundered by our
enemies, and our sanctuary made desolate for three years and six
months. And what need I bring any more examples? Indeed what can it be
that hath stirred up an army of the Romans against our nation? Is it not
the impiety of the inhabitants? Whence did our servitude commence? Was
it not derived from the seditions that were among our forefathers, when
the madness of Aristobulus and Hyrcanus, and our mutual quarrels,
brought Pompey upon this city, and when G-d reduced those under
subjection to the Romans who were unworthy of the liberty they had
enjoyed? After a siege, therefore, of three months, they were forced to
surrender themselves, although they had not been guilty of such offenses,
with regard to our sanctuary and our laws, as you have; and this while
they had much greater advantages to go to war than you have. Do not we
know what end Antigonus, the son of Aristobulus, came to, under whose
reign G-d provided that this city should be taken again upon account of

the people's offenses? When Herod, the son of Antipater, brought upon us
Sosius, and Sosius brought upon us the Roman army, they were then
encompassed and besieged for six months, till, as a punishment for their
sins, they were taken, and the city was plundered by the enemy. Thus it
appears that arms were never given to our nation, but that we are always
given up to be fought against, and to be taken; for I suppose that such as
inhabit this holy place ought to commit the disposal of all things to G-d,
and then only to disregard the assistance of men when they resign them-
selves up to their Arbitrator, who is above. As for you, what have you
done of those things that are recommended by our legislator? and what
have you not done of those things that he hath condemned? How much
more impious are you than those who were so quickly taken! You have
not avoided so much as those sins that are usually done in secret; I mean
thefts, and treacherous plots against men, and adulteries. You are
quarrelling about rapines and murders, and invent strange ways of
wickedness. Nay, the temple itself is become the receptacle of all, and this
Divine place is polluted by the hands of those of our own country; which
place hath yet been reverenced by the Romans when it was at a distance
from them, when they have suffered many of their own customs to give
place to our law. And, after all this, do you expect Him whom you have so
impiously abused to be your supporter? To be sure then you have a right
to be petitioners, and to call upon Him to assist you, so pure are your
hands! Did your king [Hezekiah] lift up such hands in prayer to G-d
against the king of Assyria, when he destroyed that great army in one
night? And do the Romans commit such wickedness as did the king of
Assyria, that you may have reason to hope for the like vengeance upon
them? Did not that king accept of money from our king on this condition,
that he should not destroy the city, and yet, contrary to the oath he had

*taken, he came down to burn the temple? while the Romans do demand no
more than that accustomed tribute which our fathers paid to their fathers;
and if they may but once obtain that, they neither aim to destroy this
city, nor to touch this sanctuary; nay, they will grant you besides, that
your posterity shall be free, and your possessions secured to you, and will
preserve our holy laws inviolate to you. And it is plain madness to expect
that G-d should appear as well disposed towards the wicked as towards
the righteous, since he knows when it is proper to punish men for their
sins immediately; accordingly he brake the power of the Assyrians the
very first night that they pitched their camp. Wherefore, had he judged
that our nation was worthy of freedom, or the Romans of punishment, he
had immediately inflicted punishment upon those Romans, as he did upon
the Assyrians, when Pompey began to meddle with our nation, or when
after him Sosius came up against us, or when Vespasian laid waste
Galilee, or, lastly, when Titus came first of all near to this city; although
Magnus and Sosius did not only suffer nothing, but took the city by force;
as did Vespasian go from the war he made against you to receive the
empire; and as for Titus, those springs that were formerly almost dried
up when they were under your power since he is come, run more plentifully than they did before; accordingly, you know that Siloam, as well as
all the other springs that were without the city, did so far fail, that water
was sold by distinct measures; whereas they now have such a great
quantity of water for your enemies, as is sufficient not only for drink
both for themselves and their cattle, but for watering their gardens also.
The same wonderful sign you had also experience of formerly, when the
forementioned king of Babylon made war against us, and when he took
the city, and burnt the temple; while yet I believe the Jews of that age were
not so impious as you are. Wherefore I cannot but suppose that G-d is fled*

out of his sanctuary, and stands on the side of those against whom you fight. Now even a man, if he be but a good man, will fly from an impure house, and will hate those that are in it; and do you persuade yourselves that G-d will abide with you in your iniquities, who sees all secret things, and hears what is kept most private? Now what crime is there, I pray you, that is so much as kept secret among you, or is concealed by you? nay, what is there that is not open to your very enemies? for you show your transgressions after a pompous manner, and contend one with another which of you shall be more wicked than another; and you make a public demonstration of your injustice, as if it were virtue. However, there is a place left for your preservation, if you be willing to accept of it; and G-d is easily reconciled to those that confess their faults, and repent of them. O hard-hearted wretches as you are! cast away all your arms, and take pity of your country already going to ruin; return from your wicked ways, and have regard to the excellency of that city which you are going to betray, to that excellent temple with the donations of so many countries in it. Who could bear to be the first that should set that temple on fire? who could be willing that these things should be no more? and what is there that can better deserve to be preserved? O insensible creatures, and more stupid than are the stones themselves! And if you cannot look at these things with discerning eyes, yet, however, have pity upon your families, and set before every one of your eyes your children, and wives, and parents, who will be gradually consumed either by famine or by war. I am sensible that this danger will extend to my mother, and wife, and to that family of mine who have been by no means ignoble, and indeed to one that hath been very eminent in old time; and perhaps you may imagine that it is on their account only that I give you this advice; if that be all, kill them; nay, take my own blood as a reward, if it may but procure

your preservation; for I am ready to die, in case you will but return to a
sound mind after my death."

As Josephus was speaking thus with a loud voice, the seditious would
neither yield to what he said, nor did they deem it safe for them to alter
their conduct; but as for the people, they had a great inclination to desert
to the Romans; accordingly, some of them sold what they had, and even
the most precious things that had been laid up as treasures by them, for
every small matter, and swallowed down pieces of gold, that they might
not be found out by the robbers; and when they had escaped to the
Romans, went to stool, and had wherewithal to provide plentifully for
themselves; for Titus let a great number of them go away into the
country, whither they pleased. And the main reasons why they were so
ready to desert were these: That now they should be freed from those
miseries which they had endured in that city, and yet should not be in
slavery to the Romans: however, John and Simon, with their factions, did
more carefully watch these men's going out than they did the coming in of
the Romans; and if any one did but afford the least shadow of suspicion
of such an intention, his throat was cut immediately."[144]

This long and contrived speech is almost definitely a poetic piece
of prose rather than a true statement of what he said.

It also probably overstates the degree to which people listened
to Josephus, considering the fact that Josephus himself wrote this
account.

The primary indication that this long speech was ineffective
is that nobody actually listened to it, they chose to fight on and
continue their last stand against Roman occupation.

A speech was ultimately never going to work, the people defending Jerusalem knew that they were in a dire and hopeless position,

but they fought anyway because in their eyes the preservation of the legacy of the Jews was more important than their material happiness.

Josephus seemed to forget this and ended up alienating himself from the other Jews, he was seen as cowardly and immoral. He was in their eyes a traitor.

It is undiplomatic to accuse a historian of being a traitor, especially when I have used so much of his work to inform the words of this one, but it would be remiss of me not to point out the deep hypocrisy of claiming to support Judaism and being a servant of the most ardently antisemitic political entity of the time.

Titus continued his siege and began having civilians crucified to scare the Jews into submission. This seemed to only increase their resolve to resist Rome.

In the end the Antonia fortress to the north of the temple collapsed and Titus used this passage to enter the temple with his men.

On the 9th of Av Titus and his men entered the temple and ruined it completely. The temple was levelled and burned, raided of its ancient treasures and brought to nothing but rubble.

From the 9th of Av, in 70CE this tragic day would be known as Tisha B'av, the primary Jewish holiday related to mourning the losses of the first and second temples.

For his crime Titus is remembered as the chief devil of the Romans, and he is still hated by many. Titus even sacrificed a pig on the altar

The arch of Titus in Rome commemorates this atrocity and contains the only known image of what the menorah looked like. It was illegal under Jewish law to walk beneath the arch of Titus until 1948 and many Jews still refuse to do so.

There would be no third temple, not as of yet anyway.

The justification Josephus gave for the destruction of the temple was as follows.

"They slew certain of their own enemies, and were subservient to other men for money; and slew others, not only in remote parts of the city, but in the temple itself also; for they had the boldness to murder men there, without thinking of the impiety of which they were guilty. And this seems to me to have been the reason why G-d, out of his hatred of these men's wickedness, rejected our city; and as for the temple, he no longer esteemed it sufficiently pure for him to inhabit therein, but brought the Romans upon us, and threw a fire upon the city to purge it; and brought upon us, our wives, and children, slavery, as desirous to make us wiser by our calamities."[145]

Simply put, because murders had taken place in the temple at the hands of some Jews, the Jews in general were (according to Josephus) not worthy of the Lord's presence, nor was their temple Holy enough for him to occupy it any longer.

This is obviously a questionable rationale, but it stems from the position Flavius Josephus was in. He had been adopted by the very family that destroyed his country.

He was trying to strike a balance between and attempting to reconcile two polar opposites.

His Jewish roots and his Roman branches constantly battled. This war within himself is evidenced by how much he contradicts himself in supporting Rome and supporting Jewish culture and religious traditions. Josephus scolds the impious apart from his adoptive Flavian family.

This discounts Josephus' objectivity, but it also enhances our understanding of what Josephus lived through, and how he tried to rationalise the brutal realities he was faced with.

John of Gischala and Simon bar Giora were forced to meet with Titus and discuss the terms of a possible surrender.

Both of these men knew they had no chance, but they kept going anyway. They were the masters of this defence in good times and bad, in victory and defeat.

Simon had once been a poor man and was now the final defender of the city. John had once been a criminal and a petty murderer; he was now the final defender of the city.

John of Gischala may have been a criminal, a cutthroat and a fiend but on this day, he was a Jew first and foremost. He made a valiant last stand in defence of his city, keeping to the oath he had sworn.

He was in many ways like Herod Agrippa I, a swindler who ended up being honourable when history came calling.

Both of these men were not anyone's first choice, or even their second, but when they were called upon, they chose not to lay down their arms in submission.

The battle thereafter was slow and brutal, the fighting took place in the streets, in the homes of the Jews, in all the places of the lower portion of the city.

John and Simon were held captive and taken along with the relics of the temple to be marched around the streets of Rome, to be gawked at and mocked. The Romans had won, and they had almost destroyed Jerusalem completely.

It would still take another 3 years for the entire rebellion to be crushed.

15

Chapter 15- Flavian Rule and the Fate of the Jews

With the Jews defeated Vespasian now had total control over the empire. He was a notoriously productive Emperor as they go. He didn't take power simply for its own sake, but to do something of note with it.

From 69CE to 79CE Vespasian ruled the empire better than almost anyone else of his day, although there was a fairly slim margin for defining 'better'.

Not being murdered in a coup or putting his own relatives to death qualifies him enough for such a description.

Vespasian is known for building the Colosseum, or as it was officially known the Flavian Amphitheatre, but few people know the truth of how it was built.

The Emperor used Jewish slaves to build the Colosseum and used the money raised from Jerusalem to pay for it.

The irony of the Jews being the forced labourers who built one of Rome's most famous marvels is not lost in posterity. This underpins the relationship between the Jews and the Romans.

For all their mutual hatred and violence there would be no Rome without the Jews, just as modern Judaism would not exist in the form it now takes without the Romans.

Vespasian may have destroyed, enslaved and ravaged the Jews but he ended up making them who they are today. The biggest difference is in how these legacies survived.

Vespasian's legacy survived in stone, Judaism survived as an entire identity and way of life.

In other words, even though the Romans won militarily they ultimately didn't survive whilst the Jews live on in spite of and partially because of the Romans.

Most sources stop recounting the war at the point of Jerusalem's fall, but in fact there was a great deal of guerrilla warfare that lasted all the way up to 73CE.

There was a last stand at Masada. The very same fort built by Herod to defend against the Jews was now used by the Jews to repel the Romans.

The occupants were a group known as the Sicarii. Without describing their crimes in depth their name derived from the swords they used to murder people going from Nabataea to Judea.

This says more about them than anything else. For reference they were considered too extreme even by the Zealots.

The Sicarii essentially committed a form of suicide that involved being slowly sieged by the Romans.

"Since we, long ago, my generous friends, resolved never to be servants to the Romans, nor to any other than to G-d himself, who alone is the true and just Lord of mankind, the time is now come that obliges us to make

that resolution true in practice. And let us not at this time bring a reproach upon ourselves for self-contradiction, while we formerly would not undergo slavery, though it were then without danger, but must now, together with slavery, choose such punishments also as are intolerable; I mean this, upon the supposition that the Romans once reduce us under their power while we are alive. We were the very first that revolted from them, and we are the last that fight against them; and I cannot but esteem it as a favor that G-d hath granted us, that it is still in our power to die bravely, and in a state of freedom, which hath not been the case of others, who were conquered unexpectedly. It is very plain that we shall be taken within a day's time; but it is still an eligible thing to die after a glorious manner, together with our dearest friends. This is what our enemies themselves cannot by any means hinder, although they be very desirous to take us alive. Nor can we propose to ourselves any more to fight them, and beat them. It had been proper indeed for us to have conjectured at the purpose of G-d much sooner, and at the very first, when we were so desirous of defending our liberty, and when we received such sore treatment from one another, and worse treatment from our enemies, and to have been sensible that the same G-d, who had of old taken the Jewish nation into his favor, had now condemned them to destruction; for had he either continued favorable, or been but in a lesser degree displeased with us, he had not overlooked the destruction of so many men, or delivered his most holy city to be burnt and demolished by our enemies. To be sure we weakly hoped to have preserved ourselves, and ourselves alone, still in a state of freedom, as if we had been guilty of no sins ourselves against G-d, nor been partners with those of others; we also taught other men to preserve their liberty. Wherefore, consider how G-d hath convinced us that our hopes were in vain, by bringing such distress upon us in the

desperate state we are now in, and which is beyond all our expectations;
for the nature of this fortress which was in itself unconquerable, hath not
proved a means of our deliverance; and even while we have still great
abundance of food, and a great quantity of arms, and other necessaries
more than we want, we are openly deprived by G-d himself of all hope of
deliverance; for that fire which was driven upon our enemies did not of
its own accord turn back upon the wall which we had built; this was the
effect of G-d's anger against us for our manifold sins, which we have been
guilty of in a most insolent and extravagant manner with regard to our
own countrymen; the punishments of which let us not receive from the
Romans, but from G-d himself, as executed by our own hands; for these
will be more moderate than the other. Let our wives die before they are
abused, and our children before they have tasted of slavery; and after we
have slain them, let us bestow that glorious benefit upon one another
mutually, and preserve ourselves in freedom, as an excellent funeral
monument for us. But first let us destroy our money and the fortress by
fire; for I am well assured that this will be a great grief to the Romans,
that they shall not be able to seize upon our bodies, and shall fail of our
wealth also; and let us spare nothing but our provisions; for they will be a
testimonial when we are dead that we were not subdued for want of
necessaries, but that, according to our original resolution, we have
preferred death before slavery."[146]

The Sicarii had all the basic qualities of a cult. They had a charismatic leader, extreme aims and eventually committed ritual suicide together rather than surrendering.

Ironically the notion of suicide as being honourable was a far more Roman quality, so it is almost as if Josephus reimagined this story to garner sympathy from a predominantly Roman audience.

The account from Josephus' work is probably an exaggeration if not a complete fabrication.

So, it is either the case that the Sicarii made their last stand, and in doing so proved themselves to be a cult or that the whole thing was fabricated to make the story more in line with Roman views on death and the afterlife.

The Jews who had been captured largely ended up in a portion of Germany known as Agri Decumates or אַשְׁכְּנַז in Hebrew.

Ashkenaz as it was called was a small border region where Vespasian offered his veterans from the Jewish war plots of land.

These soldiers had Jewish slaves who came to this region and the term for European Jews (Ashkenazim) became eponymous with this region.

To raise funds for the Roman state Vespasian used creative methods. Among other things he taxed the public toilets of Rome and clamped down on corruption.

This anti-corruption stance mainly existed because the Emperor didn't want other people embezzling public money. This rule was not applied to the state itself because Vespasian used his position to centralize his corruption by gaining monopolistic control of certain industries.

As well as this his son Titus continued an affair with Berenice (the daughter of Agrippa I and sister of Agrippa II). Although these Jews had been loyal to Rome during the war Titus had to send her back to Judaea for fear of public backlash.

The insecurity the Flavians held over their public image never really died down, they were not descendants of Augustus so their only claim to legitimacy came from their successes.

Although they had these in abundance, they were careful not to do anything that would excessively antagonise their opponents.

This involved a careful and rather elaborate use of propaganda and public displays of power.

They portrayed themselves as the only capable rulers Rome had available and illustrated this with public works and printed similar propaganda on their coins.

Titus was upset about the tax on public urination and Vespasian used his remarkable wit to counter.

"And to Titus, who was angry at the tax on urinating, which was appointed along with the rest, he replied, as he picked up some gold pieces that were the product of it: "See, my child, if they smell at all.""[147]

Vespasian liked making jokes, he had been forged in the harsh fires of the Roman army.

Good humour was an important method of earning the love of his soldiers, they didn't respond to serious speeches so much as to banter.

The Emperor always made jokes, in some ways (as illustrated above) he used jokes as a defence mechanism to deprive his critics of credibility. It is much harder to stay mad at someone who makes you laugh.

Vespasian was an old man when he took the throne and fell gravely ill ten years after his accession.

The Emperor died of a severe case of dysentery. He stood up and uttered his final words.

Vae, puto deus fio.[148]

In English this means *"Dear me, I think I'm becoming a G-d."* With these words he died, after 10 years of fairly stable rule.

Titus succeeded his father in 79CE, and it was initially feared that because of his youth and reported affair with Berenice he would become another bad Emperor.

He assuaged these fears by abolishing the treason trials in good faith. These trials had become a problematic political tool used for violence and repression. He saw these trials as a glib measure on the part of prior Emperors and wanted a fresh start which involved free speech being allowed.

"It is impossible for me to be insulted or outraged in any way. I do naught that deserves censure and I care not for what is falsely reported. As for the Emperors that are dead and gone, they will avenge themselves in case any one does them wrong, if in very truth they be heroes and possess some power."[149]

With these words Titus began an age of unprecedented personal freedom for the Romans.

This was the single greatest time in Roman history for independent thought and the expression of it.

Titus' first great test as a leader was the emergence of a pretender claiming to be Nero. This man took his followers to Parthia and was received well by the Parthians because of the inconvenience this caused for Titus.

This false claimant eventually got himself killed when he was found to be an imposter, but the damage was lasting.

In the first year of his reign the greatest and most cataclysmic event of his reign took place.

When Pompeii was destroyed the Jewish community therein was lost too. We know that such a community existed because there was a piece of graffiti linking the unfortunate fate of Pompeii to that of the cities of Sodom and Gomorrah.

This is direct proof that Jewish slaves occupied Pompeii and they obviously had enough of an impact to leave a mark on the city before Vesuvius erupted.

The fact that someone wrote this also indicates that the Jews found a certain measure of levity before the end, seeing this destruction as the Lord's wrath against the people who had destroyed the temple.

One cannot help but see an element of irony in the fact that these Romans suffered a similar fate to the Jews of Jerusalem, but regarding it as some divine act of vengeance and expressing joviality about it shall not cause the temple to sprout back into existence.

Nor will it cause the Jews to rise from the dead, it only makes us as bad as the Romans were.

In fairness to Emperor Titus, he did initiate a full-scale relief effort to rescue the masses and provide people with resources necessary for their survival.

Titus never slew anyone on any false charge, nor did he allow the treason trials to continue.

Only two years after taking power Titus died of a fever. His death is shrouded in mystery, he was only a young man, but he died, nonetheless.

This was probably some sort of infection, but the Talmud claims that it was divine wrath meted out to him because of the destruction of the temple. The Talmud speaks at length of his crimes and often exaggerates them for theatrical value.

מֶה עָשָׂה תָּפַשׂ זוֹנָה בְּיָדוֹ וְנִכְנַס לְבֵית קָדְשֵׁי הַקֳּדָשִׁים וְהִצִּיעַ סֵפֶר
תּוֹרָה וְעָבַר עָלֶיהָ עֲבֵירָה וְנָטַל סַיִּיף וְגִידֵּר אֶת הַפָּרוֹכֶת וְנַעֲשָׂה נֵס
וְהָיָה דָּם מְבַצְבֵּץ וְיוֹצֵא וּכְסָבוּר הָרַג אֶת עַצְמוֹ שֶׁנֶּאֱמַר שָׁאֲגוּ צוֹרְרֶיךָ
בְּקֶרֶב מוֹעֲדֶיךָ שָׂמוּ אוֹתוֹתָם אוֹתוֹת

"What did Titus do when he conquered the Temple? He took a prostitute with his hand, and entered the Holy of Holies with her. He then spread out a Torah scroll underneath him and committed a sin, i.e., engaged in

sexual intercourse, on it. Afterward he took a sword and cut into the
curtain separating between the Sanctuary and the Holy of Holies. And a
miracle was performed and blood spurted forth. Seeing the blood, he
mistakenly thought that he had killed himself. Here, the term himself is a
euphemism for G-d. Titus saw blood issuing forth from the curtain in
G-d's meeting place, the Temple, and he took it as a sign that he had
succeeded in killing G-d Himself. As it is stated: "Your enemies roar in the
midst of Your meeting place; they have set up their own signs for
signs"[150]

The Talmudic writers allege that Titus copulated with a prostitute in the temple itself before destroying it. This wanton villainiza-
tion underpins Jewish perspectives on Titus.

Bearing in mind that Roman sources claim that Titus was kind
and virtuous it is probably the case that Titus was somewhere between a paragon and a complete monster. Perhaps he was even both
of these things at the same time.

The Talmud claims that a gnat infested Titus' brain as punishment for his sinful behaviour, although this doesn't seem scientific
nor is it corroborated by other sources.

עָלָה לַיַּבָּשָׁה וְתַעֲשֶׂה עִמָּהּ מִלְחָמָה עָלָה לַיַּבָּשָׁה בָּא יַתּוּשׁ וְנִכְנַס
בְּחוֹטְמוֹ וְנִקֵּר בְּמוֹחוֹ שֶׁבַע שָׁנִים יוֹמָא חַד הֲוָה קָא חָלֵיף אַבָּבָא דְּבֵי
נַפָּחָא שְׁמַע קָל אַרְזַפְתָּא אִישְׁתִּיק אֲמַר אִיכָּא תַּקַּנְתָּא כָּל יוֹמָא
מַיְיתוּ נַפָּחָא וּמָחוּ קַמֵּיהּ לְגוֹי יָהֵיב לֵיהּ אַרְבַּע זוּזֵי יִשְׂרָאֵל אֲמַר לֵיהּ
מִיסַּתְיֵךְ דְּקָא חָזֵית בְּסָנְאָךְ עַד תְּלָתִין יוֹמִין עֲבַד הָכִי מִכַּאן וְאֵילָךְ
כֵּיוָן דְּדָשׁ דָּשׁ

"The Gemara resumes its story about Titus. The Divine Voice continued:
Go up on dry land and make war with it. He went up on dry land, and a

gnat came, entered his nostril, and picked at his brain for seven years. Titus suffered greatly from this until one day he passed by the gate of a blacksmith's shop. The gnat heard the sound of a hammer and was silent and still. Titus said: I see that there is a remedy for my pain. Every day they would bring a blacksmith who hammered before him. He would give four dinars as payment to a gentile blacksmith, and to a Jew he would simply say: It is enough for you that you see your enemy in so much pain. He did this for thirty days and it was effective until then. From that point forward, since the gnat became accustomed to the hammering, it became accustomed to it, and once again it began to pick away at Titus's brain.[151]

Many Roman sources also claim that Domitian was plotting against the Emperor, but this seems a little bit spurious and (as we will find out later) Domitian was not well-liked by the Senatorial class which wrote many of these historical sources.

"Titus, as he expired, said: "I have made but one error." What this was he did not reveal, and no one else feels quite sure about it."[152]

These were Titus' alleged last words, and as Dio reports we do not know which mistake he was referring to.

Domitian became Emperor in 81CE and earned the ire of the Senate during his reign to such a point of severity that they had him murdered.

This new Emperor was known for being gifted and capable in ways that his brother and father could only dream of. Vespasian had been a reckless spender and Titus had been much the same.

Domitian was slated for a good and effective reign. Domitian was 12 years younger than his brother so he was 10 years younger than Titus had been when he became Emperor, this meant that his reign would last an exceptionally long time or at least that it should have.

The first act of Domitian's rule was to have Titus declared a G-d by the Senate.

His reign is described in negative terms by the Senate but in practice he ended up being heavily popular. This passage from Suetonius is a good example of how the Senators ended up focussing excessively on his negative qualities.

"Young girls also ran races in the Stadium, at which he presided in his sandals, dressed in a purple robe, made after the Grecian fashion, and wearing upon his head a golden crown bearing the effigies of Jupiter, Juno, and Minerva; with the flamen of Jupiter, and the college of priests sitting by his side in the same dress; excepting only that their crowns had also his own image on them."[153]

Note that this passage is recounting how Domitian hosted games for the people, but it gives more focus to how he dressed implying that he was being excessive with what he wore.

An Emperor would be expected to wear fine clothes, but in the case of Domitian sources use this against him.

Suetonius was a Senator and Cassius Dio was also a Senator, the fact that Domitian suppressed the powers of the Senate and was eventually killed by them probably explains why they were so ardently opposed to him in just about every single way.

It seems from the indications of historical sources that Domitian was a populist at heart, and that he used acts of public good to promote his image. He gave gifts to the public at the expense of the Senators.

It is even said that he threw tickets for Gladiatorial games which were meant for the upper classes into the common portion of the arena.

Domitian also became extremely notorious for his building projects, which largely involved making repairs on buildings that were damaged during the string of fires that impacted the city of Rome.

Unlike Titus and Vespasian Domitian stated clearly from the beginning that he was the Lord and master of the Senate and that they were subservient to him.

He wanted to return to an Augustan model of government and saw the Senate as nothing but a corrupted roadblock stopping him from achieving his goals.

Domitian can best be regarded as a conservative in the body of a libertine. Although he extoled the same harsh virtues as Augustus, he was in practice susceptible to lust.

For instance, he was besotted with a eunuch called Earinus yet he banned the practice of castration and tried to portray the use of eunuchs for sexual purposes as immoral.

It is said that his brother Titus enjoyed eunuchs, so Cassius Dio asserts that Domitian did this as an insult to Titus' memory.

Eunuchs were common in Rome at this time, they acted as non-threatening servants. They were also useful for sex acts because they were not able to take the active role in homosexual relationships.

Homosexuality was not regarded as unfeminine so long as you were taking the active role, the same was true of heterosexual relationships as well.

Sex and morality were heavily associated in the Roman world. Sexual perversion was directly associated with poor governance, and one always came with the other. The negative portrayal of Domitian's hypocrisy regarding eunuchs indicates just how much the Senatorial historians wanted to smear Domitian.

In many ways Domitian was right about the Senate. The Senate had propped up a number of unworthy Emperors and could only really be controlled through fear.

"He was elected consul for ten years in succession, and first and only censor for life of all private citizens and Emperors."[154]

Emperors who had tried to befriend the Senate usually didn't last long. The ideal balance was something between fear and love. Domitian's failure was that he underestimated the Senate and took many roles (as is stated above) for himself.

As Censor Domitian presided over public morals and tried to go in a more socially conservative direction.

If an Emperor followed Caligula's model and tormented the Senators they would surely die, and if an Emperor did as Titus did and let them all go, he would just end up accomplishing nothing.

Domitian wanted to throw this balance out of the window and establish a new order. He was almost radically Conservative. He wanted an absolute government with the Emperor as the head of state and head of government with the Senate as an irrelevant rubber stamp.

This happened after Domitian's death, although it took far longer than he had wanted and coincided with the decline of Roman authority, so it was too little and too late.

Domitian often reduced taxes for the poor whilst raising them for the Senators.

Domitian tried to decrease inflation by increasing the silver purity of his coins from 90% to 98%. Despite having to decrease it later he still maintained a consistent anti-inflation economic stance during his reign.

Doing this decreased the amount of money he had readily available at any given time but avoided an economic spiral which made it a prudent move in the long term.

Later Emperors often devalued the coinage so that they could pay exorbitant amounts of money to the army which ultimately made Roman coins worthless. Domitian's focus on economic stability marks him as one of the best Emperors Rome ever had.

Most people who wore the purple were too short-sighted and opportunistic to do something that would damage themselves for the good of the empire at large.

This was another example of Domitian's more conservative economic policies. The one area Domitian strayed from Conservatism in was his populism.

Rather than pandering to the elite Domitian pandered to the common people. A truly Conservative person would have defended the Senate and earned their love.

This marriage of Conservatism both economic and social with a heavily populist agenda is highly effective in today's democratic states, but in ancient Rome it put a target on Domitian's back.

Domitian had been in Rome when the Year of 4 Emperors occurred. He had seen the Senate roll over and turn on every Emperor one after the other, so one can imagine the contempt he felt for them.

Domitian refused to give political offices to the rich and powerful, he focussed on crushing political corruption and nepotism so aggressively that it almost ceased to be an issue.

What seems more likely than the notion that Domitian was a tyrant is that he was a victim of his own success. That in crushing corruption he gave the corrupt a reason to crush him.

One thing we can infer about Domitian is his passionate nature, he was often governed by his emotions which probably explains his aggressive anti-Senatorial stance.

Unlike most Roman royals Domitian married purely for love. He chose Domitia Longina as his wife.

Through what can best be described as intense political wrangling he was able to convince his father to let him marry this girl instead of his niece Julia Flavia.

The husband of Longina had to divorce her so that she could marry Domitian. The love life of this imperial couple could be described as both rocky and passionate. They had a number of fights but always seemed to forgive each other for their iniquities.

Some also claim that Titus had an affair with Domitian's wife, and that for this slight he killed his brother. This theory doesn't seem to hold much weight but theories without much proof that tell a good story often stick even if they aren't very substantive.

It is said that Domitia Longina fell for an actor called Paris and that when Domitian found out he sent her away, but later allowed her to return to him out of the earnestness of his love.

According to Suetonius he murdered Paris in public and had an affair with his niece. This last point seems contrived and impossible; Domitian had willingly avoided marrying his niece so he could marry Longina so it doesn't seem logical that he would then sleep with the same woman he had rejected before.

Either way, Domitian welcomed Longina back and they had a happy marriage after this incident. It seems that in his rashness he had his wife banished, but that in the end he decided to forgive her.

An Emperor does not need to feign forgiveness. If he had truly held a grudge, he could have just killed his wife and replaced her with someone else.

Their only son had died in infancy so the fact that Domitian didn't simply divorce her for a more fertile woman points to the fact that he loved her a great deal, even after the alleged incident with Paris.

Another indication of his devotion to his wife comes from how he reacted to insults directed at the couple. He had her ex-husband killed for making jokes about their relationship and had a writer put to death for producing a comedic play (farce) about their marriage.

It is not often that a man has people murdered for insulting a woman he doesn't have affection for.

At some point in the 90sCE Herod Agrippa II died, marking the end of the final Hasmonean and Herodian King of the Jews. There would not be another officially recognised head of state for the Jews until 1949 when Chaim Weizmann became Israel's first President.

So it was that Domitian presided over the end of Jewish self-rule. The Sanhedrin was also moved to the city of Jamnia since Jerusalem was all but destroyed.

This period can best be described as the Sanhedrin's death preparations. It no longer governed the Jews so it could only function as a means of preserving the Jewish religion. It made important contributions to the modern Jewish religion from Jamnia and codified a lot of the rules and systems that Judaism relied on to survive.

In 85CE it declared Theudas, Yehoshua and Judas of Gamala to be false messianic claimants.

Though it was largely accepted that none of these men were the true messiah in Jewish circles doing this marked a formal and lasting separation between Christianity and Judaism.

In many ways this was the first time these two religions were separated in a formal context.

The temple was gone and Yehoshua was declared to be a false messiah, so Christians no longer adhered to their Jewish roots. Domitian allegedly persecuted the Christians heavily.

Eusebius claims that Domitian prosecuted the Jews as well, but beyond high taxes there is not much evidence that Domitian was religiously intolerant.

Christianity was largely as successful as it was because when faced with destruction, it used the concept of martyrdom to come back stronger. A religious sect that only gets more powerful when you persecute it will inevitably become a force to be reckoned with.

It would take another 2 centuries however for the Christians to become the chief religious group of the Roman world.

In military affairs Domitian was more mediocre than he was in the domestic field. He increased the pay of the soldiery by 33% and involved himself in several conflicts.

He first launched a campaign against the Chatti, a Germanic tribe and then against the Suebi another Germanic tribe. He did this to consolidate the Roman defence against Germanic tribes and to promote himself as a defender of the empire.

The Limes Germanicus was a defensive system of fortifications which Domitian put up to cover the gap between the Rhine and the Danube, this was an important step because it deprived the tribes of an easy route into Roman lands.

Domitian also had Gnaeus Julius Agricola expand Roman rule into most of Scotland. The campaign was successful and is very well documented because the historian Tacitus was Agricola's son-in-law.

He served until 85CE and also discovered Ireland, although he deemed it to be unworthy of Roman conquest.

In 85CE the most memorable conflict of Domitian's reign took place. The King of Dacia Decebalus invaded the empire and killed a great many of its civilians in the border regions.

The Kingdom of Dacia encompassed modern Romania and some parts of Hungary. It was very rich in natural resources including gold which made it a key target for Roman expansion.

Initially the Romans pushed them back, but the Praetorian Prefect was sent to Dacia and killed there.

The eagle standard of the Praetorians was stolen, which was a great blow to Roman prestige.

In the end despite having the upper hand Domitian was forced into a humiliating peace agreement. Decebalus got a great deal of money from this which he used to strengthen his anti-Roman defences.

Domitian had to make peace because he was being harangued by Germanic tribes so he couldn't split his forces between two conflicts.

The Emperor spent the rest of his reign preparing for a war with Dacia, but he died before he could launch one.

A more pressing concern was the Senatorial plot developing in Germany. Lucius Saturninus the governor of Germania Superior raised a legion against the Emperor with the help of a string of Senators.

A Spanish general named Trajan was sent to deal with the uprising and Domitian came in person to defeat the rebels as well.

The rebels had hoped for help from the Chatti but the tribesmen never came, so they were soundly defeated. All the documents linking Senators to the rising were destroyed before Saturninus was captured and executed brutally.

By the time he had reigned 15 years the Senate felt it was necessary to kill him.

"The day before his death, he ordered some dates, served up at table, to be kept till the next day, adding, "If I have the luck to use them." And turning to those who were nearest him, he said, "To-morrow the moon in Aquarius will be bloody instead of watery, and an event will happen, which will be much talked of all the world over." About midnight, he was so terrified that he leaped out of bed. That morning he tried and passed sentence on a soothsayer sent from Germany, who being consulted about

the lightning that had lately happened, predicted from it a change of government. The blood running down his face as he scratched an ulcerous tumour on his forehead, he said, "Would this were all that is to befall me!" Then, upon his asking the time of the day, instead of five o'clock, which was the hour he dreaded, they purposely told him it was six. Overjoyed at this information; as if all danger were now passed, and hastening to the bath, Parthenius, his chamberlain, stopped him, by saying that there was a person come to wait upon him about a matter of great importance, which would admit of no delay. Upon this, ordering all persons to with- draw, he retired into his chamber, and was there slain."[155]

Long ago Domitian had heard a prophecy that he would die in the middle of the day. During this time of day, he was uneasy and kept his guard up.

Suetonius reports that the chief G-ddess Domitian revered, Minerva came to him in a dream and told him she could no longer offer him her protection a few days before his assassination.

He asked one of his servants what the time was and (this man being among the plotters) lied, saying that the time had passed.

Domitian went to start his work when Stephanus (a servant of his niece) came for an audience with a bandage around his arm. He claimed that he had a document detailing a Senatorial plot against him.

The Emperor grabbed the paper and carefully read it. It was this very diligence that condemned him, for the wounded man took a knife from under his bandages and stabbed Domitian.

The two fought and Domitian killed Stephanus, but the damage was already done.

The other plotters came in to finish him off. He could not repel them in such great numbers.

Some sources claim that Domitian's wife had plotted against him by passing a list of those condemned to death to Domitian's assassins, but this is probably a copied event from the reign of Commodus.

Commodus' mistress is said to have also passed a list of names to his enemies which seems to indicate that Longina was simply demonized by the very same Senatorial class that killed her husband.

After Domitian's death his wife never remarried and despite living until the 130sCE she always referred to herself as his wife in all official capacities.

This was quite literally illegal considering the damnatio memoriae issued against Domitian.

All records of his rule and all images of him were meant to be removed, so even referring to herself as his wife was dangerous.

She didn't care, because no matter what the questionable ancient sources say she was always in love with her husband.

It was with all of this that the Flavians lost power after 27 years of nearly unchallenged authority.

One of the most notable and profound quotes attributed to Domitian is this. He complained of his early onset of baldness, and this was his remark.

"Remember that nothing is more fascinating than beauty, but nothing of shorter duration."[156]

Josephus died not long after Domitian, by the time the Flavians lost power in 96CE most of the people who remembered the Jewish War were dead.

The generation of men and women from Vespasian's reign were mostly gone, a new generation and a new dynasty inherited the

Roman world and, in many ways, repeated the mistakes of their elders.

Domitian was replaced with an old Senator called Nerva. It was probably the case that Nerva had been involved in the assassination.

This is because of the fact that he was acclaimed despite (and also because of) being a weak old man.

He was chosen in large part because people knew his reign would be short, and that he would not be able to make as many enemies as Domitian had.

Nerva was never as popular or accomplished as Domitian, and he only reigned for 2 years.

He was picked because he couldn't do as much, he was the obvious choice for a Senatorial class that wanted a pliable and weak imperial presence instead of the efficient autocrat Domitian had been.

A more obvious choice would have been an opponent of Domitian, so the fact that Nerva was picked for the purple shows that the Senate was also aware of appearances. He was not outwardly involved in the plot but was at least aware that it was taking place.

In a way choosing someone like Nerva was a compromise. It made very few people happy, but in doing so didn't earn the total contempt of anyone.

Nerva also had no children. Normally this would be problematic as it would leave the succession unclear, but in this case, it made Nerva nearly powerless.

This was a massive advantage for those who wanted to limit the powers of Emperors.

The Senate immediately passed a damnatio memoriae against Domitian. They erased public records of him, destroyed his coins and broke down his statues and revoked his honours. The fact that there are still many records of Domitian and many statues of him shows how ineffective this was. Geta, who was the next Emperor to suffer a damnatio memoriae has far fewer surviving images or records because he had not reigned for very long, and also because his brother Caracalla ruthlessly enforced the order.

Nerva allowed the damning of Domitian's memory without any reservations, which implies that he was either too weak to stop it or just didn't care.

The army was completely outraged. They quite literally held Nerva hostage and forced him to hand the assassins over in 97CE.

The Praetorian guard itself executed the assassins and Nerva could do nothing to stop them.

Nerva never had time to accomplish anything noteworthy because in 98CE he died of a stroke. The thing he is remembered for (and the reason he is described as one of the 5 good Emperors) is that he adopted Trajan as his heir.

Trajan was the descendant of Italian settlers in Roman Spain, and so he became the first Roman Emperor not to be an Italian.

When Roman Emperors are ranked against one another Trajan often comes out as the best, and there is good reason for this.

Trajan pleased the Senate by offering them enhanced powers and honouring their position in the empire, for most things he requested their approval and often got it without any issues.

Roman Emperors were by default dictators, but Trajan chose to turn Rome into the oligarchy it had traditionally been rather than an autocratic regime.

He democratised the empire in so far as he expanded the dictatorship from himself to the aristocracy at large.

This is illustrated by the level of positivity expressed towards him by Senatorial sources.
Cassius Dio for instance described his purge of the mutineers against Nerva in an elegantly avoidant way.

"He sent for Aelianus and the Pretorians who had mutinied against

Nerva, pretending that he was going to employ them in some way, and relieved the world of their presence."[157]

He admits that Trajan purged his potential enemies early on but does so in a way that paints Trajan positively. If a more hated Emperor like Domitian had done this at the start of his reign there would be no end to Dio's complaints and condemnations.

Despite this obvious bias Dio is still useful for assessing events and more importantly what the Senate actually thought of different Emperors.

This is necessary for historical analysis because it explains both the successes and failures of those who wore the purple.

Trajan had his vices as well, but these are written off by his supporters because he didn't let any of this impact his quality as a leader.

"I know well enough that he was given to wine and boys, but if he had ever committed or endured any base or wicked deed as a result of this, he would have incurred censure. As the case stood, he drank all the wine he wanted, yet remained sober, and his pursuit of pederasty [sexual relations between a man and young boy] harmed no one."[158]

Trajan was by modern standards a paedophile but having intercourse with young boys was considered an entirely normal and acceptable thing to do. It is also unclear if Dio is referring to young adults or literal children.

It was a very widespread practice and people often did it as a rite of passage. Trajan was married to a wife that was very popular both with the public and the Senate so what he got up to in his leisure time didn't ruffle any feathers. Even later Christian (homophobic) sources praised Trajan despite his acts of homosexuality.

Between 101CE and 102CE Trajan made war with Decebalus and saw much more success than his predecessors. In this first war Trajan managed to decisively defeat Decebalus at Tapae and a number of other battles.

The Dacians lost and were forced to cede some land and pay for the construction of a bridge between Rome and Dacia across the Danube. This now gave the Romans a direct route for invasion which they hoped would prevent further conflict.

In 105CE another war with Dacia began, and this time Trajan took no prisoners. He launched a full-scale offensive and marched towards Sarmizegetusa, the capital of the Dacian Kingdom.

In 106CE Trajan took Sarmizegetusa and Decebalus killed himself to avoid capture. Dacia was annexed as a Roman province which officially brought Rome to the peak of its territorial expanses.

Never again would Rome be as large as it was. There was a large pivot in Rome's foreign policy after Dacia's annexation. Rome was now so large that expansion was impossible, Rome no longer wanted to enlarge itself, it just wanted to consolidate what it already had.

Much like a puzzle Rome was complete. Future Emperors would have to use their resources to defend this puzzle from others and keep the pieces intact. If anything, the expansion of the empire was a liability.

There simply weren't enough resources to keep the empire from being invaded and Rome needed to constantly keep a careful eye on the borders.

A bigger empire was a bigger target and eventually Rome became so fragmented that it couldn't maintain itself.

Despite having made Rome larger Trajan didn't make it any safer, he actually sealed its fate of terminal decline from then on.

Dacia was also impossible to defend. It was a soft protrusion poking out from Rome's belly, it was too mountainous to be easily defended and there were constant attacks from bordering tribes.

This province may have been wealthy and a prestige boost for Trajan, but it was ultimately more trouble than it was worth.

Trajan had an extravagant triumph for his Dacian victories. He was also known for being very down-to-earth. He would often randomly go to dinner in the homes of his friends without guards and he would make himself at home.

He didn't take himself too seriously and often behaved respectfully even to those of a much lower status.

In the same year as the Dacian victory Trajan annexed the Nabatean Kingdom, connecting Rome to the Arabian Peninsula.

Next Trajan made war with the Parthians in 113CE. The King of Parthia had installed his nephew as King of Armenia which was reason enough for Trajan to make war with them.

Armenia was a client Kingdom of Rome and was an essential buffer state between the two powers so the presumption that the Parthians could choose an Armenian monarch gave Trajan a solid justification to invade the Parthians and Armenians.

Parthia lost this war in a spectacular fashion, and Trajan expanded the empire all the way to modern Kuwait. Babylon was taken, monuments were erected, and the Parthians had to cede a lot of their western territory.

In this war Lusius Quietus proved himself just as he had done in the Dacian wars. Quietus was a Berber from modern Morocco and became one of Trajan's most trusted officers.

The victory in Parthia set the stage for the Kitos war in 115CE. This war would be far more violent than the previous Jewish wars and Quietus would ultimately be sent as the chief architect of the Roman offensive.

16

Chapter 16- The Kitos War

After the first Roman-Jewish war the Jews migrated to other parts of the Mediterranean.

Despite their enslavement and diaspora, they actually increased in number in places like Egypt and Cyprus.

They weren't quite the majority outside of Judaea, but they were such a sizeable minority that they held a great deal of sway in these regions of the empire.

The Parthian war depleted the Roman garrisons in the eastern provinces which set the perfect scene for a full-scale revolt.

Despite the destruction of the temple Jewish identity continued and calls for emancipation increased. The Jews in diaspora forgot the defeat they had previously endured and their desire for freedom began to overtake their fear of Roman reprisals.

When the Romans invaded Parthia most of the Babylonian Jewry chose to side with the Parthians. Parthia was considerably more tolerant of Jews than Rome, so it was natural for them to favour the side which was the least likely to oppress them.

Rome had issued a number of edicts and taxes to suppress the Jews and limit their personal freedoms. One such tax was the Fiscus Judaicus.

The Fiscus Judaicus was the most immoral tax Rome ever threw at their Jewish subjects. The money that had once been paid by Jews for the preservation of the temple was now given to the Emperor for the preservation of the temple of Jupiter.

This affront made the Jews furious, furious enough to risk everything in another rebellion.

In a way the Kitos war was completely inevitable because of the indignities Rome rained down on the Jews.

When a population suffers so immensely that they would choose to slaughter and be slaughtered rather than enduring it any longer this points to a tremendous lack of morality on the part of the oppressor.

In the year 115CE Andreas Lukuas declared himself to be a King of the Jews and the Davidic messiah.

He began an open revolt against Roman rule in his local city of Cyrene where the Greek population was put to death.

This is how Eusebius of Caesarea described the outbreak of the conflict.

"For in Alexandria and in the rest of Egypt, and also in Cyrene, as if incited by some terrible and factious spirit, they rushed into seditious measures against their fellow-inhabitants, the Greeks. The insurrection increased greatly, and in the following year, while Lupus was governor of all Egypt, it developed into a war of no mean magnitude."[159]

The chief historical records available to us are of Roman origin. Eusebius was a Roman Christian of the later empire so his limited accounts must be taken with a grain of salt.

Marcus Lupus the governor of Egypt was forced to flee because of how rapid Lukuas' advance was.

He managed to sack Alexandria as well as most of the Egyptian coastline, the breadbasket of the empire was all but lost in a blink of an eye.

Many supported his claims of messiahship and riots broke out all over the east. Artemion of Cyprus raised the Jews in revolt and killed over 240,000 non-Jews on the island.

Many of the Jews in these other areas of the empire had been the same rebels (and their descendants) who had fought against Vespasian and Titus. There was a latent rage in the Jewish community that was continuously aggravated until it simply reached a breaking point.

Cassius Dio also claimed that the Jews committed cannibalism and used the corpses of the dead for unspeakable things.

"Meanwhile the Jews in the region of Cyrene had put one Andreas at their head and were destroying both the Romans and the Greeks. They would cook their flesh, make belts for themselves of their entrails, anoint themselves with their blood, and wear their skins for clothing. Many they sawed in two, from the head downwards. Others they would give to wild beasts and force still others to fight as gladiators. In all, consequently, two hundred and twenty thousand perished. In Egypt, also, they performed many similar deeds, and in Cyprus under the leadership of Artemio.

There, likewise, two hundred and forty thousand perished. For this reason no Jew may set foot in that land, but even if one of them is driven upon the island by force of the wind, he is put to death. Various persons took part in subduing these Jews, one being Lusius, who was sent by Trajan."[160]

Apart from being a complete and obvious lie this does illustrate the degree to which the Romans demonized the Jews. Judaism has always had an intense notion of piety and cleanliness.

Jewish rites and rituals are often centred around the belief that human corpses are unclean and that defiling a corpse is immoral, so these allegations are not only a falsehood they directly go against Jewish beliefs.

The fact that Dio thought he could get away with these blatant lies illustrates just how little the Romans understood the Jewish world. It was easy to demonize them because their views were so remote from Roman ones.

This is one reason I believe that the Jews were such an easy target for Roman cruelty. It was far easier to label them in negative terms because the average Roman would not have known enough about the Jews to correct such stories.

Trajan was very unwell by this time. He had suffered a severe stroke and was nearly paralysed.

Because Trajan was unwell, he sent Lusius Quietus (Kitos) to slay the rebels. Kitos is the Greek version of Quietus which is why this war is referred to as the Kitos War.

By the time Trajan died in 117CE most of Egypt including the coast and the interior had been taken by the rebels.

It is said that because Trajan had not formally adopted Hadrian as his heir his wife Pompeia Plotina hid Trajan's death from the officials so she could forge a document declaring Hadrian as the heir.

Hadrian had always been the obvious heir. He too was a Spaniard and was married to Trajan's niece. He was the closest relative

Trajan had and had been groomed to inherit the empire for quite some time.

Hadrian ascended to the throne in 117CE at the age of 41. This was the perfect age. He was young enough to run the empire well but old enough that he wouldn't stick around for too long.

Much like Trajan the new Emperor was very skilled in military affairs. But he was far less merciful than his predecessor and purged certain officials for personal gain.

Lusius Quietus defeated the revolt and Lukuas tried to flee to the Sanhedrin in Jamnia for protection.

Quietus hunted the rebels to Lydda where they were soundly defeated. Soon after this Hadrian had Quietus killed. This was probably because of his popularity and closeness with the previous Emperor.

He was a potential rival that Hadrian purged to avoid having to worry about any plots.

Hadrian was still too fresh in his office to continue a war, trying to pacify the Jews would have put him in a difficult position and he needed to get to Rome to avoid political intrigues while he was away on campaign.

Hadrian essentially reversed the diaspora by sending the Jews back to Judaea as to avoid more racially motivated conflicts, and he also banned them altogether from entering Cyprus.

The Alexandrine Synagogue was destroyed and Jewish roots in other parts of the empire were plucked up using brutal force.

To call this a peace agreement implies that it had a lasting impact. It was nothing of this sort, he simply delayed the conflict for personal political reasons. He probably knew that there would be more conflict in the future and that he would have to 'finish the job'.

This was a task he most certainly completed.

The Kitos war is often overlooked because of some key factors. Firstly, it did not last very long. Secondly, it was followed later with a far greater conflict. Thirdly, it is very poorly documented, and sources can barely agree on any of the details of the events.

It is something of a footnote in most cases, but it was important because of the horrors it ended up creating.

If anything is to be remembered about the Kitos war it is that not every Jewish-Roman conflict ended in a total Jewish defeat. The Jews fought back far more fiercely than most people would assume from looking at the resulting diaspora of the Jewish people.

The Roman state was pushed to its limits by the rancour of the Jews, even though the Jews were always on the back foot the playing field was levelled by just how disruptive and ferocious the Jewish resistance was.

17

Chapter 17- Bar Kochba

Hadrian began his reign as an intensely controversial figure. He was disliked by the Senatorial class and the feeling was often mutual.

He is generally a revered figure, but most sources forget just how much contempt the Senators held him in. One reason for his popularity was that he had the debt documents of the past 15 years burned in public and forgave the debts of all Romans.

Having your debts magically erased is bound to make you like someone even if they have a fairly poor personality.

The Emperor was partially hated because of his love of Hellenistic culture, he revered the Greeks and took on most of their mannerisms. Despite Rome borrowing heavily from Greek culture this was still considered an affront to the Senators, who regarded themselves as the traditional defenders of Roman culture.

Hadrian granted certain rights to the Greeks that other imperial subjects did not have.

Hadrian was also gay and was extremely well known for it. His lover Antinous was by far his favourite, and he lavished gifts on the young Greek.

He took Antinous with him everywhere and glorified him in every way he could. An event which rocked Hadrian for the rest of his life was poor Antinous' death.

In 130CE Antinous drowned and in his immense grief Hadrian had him deified. To this day there are more surviving statues of Antinous than of any other Roman.

The grief Hadrian endured seems to have changed him, his penchant for angry outbursts seems to have intensified.

In Judaea other things were taking place that coincided with Hadrian's rule.

We will now talk of Rabbi Akiva, the most prominent Jewish intellectual of this era.

He was born the son of converts, and he was illiterate even by the age of 40. His wife's father disowned her for marrying an illiterate man and the couple were forced to live in a house with nothing but straw for bedding. Such unfortunate beginnings created a great man regardless these obstacles.

The Talmud recounts Akiva's journey to becoming a Rabbi.

אָמְרָה לֵיהּ זִיל הֱוֵי בֵּי רַב אָזַל תַּרְתֵּי סְרֵי שְׁנִין קַמֵּי דְּרַבִּי אֱלִיעֶזֶר וְרַבִּי
יְהוֹשֻׁעַ לְמִישְׁלַם תַּרְתֵּי סְרֵי שְׁנִין קָא אָתָא לְבֵיתֵיהּ שְׁמַע מִן אֲחוֹרֵי
בֵּיתֵיהּ דְּקָאָמַר לַהּ חַד רָשָׁע לִדְבֵיתְהוּ שַׁפִּיר עָבֵיד לִיךְ אֲבוּךְ חֲדָא
דְּלָא דָּמֵי לִיךְ וְעוֹד [שַׁבְקָךְ] אַרְמְלוּת חַיּוּת כּוּלְּהוֹן שְׁנִין אָמְרָה לֵיהּ אִי
צָיֵית לְדִילִי לֵיהֱוֵי תַּרְתֵּי סְרֵי שְׁנִין אַחְרָנְיָיתָא אֲמַר הוֹאִיל וִיהַבַת לִי
רְשׁוּתָא אֶיהְדַר לַאֲחוֹרֵי הֲדַר אָזַל הֲוָה תַּרְתֵּי סְרֵי שְׁנֵי אַחְרָנְיָיתָא

"She said to him: Go and be a student of Torah. He went and studied Torah for twelve years before Rabbi Eliezer and Rabbi Yehoshua. At the completion of the twelve years, he was coming home when he heard from

behind his house that one wicked person was saying to his wife: Your
father behaved well toward you. He was right to disinherit you. One
reason is that your husband is not similar to you, i.e., he is not suitable
for you. And furthermore, he has left you in widowhood in his lifetime
all these years. She said to him: If he listens to me, he should be there for
another twelve years. Rabbi Akiva said: Since she has given me permis-
sion through this statement, I will go back and study more. He turned
back and went to the study hall, and he was there for another twelve
years."[161]

It is said that through semi-supernatural means Akiva became very
wealthy. He is said to have used this wealth for the benefit of
others rather than for his own comforts.
In another instance Akiva was accompanied by an assortment of
prominent Rabbis as they ventured to Jerusalem's remains to pay
their respects for what they had all lost.

וכבר היה ר"ג ורבי אלעזר בן עזריה ורבי יהושע ורבי עקיבא
מהלכין בדרך ושמעו קול המונה של רומי מפלטה [ברחוק] מאה
ועשרים מיל והתחילו בוכין ורבי עקיבא משחק אמרו לו מפני מה
אתה משחק אמר להם ואתם מפני מה אתם בוכים אמרו לו הללו
כושיים שמשתחוים לעצבים ומקטרים לעבודת כוכבים יושבין בטח
והשקט ואנו בית הדום רגלי אלהינו שרוף

"Apropos tribulations of exile and hope for redemption, the Gemara
relates: And it once was that Rabban Gamliel, Rabbi Elazar ben Azarya,
Rabbi Yehoshua, and Rabbi Akiva were walking along the road in the
Roman Empire, and they heard the sound of the multitudes of Rome
from Puteoli at a distance of one hundred and twenty mil. The city was so

large that they were able to hear its tumult from a great distance. And the
other Sages began weeping and Rabbi Akiva was laughing. They said to
him: For what reason are you laughing? Rabbi Akiva said to them: And
you, for what reason are you weeping? They said to him: These gentiles,
who bow to false g-ds and burn incense to idols, dwell securely and
tranquilly in this colossal city, and for us, the House of the footstool of
our G-d, the Temple, is burnt

באש ולא נבכה אמר להן לכך אני מצחק ומה לעוברי רצונו כך
לעושי רצונו על אחת כמה וכמה

by fire, and shall we not weep? Rabbi Akiva said to them: That is why I
am laughing. If for those who violate His will, the wicked, it is so and
they are rewarded for the few good deeds they performed, for those who
perform His will, all the more so will they be rewarded.

שוב פעם אחת היו עולין לירושלים כיון שהגיעו להר הצופים קרעו
בגדיהם כיון שהגיעו להר הבית ראו שועל שיצא מבית קדשי
הקדשים התחילו הן בוכין ור"ע מצחק אמרו לו מפני מה אתה
מצחק אמר להם מפני מה אתם בוכים אמרו לו מקום שכתוב בו
(במדבר א, נא) והזר הקרב יומת ועכשיו שועלים הלכו בו ולא
נבכה

The Gemara relates another incident involving those Sages. On another
occasion they were ascending to Jerusalem after the destruction of the
Temple. When they arrived at Mount Scopus and saw the site of the
Temple, they rent their garments in mourning, in keeping with halakhic
practice. When they arrived at the Temple Mount, they saw a fox that
emerged from the site of the Holy of Holies. They began weeping, and

Rabbi Akiva was laughing. They said to him: For what reason are you
laughing? Rabbi Akiva said to them: For what reason are you weeping?
They said to him: This is the place concerning which it is written: "And
the non-priest who approaches shall die" (Numbers 1:51), and now foxes
walk in it; and shall we not weep?

אמר להן לכך אני מצחק דכתיב (ישעיהו ח, ב) ואעידה לי עדים
נאמנים את אוריה הכהן ואת זכריה בן יברכיהו וכי מה ענין אוריה
אצל זכריה אוריה במקדש ראשון וזכריה במקדש שני אלא תלה
הכתוב נבואתו של זכריה בנבואתו של אוריה

Rabbi Akiva said to them: That is why I am laughing, as it is written,
when G-d revealed the future to the prophet Isaiah: "And I will take to Me
faithful witnesses to attest: Uriah the priest, and Zechariah the son of
Jeberechiah" (Isaiah 8:2). Now what is the connection between Uriah and
Zechariah? He clarifies the difficulty: Uriah prophesied during the First
Temple period, and Zechariah prophesied during the Second Temple
period, as he was among those who returned to Zion from Babylonia.
Rather, the verse established that fulfillment of the prophecy of Zechariah
is dependent on fulfillment of the prophecy of Uriah.

באוריה כתיב (מיכה ג, יב) לכן בגללכם ציון שדה תחרש [וגו']
בזכריה כתיב (זכריה ח, ד) עוד ישבו זקנים וזקנות ברחובות ירושלם
עד שלא נתקיימה נבואתו של אוריה הייתי מתירא שלא תתקיים
נבואתו של זכריה עכשיו שנתקיימה נבואתו של אוריה בידוע
שנבואתו של זכריה מתקיימת בלשון הזה אמרו לו עקיבא ניחמתנו
עקיבא ניחמתנו:

In the prophecy of Uriah it is written: "Therefore, for your sake Zion

shall be plowed as a field, and Jerusalem shall become rubble, and the
Temple Mount as the high places of a forest" (Micah 3:12), where foxes
are found. There is a rabbinic tradition that this was prophesied by Uriah.
In the prophecy of Zechariah it is written: "There shall yet be elderly men
and elderly women sitting in the streets of Jerusalem" (Zechariah 8:4).
Until the prophecy of Uriah with regard to the destruction of the city was
fulfilled I was afraid that the prophecy of Zechariah would not be ful-
filled, as the two prophecies are linked. Now that the prophecy of Uriah
was fulfilled, it is evident that the prophecy of Zechariah remains valid.
The Gemara adds: The Sages said to him, employing this formulation:
Akiva, you have comforted us; Akiva, you have comforted us."[162]

In the book of Isaiah, the High Priest Uriah prophesied that the
temple would be destroyed and that foxes would occupy it. When
Akiva saw the prophecy confirmed by a fox wandering into the
remains of the temple, he could do nothing but laugh.

To Akiva this was a thing worthy of celebration, for it indicated
that the prophecies related to the messiah must also be true.

He was not laughing out of cruelty or contempt, but because he
knew that the Jews would have the last laugh.

The other Rabbis wept at the desecration of the temple, but
Akiva saw the bigger picture. He knew of the revenge that would
come.

'Akiva you have comforted us' was their reply to his conjectures.
Comfort was precisely what the Jewish people needed in such a
time of misery.

But in Akiva's mind and the minds of many others their only
consolation was the notion of retribution.

Akiva also became the chief giver of alms to the poor.[163] This is evidence of Akiva's dedication to helping the less fortunate and shows that he had something of a common touch.

This made his involvement in the Bar Kochba revolt a useful contribution. He did something that Rabbis at the time were known for, he generated a politically conscious Jewish religious movement.

This could be compared to Liberation Theology, the politically conscious Catholic movement in South America which advocated intensely for the rights of the poor.

Akiva was advocating for the freedom of the Jewish people as a religious obligation. This was a commonly held belief but Akiva's influence on public opinion cannot be overstated.

The Talmud reports that Akiva considered Bar Kochba to be the true messiah and that he died for this belief.

Akiva is said to have died in prison after a number of years of incarceration rather than being killed immediately like so many others.

ת"ר אין מעברין את השנה לא משנה לחברתה ולא שלש שנים זו אחר זו אמר רבי שמעון מעשה ברבי עקיבא שהיה חבוש בבית האסורים ועיבר שלש שנים זו אחר זו אמרו לו משם ראיה ב"ד ישבו וקבעו אחת אחת בזמנה

"The Sages taught in a baraita (Tosefta 2:4): The court may not intercalate the year from one year to another, and it does not intercalate three successive years, one directly after the other. Rabbi Shimon says: There was an incident involving Rabbi Akiva at the time when he was incarcerated in prison, and he intercalated three years, one after the other. The Sages said to Rabbi Shimon: Is there any proof from there? Rabbi

Akiva merely made the calculations, but a special court sat and established each one at its time."

Though the topic of this passage is not specifically related to Akiva, it does reference him being subjected to imprisonment rather than immediately being put to death.

Still, we know he probably died around the year 132CE which shows that he was either killed by the Romans or allowed to die in the harsh conditions of his prison before the revolt began.

His contributions far outlived him, and even today he is regarded as a paragon of wisdom and inspires the social consciousness of modern Jews.

His quest for preserving his identity and the identities of his countrymen ultimately succeeded, even if the revolt did not.

Another surprising contribution to the rebellion was Josephus' work. Although he had for many years been a puppet of the Romans in his later years, he scorned them. He was long dead when the Bar Kochba revolt began but his last work greatly inspired the Jewish spirit of liberation.

Flavius Josephus wrote one work as an old man which in some ways redeemed his previous publications of flattery. Against Apion was a seminal piece written to disavow antisemitic Roman beliefs which Apion had popularised with his slanderous works.

Josephus was old and established enough to make his true feelings known. He railed against Hellenism more aggressively than his Roman overlords would have allowed in his youth.

"And now, in the first place, I cannot but greatly wonder at those men, who suppose that we must attend to none but Grecians, when we are inquiring about the most ancient facts, and must inform ourselves of their

truth from them only, while we must not believe ourselves nor other men;
for I am convinced that the very reverse is the truth of the case."[164]

Though Apion's works are lost we can infer that he claimed that the Tanakh was not historically accurate. Josephus criticizes the arrogance of assuming that Hellenistic sources are the only ones that matter and defends the Tanakh's historicity.

In his last work Josephus implicitly defends Jewish martyrdom and the notion of Jewish emancipation.

"For we have not an innumerable multitude of books among us, disagree-ing from and contradicting one another, [as the Greeks have,] but only twenty-two books, which contain the records of all the past times; which are justly believed to be divine; and of them five belong to Moses, which contain his laws and the traditions of the origin of mankind till his death. This interval of time was little short of three thousand years; but as to the time from the death of Moses till the reign of Artaxerxes king of Persia, who reigned after Xerxes, the prophets, who were after Moses, wrote down what was done in their times in thirteen books. The remaining four books contain hymns to G-d, and precepts for the conduct of human life. It is true, our history hath been written since Artaxerxes very particularly, but hath not been esteemed of the like authority with the former by our forefathers, because there hath not been an exact succession of prophets since that time; and how firmly we have given credit to these books of our own nation is evident by what we do; for during so many ages as have already passed, no one has been so bold as either to add any thing to them, to take any thing from them, or to make any change in them; but it is become natural to all Jews immediately, and from their very birth, to esteem these books to contain Divine doctrines, and to persist in them,

and, if occasion be willingly to die for them. For it is no new thing for our captives, many of them in number, and frequently in time, to be seen to endure racks and deaths of all kinds upon the theatres, that they may not be obliged to say one word against our laws and the records that contain them; whereas there are none at all among the Greeks who would undergo the least harm on that account, no, nor in case all the writings that are among them were to be destroyed; for they take them to be such discourses as are framed agreeably to the inclinations of those that write them; and they have justly the same opinion of the ancient writers, since they see some of the present generation bold enough to write about such affairs, wherein they were not present, nor had concern enough to inform themselves about them from those that knew them; examples of which may be had in this late war of ours, where some persons have written histories, and published them, without having been in the places concerned, or having been near them when the actions were done; but these men put a few things together by hearsay, and insolently abuse the world, and call these writings by the name of Histories."[165]

This is as clear as it gets. Josephus claims (in contradiction to his other works) that the Jews were willing to die in the defence of their religion and customs, and in no small way glorifies these people as heroic rather than foolish.

Nothing can fully redeem Josephus' hypocrisies in The Jewish War and the Antiquities of the Jews but Against Apion goes a long way in doing that.

The greatest falsehood Apion popularised was the idea of blood libels. To a Roman the claims of blood libel would have been horrifying despite how flagrantly untrue they were.

"He adds another Grecian fable, in order to reproach us. In reply to which,

it would be enough to say, that they who presume to speak about Divine worship ought not to be ignorant of this plain truth, that it is a degree of less impurity to pass through temples, than to forge wicked calumnies of its priests. Now such men as he are more zealous to justify a sacrilegious king, than to write what is just and what is true about us, and about our temple; for when they are desirous of gratifying Antiochus, and of concealing that perfidiousness and sacrilege which he was guilty of, with regard to our nation, when he wanted money, they endeavor to disgrace us, and tell lies even relating to futurities. Apion becomes other men's prophet upon this occasion, and says that "Antiochus found in our temple a bed, and a man lying upon it, with a small table before him, full of dainties, from the [fishes of the] sea, and the fowls of the dry land; that this man was amazed at these dainties thus set before him; that he immediately adored the king, upon his coming in, as hoping that he would afford him all possible assistance; that he fell down upon his knees, and stretched out to him his right hand, and begged to be released; and that when the king bid him sit down, and tell him who he was, and why he dwelt there, and what was the meaning of those various sorts of food that were set before him the man made a lamentable complaint, and with sighs, and tears in his eyes, gave him this account of the distress he was in; and said that he was a Greek and that as he went over this province, in order to get his living, he was seized upon by foreigners, on a sudden, and brought to this temple, and shut up therein, and was seen by nobody, but was fattened by these curious provisions thus set before him; and that truly at the first such unexpected advantages seemed to him matter of great joy; that after a while, they brought a suspicion him, and at length astonishment, what their meaning should be; that at last he inquired of the servants that came to him and was by them informed that it was in order to the fulfilling a law of the Jews, which they must not tell him, that he was thus fed; and that they did the same at a set time every year: that they used to catch a Greek foreigner, and fat him thus up every year, and then lead him to a certain wood, and kill him, and sacrifice with their accustomed solemnities, and taste of his entrails, and take an oath upon this sacrificing a Greek, that they would ever be at enmity with the Greeks; and that then they threw the remaining parts of the miserable wretch into a certain pit." Apion adds further, that, "the man said there were but a few days to come ere he was to be slain, and implored of Antiochus that, out of the reverence he bore to the Grecian g-ds, he would disappoint the snares the Jews laid for his blood, and would deliver him from the miseries with which he was encompassed." Now this is such a most tragical fable as is full of nothing but cruelty and impudence; yet does it not excuse Antiochus of his sacrilegious attempt, as those who write it in his vindication are willing to suppose; for he could not presume beforehand that he should meet with any such thing in coming to the temple, but must have found it unexpectedly. He was therefore still an impious person, that was given to unlawful pleasures, and had no regard to G-d in his actions. But [as for Apion], he hath done whatever his extravagant love of lying hath dictated to him, as it is most easy to discover by a consideration of his writings; for the difference of our laws is known not to regard the Grecians only, but they are principally opposite to the Egyptians, and to some other nations also for while it so falls out that men of all countries come sometimes and sojourn among us, how comes it about that we take an oath, and conspire only against the Grecians, and that by the effusion of their blood also? Or how is it possible that all the Jews should get together to these sacrifices, and the entrails of one man should be sufficient for so many thousands to taste of them, as

Apion pretends? Or why did not the king carry this man, whosoever he
was, and whatsoever was his name, [which is not set down in Apion's
book,] with great pomp back into his own country? when he might
thereby have been esteemed a religious person himself, and a mighty lover
of the Greeks, and might thereby have procured himself great assistance
from all men against that hatred the Jews bore to him. But I leave this
matter; for the proper way of confuting fools is not to use bare words, but
to appeal to the things themselves that make against them. Now, then, all
such as ever saw the construction of our temple, of what nature it was,
know well enough how the purity of it was never to be profaned; for it
had four several courts encompassed with cloisters round about, every one
of which had by our law a peculiar degree of separation from the rest.
Into the first court every body was allowed to go, even foreigners, and
none but women, during their courses, were prohibited to pass through it;
all the Jews went into the second court, as well as their wives, when they
were free from all uncleanness; into the third court went in the Jewish
men, when they were clean and purified; into the fourth went the priests,
having on their sacerdotal garments; but for the most sacred place, none
went in but the high priests, clothed in their peculiar garments. Now there
is so great caution used about these offices of religion, that the priests are
appointed to go into the temple but at certain hours; for in the morning,
at the opening of the inner temple, those that are to officiate receive the
sacrifices, as they do again at noon, till the doors are shut. Lastly, it is not
so much as lawful to carry any vessel into the holy house; nor is there any
thing therein, but the altar [of incense], the table [of shew-bread], the
censer, and the candlestick, which are all written in the law; for there is
nothing further there, nor are there any mysteries performed that may
not be spoken of; nor is there any feasting within the place. For what I

have now said is publicly known, and supported by the testimony of the whole people, and their operations are very manifest; for although there be four courses of the priests, and every one of them have above five thousand men in them, yet do they officiate on certain days only; and when those days are over, other priests succeed in the performance of their sacrifices, and assemble together at mid-day, and receive the keys of the temple, and the vessels by tale, without any thing relating to food or drink being carried into the temple; nay, we are not allowed to offer such things at the altar, excepting what is prepared for the sacrifices."[166]

The Jews were portrayed as bloodthirsty monsters who fed on the blood of the innocent. Even Christians and modern antisemitic Muslims believe in this lie. Hamas even promoted it in their charter until 2017.

Perennial persecutions of the Jews continued long after the fall of Rome on the basis of this lie. It is arguably the single most damaging antisemitic canard in world history.

The fact that Josephus risked his life and position to point out Apion's foolishness shows that even if he strayed from his heritage for a while, he was still a devoted Jew and cared for his fellow Jews.

In many ways his surrender to Roman life was a ploy. Some would call him selfish or treacherous for giving up on his people to save himself, but in many ways, he was trying to set an example of how they could escape persecution.

He wanted to blend in (and for others to do so) because at the end of the day it is better to fail at living by your principles than to die by them.

Regardless of how one feels about Josephus I feel it is important to reference this contribution of his, and how it illustrates his latent loyalty to the cause of Jewish liberation.

It was these men, Akiva and Josephus who set down the intellectual bedrock that begot the Bar Kochba revolt.

Hadrian's early mission was to consolidate Trajan's gains so he made client kingdoms out of the provinces in the Parthian sphere because he couldn't sustain such gains.

Trajan had used half of Rome's army to take these lands in the first place. Occupying this much land would simply be too great of a risk to Rome's other holdings. It was far better in Hadrian's eyes to quit while he was ahead.

Cashing in now was probably the best decision. Roman foreign policy was no longer about expansion but about keeping Rome together.

This was nearly impossible to do. There simply weren't enough people in the empire to defend all of the borders sufficiently.

The best Hadrian could do was to build defensive forts and walls in key areas to make it clear that Rome wasn't going to get any bigger.

This was why Hadrian built his famous wall in the north of England. He built the wall in about 122CE and from then on expansion into Scotland was considered more of a pipe dream than a serious proposition.

It was just not worth taking. The manpower and resources needed to control a province did not make up for the thinning out of the Roman army or the loss of resources in crushing revolts.

If Trajan had been the conqueror, then Hadrian was the consolidator. This strategy was far more fiscally sound than Trajan's had been, and it prevented Rome from getting too big for its boots.

Hadrian's initial policy towards the Jews was to simply live and let live. He didn't see the utility in starting a war when he could probably have just left them to their own devices.

He tried to make peace by rebuilding Jerusalem, but his promises were a shallow deception.

This was what created the rebellion. Hadrian did not rebuild Jerusalem for the Jews, but for himself. He renamed it Aelia Capitolina in 132CE.

Hadrian's full name was Pulius Aelius Hadrianus so he was naming Jerusalem after himself and the G-d Jupiter.

He also built a temple to Jupiter where the Holy temple had been and didn't give the city any walls, so the Romans would not have to besiege the city like last time. Hadrian also angered the Christians by building a temple to Venus on the hill Yehoshua had been crucified on.

This incensed the Jews so severely that they rallied around one man as their leader. Though Herod Agrippa II was formally the last Jewish head of state Simon Bar Kochba was unofficially the last as he declared himself both messiah and Nasi of Israel.

The war with Bar Kochba is commonly regarded as the Second Roman-Jewish war despite the previous Kitos rebellion.

Hadrian's changeability is probably evidence of some level of mental instability. For all his virtues as a leader he had an anger management problem, delusions of grandeur and a strong belief in the supremacy of Greek culture over any other sort of worldview.

He was at heart a colonialist; this made another Jewish-Roman war completely inevitable.

In light of Hadrian's slights against the Jews Rabbi Akiva sent word to the Jews of other nations and proclaimed that Simon Bar Cosiba was the Jewish messiah and called on them to rise in revolt against their Roman overlords.

Bar Cosiba was known by the name Bar Kochba which was a reference to a passage from the book of Numbers.

"I see Him, but not now;
I behold Him, but not near;
A Star shall come out of Jacob;
A Scepter shall rise out of Israel,
And batter the brow of Moab,
And destroy all the sons of tumult."
-Numbers 24:17

This passage is a messianic prophecy which was applied by Akiva to Bar Kochba, hence why he was referred to in this manner. In Hebrew Bar Kochba roughly means *'son of a star'.*

After his defeat Bar Kochba was referred to by some who were disillusioned with him as Bar Koziba. This translates roughly to *'son of a lie.'*

Many believed that Bar Kochba was a fraud and a liar when he was defeated by the Romans, and that his claims of being the messiah were nothing but a manipulative tactic he used to support his ambitious war with Rome.

We know precious little about Bar Kochba. The victors tend to write the history books, so pro-Roman accounts are the best we have. These are fairly limited in their descriptions of Jewish life because as we have observed the Romans had a very poor understanding of the Jewish world.

The accounts we have mainly honour Hadrian's skill in waging the war. But what most of these sources ignore is the fact that Bar Kochba's revolt was far more successful and well organised than the previous ones.

The fact that he was able to rally the Jews to his cause in such large numbers and create a unified military response shows that he was probably of an aristocratic origin, and that he most certainly learned from the mistakes of the past.

Rather than having multiple factions fighting under separate leaders (Simon Bar Giora and John of Gischala being prime examples of this) Bar Kochba had one army and one unified vision.

In the previous Roman-Jewish wars there was no sense of direction. The Romans inflicted less damage on the Jews than they inflicted on one another, it was simply a case of waiting for them to pick each other off.

Without civil strife the Jews couldn't simply be divided and conquered, they had to be faced head on and as one cohesive unit.

There weren't Zealots running around slaughtering government officials nor were there multiple armies like before, this was a challenge Rome had never faced.

This war was similar to the Vietnam war. Elaborate hideouts were built in caves and the Jews attacked in deceptively small numbers to throw Hadrian's forces off.

Much like the Viet Minh the Jews chose to use geography to their advantage rather than engaging in traditional warfare.

As Dio reports, the Jews across the empire made efforts to support Bar Kochba and came home to fight.

"At first the Romans made no account of them. Soon, however, all Judaea had been up-heaved, and the Jews all over the world were showing signs of disturbance, were gathering together, and giving evidence of great hostility to the Romans, partly by secret and partly by open acts; many other outside nations, too, were joining them through eagerness for gain, and the whole earth, almost, was becoming convulsed over the matter. Then, indeed, did Hadrian send against them his best generals, of who Julius Severus was the first to be despatched, from Britain, of which he

was governor, against the Jews. He did not venture to attack his opponents
at any one point, seeing their numbers and their desperation, but by
taking them in separate groups by means of the number of his soldiers
and his under-officers and by depriving them of food and shutting them
up he was able, rather slowly, to be sure, but with comparatively little
danger, to crush and exhaust and exterminate them."[167]

Though it is an unfair comparison this could be compared to how the Islamic State was able to recruit swathes of Muslims in other countries to come and fight in Syria and Iraq. The comparison is not of morals or aims but in the general fact that a great number of Jews wanted to support the cause of the rebels.

The Jews were not fighting for some bizarre and evil purpose like ISIS, but in a sense (much like ISIS) there was long-term foreign intervention that fomented an extremism in the Jewish population.

The cause of the Jews was a just and fair one. The point being made in this instance is that extremism and political violence are symptoms of oppression by foreign powers.

The USA (much like Rome) created its own enemies by stripping middle eastern countries of resources and making the political institutions of those countries extremely unstable.

Rome (much like the USA) was an empire that created its own rebellions by oppressing the Jews. It was inevitable that eventually there would be a breaking point.

The Romans ultimately knew this but continued anyway because they saw it as their duty to 'civilize' the Jews.

This is the root of colonialism in a lot of ways. The delusional belief that by oppressing others you might give them nuggets of a level of wisdom only you can attain.

Rome's downfall both moral and political came as a result of the arrogant view that their culture was the only one worth protecting.

Hadrian also allegedly banned circumcision which would have certainly angered the Jewish population as well. Trying to find a sole cause for this rebellion is something of an impossibility.

The list of things Rome did not do to cause the revolt would be far shorter. Like most large historical events this was caused by long-term issues and multiple Roman policies.

The war lasted from 132CE to 135CE. We know that Bar Kochba did well against Rome initially because he was able to capture Jerusalem and mint coins in celebration of this victory.

The greatest irony of all was that Bar Kochba had Roman coins reminted with new Jewish images. This was against Roman law and ultimately acted as a mockery of Roman rule and a celebration of Jewish identity.

Another thing of great irony is that Jerusalem was so easily captured by the rebels because it lacked walls. A city engineered to be easy for the Romans to occupy was taken because of the ultimate advantage it gave the Jews.

The Jews wiped out two whole Roman legions. We know this because the Senate made attempts to remove the existence of one of these from the public record. This shows that they were so embarrassed by their defeats that they were willing to alter history.

The Romans sent about a third of their entire military might to Judaea to finally crush the revolt.

Bar Kochba ended up having to flee with his men to the city of Betar, where the rebels were slaughtered. It is said that this messianic claimant was killed by a snake bite and his severed head was given to Hadrian.

In the aftermath of the conflict Hadrian committed large-scale genocide. He killed 580,000 Jews and cut the Jewish population by a solid margin. He also scattered a lot of the Jews thinly across the empire and even abolished Judaea as a province.

He renamed it Syria Palestina. From this point on Judaea was no longer considered the homeland of the Jews, and Jews were prohibited even from entering Jerusalem.

If there was a moment in history where the Jewish faith could have been wiped out this was it. It was going to take a lot of resilience, care, intellect and effort to maintain the Jewish identity in such harsh conditions.

The Jews refused to accept the new name of their province (which was a reference to the Biblical Philistines, naming the province as such was an act of mockery and a genocidal attempt at removing Judaism from the region's history).

It is also said that the famine that came after the war was so severe that it took the death toll up to a million. This quite literally reduced the Jewish population to such lows that it would take hundreds of years to recover.

It was a similar demographic shift to that caused by the Shoah. It decimated the population but also came close to killing the Jewish spirit altogether.

The members of the Sanhedrin shared the cruel fate of Akiva. They were tortured and killed horribly. It is said that Akiva was flayed alive, but we are not given specific details on how the members of the Sanhedrin met their fate.

So too was it a crime to celebrate Jewish holidays and observances. Judaism was brought to its knees and in some ways never recovered, not in that epoch anyway.

It was only Hadrian's death in 138CE that spared the Jews of his unthinkable cruelty.

Hadrian initially chose to make Lucius Ceionius Commodus his heir, but he died before Hadrian and his son was too young to become Emperor.

Hadrian was himself childless (probably because he was gay and didn't seem to like women in general let alone his wife) so the succession preoccupied him a great deal in his later years.

Antoninus Pius was adopted by Hadrian as the heir, and he was in turn forced to adopt Commodus' son of the same name and Marcus Aurelius as his heirs.

Both of these boys were much too young to be Emperors in their own right so Antoninus was chosen to bridge the gap between the boys and an aging Hadrian. This was Hadrian's way of eliminating bad blood between the top Senatorial families.

The royal succession now included most of the top Senatorial families, so every elite family was given a chance at having power.

Lucius Julius Ursus Servianus was Hadrian's brother-in-law and therefore the closest relative to the Emperor. He had expected his grandson to be Hadrian's heir, so he tried to overthrow the government and get him into the imperial office. His grandson was the closest genetic relative to Hadrian but in Roman politics this didn't inherently matter.

When Servianus failed, he was put to death along with his grandson. Servianus cursed Hadrian before the end.

"I am guilty of no wrong, ye; O G-ds, are well aware: and as for Hadrian I pray only this, that he may desire to die and not be able."[168]

When Hadrian neared the end the prophetic words of Servianus came true. He was in such severe bouts of pain that he begged to be killed, but no one would oblige him. He tried to kill himself multiple times, but he was thwarted in each attempt.

Some people have described his end as a punishment from the Lord, and I cannot help but agree.

"Often he would ask for poison and a sword, but no one would give them to him. As no one would obey him, although he promised money and immunity, he sent for Mastor, an Iazygian barbarian that had become a captive, whom he had employed in hunts on account of his strength and daring. Then, partly by threatening him and partly by making promises, he compelled the man to undertake the duty of killing him. He drew a colored line around a spot beneath the nipple that had been shown him by Hermogenes the physician, in order that he might there be struck a finishing blow and perish painlessly. But even this plan did not succeed, for Mastor became afraid of the project and in terror withdrew. The Emperor lamented bitterly the plight in which the disease had placed him and bitterly his powerlessness, in that he was not able to make away with himself, though he might still, even when so near death, destroy anybody else."[169]

In Cassius Dio's account Hadrian's suffering is emphasized heavily, so it is fair to say that Hadrian's suffering was unthinkable.

So it was that in 138CE Hadrian died and Antoninus Pius succeeded him as Emperor.

To conclude this chapter, I will recount the final passage of Against Apion, for it fittingly describes not only the laws of Judaism, but what those poor men and women who died in the Bar Kochba revolt were truly fighting for.

"As to the laws themselves, more words are unnecessary, for they are visible in their own nature, and appear to teach not impiety, but the truest piety in the world. They do not make men hate one another, but encour-

age people to communicate what they have to one another freely; they are
enemies to injustice, they take care of righteousness, they banish idleness
and expensive living, and instruct men to be content with what they have,
and to be laborious in their calling; they forbid men to make war from a
desire of getting more, but make men courageous in defending the laws;
they are inexorable in punishing malefactors; they admit no sophistry of
words, but are always established by actions themselves, which actions we
ever propose as surer demonstrations than what is contained in writing
only: on which account I am so bold as to say that we are become the
teachers of other men, in the greatest number of things, and those of the
most excellent nature only; for what is more excellent than inviolable
piety? what is more just than submission to laws? and what is more
advantageous than mutual love and concord? and this so far that we are
to be neither divided by calamities, nor to become injurious and seditious
in prosperity; but to contemn death when we are in war, and in peace to
apply ourselves to our mechanical occupations, or to our tillage of the
ground; while we in all things and all ways are satisfied that G-d is the
inspector and governor of our actions. If these precepts had either been
written at first, or more exactly kept by any others before us, we should
have owed them thanks as disciples owe to their masters; but if it be
visible that we have made use of them more than any other men, and if
we have demonstrated that the original invention of them is our own, let
the Apions, and the Molons, with all the rest of those that delight in lies
and reproaches, stand confuted; but let this and the foregoing book be
dedicated to thee, Epaphroditus, who art so great a lover of truth, and by
thy means to those that have been in like manner desirous to be
acquainted with the affairs of our nation."[170]

18

Chapter 18- The Decline of Rome

When Antoninus Pius took the throne in 138 CE he reversed a lot of Hadrian's most harsh policies. Hadrian was loathed by the Senatorial class, and they even wanted to declare him a public enemy and revoke his titles.

Pius refused to allow any of this, but he did change most of Hadrian's policies against the Jews.

He not only allowed the celebration of Jewish holidays but actively joined the Jews of the city of Rome in their celebrations.

Pius was considered virtuous by the Jews and for the most part he allowed life for them to go on as it had before. The only thing which did not change was the temple of Jupiter in Jerusalem and the banishment of the Jews from this city.

Some Jews saw Pius as merciful; others were not so easy to convince. This created a rift between Gamliel II the Nasi of the Sanhedrin and Shimon Bar Yochai who refused to give the Romans any credit and never ceased to criticise them.

Yochai had been a student of Rabbi Akiva and did not abandon his studies even when Akiva was jailed. He managed to get into Akiva's cell by using his father's Roman connections, he even threatened to make Akiva's imprisonment worse if he didn't continue to teach him.

חֲמִשָּׁה דְבָרִים צִוָּה רַבִּי עֲקִיבָא אֶת רַבִּי שִׁמְעוֹן בֶּן יוֹחַי כְּשֶׁהָיָה חָבוּשׁ בְּבֵית הָאֲסוּרִין. אָמַר לוֹ: רַבִּי, לַמְּדֵנִי תוֹרָה, אָמַר: אֵינִי מְלַמֶּדְךָ. אָמַר לוֹ: אִם אֵין אַתָּה מְלַמְּדֵנִי אֲנִי אוֹמֵר לְיוֹחַי אַבָּא וּמוֹסָרְךָ לַמַּלְכוּת. אָמַר לוֹ: בְּנִי, יוֹתֵר מִמַּה שֶׁהָעֵגֶל רוֹצֶה לִינַק פָּרָה רוֹצָה לְהָנִיק. אָמַר לוֹ: וּמִי בְּסַכָּנָה? וַהֲלֹא עֵגֶל בְּסַכָּנָה.

"The Gemara continues to cite similar advice dispensed by Rabbi Akiva. Rabbi Akiva commanded Rabbi Shimon ben Yoḥai to do five matters when Rabbi Akiva was imprisoned. Beforehand, Rabbi Shimon said to him: Rabbi, teach me Torah. Rabbi Akiva said to him: I will not teach you, as it is dangerous to do so at the present time. Rabbi Shimon said to him in jest: If you will not teach me, I will tell Yoḥai my father, and he will turn you over to the government. In other words, I have no means of persuading you; you are already in prison. Rabbi Akiva said: My son, know that more than the calf wishes to suck, the cow wants to suckle, but I am afraid of the danger. Rabbi Shimon said to him: And who is in danger? Isn't the calf in danger, as you are in jail and I am the one at risk?"[171]

This story as well as Yochai's fierce anti-Roman stance are reason enough for it to be said that Yochai was Akiva's intellectual successor.

Gamliel and Yochai's own students conspired to have him reported to the Roman authorities and executed because of how strong his anti-Roman polemics had become.

It is said that Yochai had to hide in a cave until Pius' death in 161CE. As a result, he was in the cave for 13 years and only left when the prophet Elijah informed him that the Emperor was dead.

וְאַמַּאי קָרוּ לֵיהּ "רֹאשׁ הַמְדַבְּרִים בְּכָל מָקוֹם"? דְּיָתְבִי רַבִּי יְהוּדָה וְרַבִּי יוֹסֵי וְרַבִּי שִׁמְעוֹן, וְיָתֵיב יְהוּדָה בֶּן גֵּרִים גַּבַּיְיהוּ. פָּתַח רַבִּי יְהוּדָה וְאָמַר: כַּמָּה נָאִים מַעֲשֵׂיהֶן שֶׁל אוּמָה זוֹ: תִּקְּנוּ שְׁוָקִים, תִּקְּנוּ גְּשָׁרִים, תִּקְּנוּ מֶרְחֲצָאוֹת. רַבִּי יוֹסֵי שָׁתַק. נַעֲנָה רַבִּי שִׁמְעוֹן בֶּן יוֹחַאי וְאָמַר: כָּל מַה שֶּׁתִּקְּנוּ, לֹא תִּקְּנוּ אֶלָּא לְצוֹרֶךְ עַצְמָן. תִּקְּנוּ שְׁוָוקִין – לְהוֹשִׁיב בָּהֶן זוֹנוֹת, מֶרְחֲצָאוֹת – לְעַדֵּן בָּהֶן עַצְמָן, גְּשָׁרִים – לִיטּוֹל מֵהֶן מֶכֶס. הָלַךְ יְהוּדָה בֶּן גֵּרִים וְסִיפֵּר דִּבְרֵיהֶם, וְנִשְׁמְעוּ לַמַּלְכוּת אָמְרוּ: יְהוּדָה שֶׁעִילָּה – יִתְעַלֶּה. יוֹסֵי שֶׁשָּׁתַק – יִגְלֶה לְצִיפּוֹרִי. שִׁמְעוֹן שֶׁגִּינָּה – יֵהָרֵג.

"In this baraita Rabbi Yehuda is described as head of the speakers in every place. The Gemara asks: And why did they call him head of the speakers in every place? The Gemara relates that this resulted due to an incident that took place when Rabbi Yehuda and Rabbi Yosei and Rabbi Shimon were sitting, and Yehuda, son of converts, sat beside them. Rabbi Yehuda opened and said: How pleasant are the actions of this nation, the Romans, as they established marketplaces, established bridges, and established bathhouses. Rabbi Yosei was silent. Rabbi Shimon ben Yoḥai responded and said: Everything that they established, they established only for their own purposes. They established marketplaces, to place prostitutes in them; bathhouses, to pamper themselves; and bridges, to collect taxes from all who pass over them. Yehuda, son of converts, went

and related their statements to his household, and those statements
continued to spread until they were heard by the monarchy. They ruled
and said: Yehuda, who elevated the Roman regime, shall be elevated and
appointed as head of the Sages, the head of the speakers in every place.
Yosei, who remained silent, shall be exiled from his home in Judea as
punishment, and sent to the city of Tzippori in the Galilee. And Shimon,
who denounced the government, shall be killed."

אֲזַל הוּא וּבְרֵיה, טְשׁוֹ בֵּי מִדְרְשָׁא. כָּל יוֹמָא הֲוָה מַתְיָא לְהוּ דְּבֵיתְהוּ
רִיפְתָּא וְכוּזָא דְמַיָא וְכָרְכִי. כִּי תְּקֵיף גְּזֵירְתָא אֲמַר לֵיה לִבְרֵיה: נָשִׁים
דַּעְתָּן קַלָּה עֲלֵיהֶן, דִּילְמָא מְצַעְרִי לַהּ וּמְגַלְיָא לָן. אֲזַלוּ טְשׁוֹ
בִּמְעַרְתָּא. אִתְרְחִישׁ נִיסָא אִיבְּרִי לְהוּ חָרוּבָא וְעֵינָא דְמַיָא, וַהֲווּ
מַשְׁלְחִי מָנַייְהוּ וַהֲווּ יָתְבִי עַד צַוַּארַייְהוּ בְּחָלָא. כּוּלֵי יוֹמָא גָּרְסִי. בְּעִידָּן
צַלוֹיֵי לָבְשִׁי מִיכַּסּוּ וּמְצַלּוּ, וַהֲדַר מַשְׁלְחִי מָנַייְהוּ כִּי הֵיכִי דְּלָא לִיבְּלוּ.
אִיתִּיבוּ תְּרֵיסַר שְׁנֵי בִּמְעַרְתָּא. אֲתָא אֵלִיָּהוּ וְקָם אַפִּיתְחָא דִמְעַרְתָּא,
אֲמַר: מַאן לוֹדְעֵיה לְבַר יוֹחַי דְּמִית קֵיסָר וּבָטֵיל גְּזֵירְתֵיה.

"Rabbi Shimon bar Yoḥai and his son, Rabbi Elazar, went and hid in the
study hall. Every day Rabbi Shimon's wife would bring them bread and a
jug of water and they would eat. When the decree intensified, Rabbi
Shimon said to his son: Women are easily impressionable and, therefore,
there is room for concern lest the authorities torture her and she reveal
our whereabouts. They went and they hid in a cave. A miracle occurred
and a carob tree was created for them as well as a spring of water. They
would remove their clothes and sit covered in sand up to their necks. They
would study Torah all day in that manner. At the time of prayer, they
would dress, cover themselves, and pray, and they would again remove
their clothes afterward so that they would not become tattered. They sat

in the cave for twelve years. Elijah the Prophet came and stood at the entrance to the cave and said: Who will inform bar Yoḥai that the Emperor died and his decree has been abrogated?"[172]

The fact that Yochai's opposition to the Romans was considered too controversial by the other Rabbis of the day shows just how much the Jewish-Roman wars impacted Jewish life.

The bar for approval had become so low that simply refraining from actively persecuting the Jews was enough for any Emperor to be immune to criticism.

It also goes to show just how little hope Jewish scholars had left for their homeland and their faith. This marked a massive change in Jewish intellectual discussions.

The Jewish religion became less about the land of Israel itself and more about celebrating the survival of the Jewish people. Holidays like Tisha B'av symbolise a certain overcoming of the melancholic reality of the Jewish exile.

Rather than accepting defeat and fading away Judaism evolved into an impervious religious movement which accepted both the joys and the tragedies of the Jewish story. A culture which had been around for thousands of years survived annihilation attempts because it was able to turn suffering into a celebration of endurance.

In fairness to the Jews who were pro-Rome the Romans had been around for well over a century and none of them could remember a time where Rome had not been in control.

Rome was a reality that would not go away anytime soon, so accepting that fact was almost a given.

Even though no revolutionary activities were fomented by Yochai he did inspire the next generation of Jewish thinkers. That was what Judaism became when it was deprived of a temple, a series of wise men making sense of a context of oppression and passing on their wisdom to subsequent Jews.

This carried on until eventually the Jews were emancipated and regained their homeland in 1948. When so many other cultures were annihilated by the Romans Judaism was preserved and only increased both in its grandness and scale.

Pius' reign was exceptionally long. At the time Augustus was the only Emperor ever to have reigned longer, and it was only much later that others managed to surpass him.

The later Roman empire was marked by a series of child Emperors who due to their youth reigned for thirty years or more, so they only really reigned longer than Pius on a technicality.

From 138CE-161CE Pius governed Rome fairly well. He is considered to be the penultimate 'good Emperor.' He was succeeded by Marcus Aurelius who of his own accord chose to make Lucius Verus his co-Emperor.

Verus was the son of Lucius Ceionius Commodus (Hadrian's original heir). The settlement of Marcus Aurelius finally brought stability to relations among the Senators. All of the main Senatorial houses had been represented in the succession and they governed Rome together, mutually borrowing each other's legitimacy.

Aurelius had married Pius' daughter Faustina and was ruling alongside Lucius Verus. This combination of noble lineage set the Nerva-Antonine dynasty up for a very stable period of rule.

Both Pius and Marcus were very popular and successful Emperors who had long reigns.

Marcus Aurelius was however impacted by a great number of crises throughout his reign and had to use much of his time and resources on reliefs for the litany of problems Rome endured under him.

He was a much-respected Philosophical thinker and chose to spend a lot of his free time with the intellectuals of the empire.

It could be said that Aurelius' only discrimination was against those who were not intellectually capable. It was for this reason that he prized intellect wherever he happened to find it, even in provinces that were traditionally overlooked.

He had thirteen children with Faustina, he evidently enjoyed his wife's company but due to the time he spent in the provinces he did not see her all too often.

Aurelius sent Verus to fight the Parthians in a war which ended in Roman victory. It is obvious that Verus was a trusted and capable commander since he was sent on his own to deal with the issue. In theory this would have been a perfect opportunity to betray Marcus and take sole control of the empire.

The Marcomanic wars preoccupied most of Aurelius' reign and he spent almost all of his time on the front combatting Germanic tribes.

He also had to deal with a pandemic of smallpox which killed a third of his army.

It killed so many people in fact that not only did Lucius Verus succumb to it, but most of the civil servants died as well. This allowed a number of relatively ignoble people such as Septimius Severus to rise through the ranks of the empire's government and gain experience.

There just weren't enough people left to effectively govern the empire unless Marcus opened up positions of power to other classes of people.

The punitive campaign against Germany occupied the rest of Aurelius' reign. The only time he spent away from Germany was out of necessity.

Due to a false rumour that Aurelius had died the governor of Egypt Avidius Cassius tried to have himself enthroned with the support of Marcus' wife Faustina.

Faustina was under the impression that her husband was dead, the only way to keep her position of influence and to protect her family was to support Cassius in the hopes that he would marry her.

Cassius was of much more noble birth than Aurelius or anyone else in the empire.

Avidius Cassius wasn't legally Jewish, but he was a Herodian descendant of the Armenian royal line and a direct descendant of Augustus.

He was therefore in the position of being a descendant of the Jewish monarchy and of the Julio-Claudian dynasty.

His attempt at usurpation was made on the false belief that Aurelius was dead. Once the Emperor found out he had Cassius (and probably Faustina) killed.

Because of the instability the attempted coup Aurelius had to do a tour of the Roman east. It was much harder for seditions to occur if he was there.

It was on this tour that Aurelius (who is referred to as Antoninus in the Talmud) met Judah the Nasi of the Sanhedrin. The pair got on extremely well and were lifelong friends and shared a great number of letters.

The irony of a Roman Emperor and a Jew becoming lifelong friends is not lost on history and the Talmud recounts a number of their intellectual disputes.

These disputes were held in good faith and Aurelius appreciated Judah's intellect. It was partially Aurelius' patronage that allowed Judah to codify a lot of the history recounted in this book in the Mishnah.

The Mishnah was not a history so much as it was a legal document of the Sanhedrin's decisions which happened to also contextualise a lot of the historical records of the Jewish world.

The main contents of their communications seem to have been Aurelius asking Judah for advice, and Judah in turn using slightly contrived metaphors to point the Emperor in the right direction.

א"ל מצערין לי חשובי [רומאי] מעייל ליה לגינא כל יומא עקר ליה
פוגלא ממשרא קמיה אמר ש"מ הכי קאמר לי את קטול חד חד
מינייהו ולא תתגרה בהו בכולהו

"Antoninus also said to Rabbi Yehuda HaNasi: Important Romans are upsetting me; what can I do about them? Rabbi Yehuda HaNasi brought him to his garden, and every day he uprooted a radish from the garden bed before him. Antoninus said to himself: Learn from it that this is what Rabbi Yehuda HaNasi is saying to me: You should kill them one by one, and do not incite all of them at once."[173]

Aurelius evidently held the Jews in higher regard than his predecessors considering the fact that he came to a Jew for advice on important personal and state matters.

הוה ליה ההוא ברתא דשמה גירא קעבדה איסורא שדר ליה
גרגירא שדר ליה כוסברתא שדר ליה כרתי שלח ליה חסא

"The Gemara relates: Antoninus had a certain daughter whose name was Gira, who performed a prohibited action, i.e., she engaged in promiscuous intercourse. Antoninus sent a rocket plant [gargira] to Rabbi Yehuda HaNasi, to allude to the fact that Gira had acted promiscuously [gar]. Rabbi Yehuda HaNasi sent him coriander [kusbarta], which Antoninus understood as a message to kill [kos] his daughter [barta], as she was liable to receive the death penalty for her actions. Antoninus sent him

leeks [karti] to say: I will be cut off [karet] if I do so. Rabbi Yehuda
HaNasi then sent him lettuce [ḥasa], i.e., Antoninus should have mercy
[ḥas] on her."174

There are a series of such scenes in the Talmud, and they paint Marcus in a very good light.

He carried on talking to Judah until his death on campaign in Germany, seemingly he died of natural causes.

In 180CE Marcus was replaced by his son Commodus. The new Emperor was the first biological son of a previous Emperor to rule the empire since Titus and Domitian.

Considering that the era of the Flavians had ended almost a century ago this was something of an odd choice and it didn't go over very well.

Commodus had grown up spoilt and vain, he didn't know what it meant to toil, or to make something of himself.

His petulance and eventual acts of madness made the Senate hate him. For one thing he named all of the months of the year after himself, and he even tried to have Rome renamed Colonia Commodiana 'the Colony of Commodus'.

Commodus reigned for 13 years and is largely remembered as a poor Emperor. He was also known to have fought as a Gladiator, and he was the highest paid Gladiator in Roman history.

He was trained by a prominent Gladiator called Narcissus and later granted this slave his freedom.

It was Narcissus who strangled him in his bath in 192CE. Commodus had planned on putting a great number of Senators and his own mistress Marcia to death and the condemned managed to catch wind of Commodus' aims.

To avoid being purged the Senators decided to have Narcissus murder the Emperor in cold blood.

He was replaced by Pertinax, one of Aurelius' generals in 193CE. Pertinax would have a very short and tragic reign, being slain just 87 days after taking office.

At the same time the Sanhedrin located itself to Tiberias as its permanent home. This sense of stability would be essential during the chaotic civil war which resulted from Commodus' death.

Pertinax's murder triggered a brutal civil war in Rome. His position was sold at an auction by the Praetorian guards and Didius Julianus became the next Emperor because he happened to be rich enough to pay the exorbitant donative they demanded.

The other claimants were Septimius Severus, Pescennius Niger and Clodius Albinus. Niger was stationed in the east and was unkind to the Jews. As a result, they largely supported Severus.

Septimius Severus marched first on Rome and had Didius Julianus murdered only 66 days after he had taken office.

For a time, Severus and Albinus made peace on the condition that Clodius would be made the heir presumptive. Niger's forces were soundly crushed, and Severus killed his entire family as an example to other would-be imperial claimants.

When Severus' son Caracalla was born in 188CE it forced Albinus to fight Severus head on. Clodius Albinus was defeated as well, and Severus became the sole master of Rome.

Severus was one of the officials who came to prominence due to the thinning of the Senatorial ranks by the Antonine plague. He was a very respected general and was also a Carthaginian.

He grew up in modern Libya and spoke Punic as his first language. Punic happened to be very similar to Hebrew so Severus probably spoke Latin with an accent.

Judah the Nasi happened to meet Severus while he was in the east and befriended him.

Severus was an admirer of Judah and when he saw the desolation of the Jews he was mortified.

He saw it as oppressive and immoral to allow the Jews to suffer any longer, so he made efforts to restore the Jewish world to its former glory.

He built a Synagogue near the temple mount and allowed the Jews to return to Jerusalem freely.

In 211CE Severus' sons Geta and Caracalla succeeded him in the running of the empire. Geta was soon murdered by his older brother Caracalla in front of their mother Julia Domna.

Caracalla is also revered by the Jews because he restored to them their lands in Judaea and granted them greater freedoms of worship.

Though the Emperor was very religious he greatly admired Judah the Nasi and gave him every resource he needed to finish the Mishnah.

One of the most important developments of Caracalla's reign was his edict on citizenship.

This made every single male in the empire a citizen. Even though he only did this so that he could start taxing the provinces more it marked a change in Rome's culture. Rather than the provinces simply being territories of the city of Rome, all the people in the empire were now truly Roman.

Judah died in 218CE after finishing his work, and Caracalla was murdered in 217CE.

Caracalla had been killed by his Praetorian Prefect Macrinus and Macrinus replaced him.

Caracalla had been waging a war against the Parthians when he died, so Macrinus was forced to sign a terrible peace deal so he could go to Rome and consolidate his power (he never got there).

Macrinus and his son Diadumenian were in turn killed by Caracalla's teenage cousin Heliogabalus who himself was murdered by his grandmother in 222CE.

Heliogabalus was the high priest of the Syrian religious cult of Elagabal *'The Lord of the Mountain'*. He radically reformed Rome's religious policies and was the first monotheist to rule the empire. He caught the ire of the Senate with these antics and also antagonised his grandmother Julia Maesa.

His younger cousin Alexander was made the heir to the throne and when Heliogabalus saw fit to try and kill him the Praetorians rose in revolt. Alexander's mother Julia Mamaea had been bribing them for some time with gold, so they were inclined to defend the young Caesar.

Heliogabalus pretended his cousin was dead to test the reaction of his guards, and in response to this Alexander and Heliogabalus were summoned to the Praetorian camp so that the guards could prove that Alexander was alive.

When they saw Alexander, they acclaimed him as their Emperor and killed Heliogabalus. This had been orchestrated by Julia Maesa.

Alexander reigned for 13 years and was by most standards a pretty good Emperor. He was seen as extremely pliable by his mother and grandmother and for the most part did whatever they said.

Alexander was tolerant of the Jews and the Christians and even befriended the early Church Father Origen.

His greatest weakness was that he was not as capable with military affairs, and he allowed his rule to be dominated by his mother Julia Mamaea.

Both mother and son were killed in 235CE by Maximinus Thrax, a Thracian officer who managed to bribe and threaten his way into getting the backing of the soldiers.

They had all been in Germany on campaign, and when Alexander tried to bribe the Germans with gold instead of facing them in battle it made the soldiers rise up against him.

Rome was in a terminal state of decline after Alexander's death. The army had become too powerful, and it had become too easy to simply bribe yourself onto the throne.

It could be said that Rome was more socially mobile when it chose adept warriors as Emperors, but in practice if anyone could do it everyone would try and in doing so, they started an endless string of civil wars.

With the death of Alexander, the Crisis of the 3rd Century began. This was a period of such extensive devastation and civil war that it ultimately caused the empire's collapse.

Thrax ruled for three years before he was deposed by the Gordians. An old African by the name of Gordian I was forced to make a claim for the throne by a mob of the public.

They had grown tired of the present administration and quite literally made him Emperor against his will.

He seems to have shown genuine reluctance to take on the role knowing how high the risk of a violent death would be for him and his family. Gordian had his son acclaimed co-Emperor and he was called Gordian II.

The Senate supported the Gordians over Thrax because he had been harsh in purging Senators.

Thrax tried to siege an Italian city called Aquileia but was killed by his own men because of his harshness and immovability. He was strict to such a degree that it turned the soldiers against him after only 3 years on the throne.

Gordian II died in battle, so his father committed suicide, leaving his grandson Gordian III as the heir apparent. Gordian III was a very young boy so he was not remotely able to rule the empire himself.

Two Senators by the name of Pupienus and Balbinus became co-Emperors with Gordian III because of his youth but they ended up both dying by the swords of each other's supporters.

They riled up the Roman masses and their supporters were so angry that in the chaos both of these Senatorial Emperors were killed.

This left a small child as Rome's Emperor. Gordian was ruled over by his mother Gordiana and a series of other advisers.

In 244CE Gordian III was murdered by his Praetorian Prefect Philip who replaced him.

Philip and his son Philip II were of Arabian origins and ruled for 9 years. Some sources claim that they were Christians because of their general sympathy for this group, but there is no direct proof of this.

The legionary Decius betrayed Philip and his son and replaced them with his own family in 249CE. He had been forced to do this by his legionaries who held a great deal of hatred in their hearts for Philip.

Decius was known for persecuting the Christians as well as the Jews because of their refusal to sacrifice animals to the Emperor. He made it a legal requirement that all Romans make sacrifices to the Emperor. For obvious reasons Jews and Christians refused this order and were killed in their thousands.

In 251CE Decius and his son Herennius Etruscus were killed in an ambush set up by Trebonianus Gallus who in turn ruled the empire with Decius' younger son Hostilian.

Hostilian died in office not long after gaining power. Gallus meanwhile met a similar end to Decius.

In 253CE he was overthrown and killed by Aemilian who was similarly overthrown by Valerian and his son Gallienus.

Valerian was a Senator of noble birth and was highly regarded. His victory came from the fact that he had the advantage of numbers when he opposed Aemilian.

By now Rome's currency was almost worthless. The continuation of the debasement of the coinage had severely crippled the economy.

Gallienus administered the west and Valerian took charge of the east. Rome was big enough that it realistically needed 2 Emperors to be administered effectively. Even when split in two holding it together was nearly impossible unless you were exceptionally skilled and exceptionally well liked.

Gallienus reformed the army to be more efficient and held off German advances whilst his father focussed on preventing the Sassanids (Successors of the Parthians) from invading the eastern provinces.

Because of the development of a new pandemic known as the Cyprian Plague the Roman armies in the east had been decimated so when Valerian faced the Parthians he was outmatched.

Cyprian the Bishop of Carthage had been executed by Valerian in 258CE and the pandemic which coincided with the death was seen as a divine punishment for Cyprian's death.

In 260CE Valerian was defeated at Edessa by Shapur I. Eventually Valerian was captured by the Parthian King and humiliated in every way.

He was forced to be a human footstool, beaten and tortured. His suffering was ended when Shapur allegedly had him flayed alive.

This left Gallienus entirely alone. The east was now in the hands of the Sassanid empire.

Gallienus was assassinated in 268CE by his own men.

Before his death the western provinces of Gaul, Britain and Hispania declared independence as the Gallic empire.

The empire was breaking down rapidly and Gallienus needed to look everywhere for allies.

Septimius Odaenathus was given command of the east because of his skill and loyalty to Gallienus. He was named as the dictator of the east and given full control over the administration of the Roman east.

Odaenathus had gained the cognomen of Septimius from the fact that his ancestors had been given it by Septimius Severus. His loyalty to Rome was therefore something of a family tradition.

He was later murdered by his wife Zenobia in a court intrigue, and she declared the creation of the Palmyrene empire (which included Judaea).

The west was under the control of a new state, the east was under the control of a new state.

Only the centre of the empire still remained, and this was not guaranteed either.

Claudius II later succeeded Gallienus and was very effective at resisting the attacks of Rome's enemies. The Goths also invaded Greece and destroyed Athens at this time. Claudius' punitive measures against them earned him the nickname Claudius Gothicus (slayer of the Goths).

Rome was beset on all sides and endured a constant string of conflicts, invasions and coups.

Claudius ended up employing a lot of men to his service who would become Emperors after him. Constantius, Diocletian, Carus and Aurelian all served under Claudius.

Under Claudius Hispania was retaken but he died in office of the Cyprian Plague. Because of this pandemic Rome was even more vulnerable and a lot of the Roman borderlands were subjected to perennial attacks.

Quintillus (Claudius' brother) briefly succeeded him before Aurelian took power. Aurelian managed to retake Gaul, Britain and the Roman east in a series of successful campaigns but after just 5 years in office he was assassinated and replaced by Tacitus.

For all of his accomplishments in defeating Zenobia and the Gallic empire he was known as restutitor orbis 'the restorer of the world'.

Tacitus died after only a year in office in 276CE which resulted in his half-brother Florianus replacing him.[175]

Probus ended up becoming Emperor after a brief struggle against Florianus and as one of Aurelian's generals he was held in high esteem by the soldiers.

In 282CE he was succeeded by Carus. Carus was struck by lightning while he was on campaign and his sons Numerian and Carinus succeeded him.

Numerian was killed in a plot by the Praetorian Prefect Afer, Carinus was killed by a usurper (Diocletian) who felt he would be better suited for imperial office.

Diocletian became Emperor in 284CE after he had Afer and Carinus killed. He ruled for many years and is regarded as one of Rome's best Emperors.

His reforms were largely unsuccessful, but he was still an exceptional leader. His first reform was to effectively establish feudalism.

He had people tied to hereditary occupations and forced them to occupy their land, they were subjects of a Dux. This later inspired the model of nobility ruling over serfs who worked on their land which they gained from their subservience to a Lord.

His second reform was decentralisation. He knew that Rome was too big to be governed by one man, so he accepted Maximian as his co-Emperor.

He also established the Roman tetrarchy. There would be an Augustus (Senior Emperor) in the east and west and two Caesars (Lesser Emperors subservient to their Augustus) to govern other areas. Rome was split into 4 semi-autonomous areas with distinct rulers.

Galerius became Diocletian's heir and Constantius Chlorus was made heir to Maximian. In theory this would split imperial responsibilities enough for Rome to be practically administered but in practice it generated a new epoch of civil wars.

Maximian and Diocletian voluntarily abdicated in 305CE for their Caesars to take their place.

This chapter does not allude very much to the complexities of all the events taking place in Rome, but to be quite blunt the Crisis of the 3rd Century deserves a history in its own right and there are already many.

Diocletian's attempts at reform ultimately failed. But from the ashes came a change that would truly cause Rome's downfall. The adoption of Christianity.

From the Tetrarchy rose Constantine I, the first Christian Emperor of the Romans and the man who ultimately did something no one would have expected. He Romanized Christianity itself.

The primary source used to compile this summary was Jerome's Chronicon, in the footnotes I have chosen not to use chapter or page numbers because so much of the Chronicon is referenced that it would be easier to assume that I used it for every referential statement.

19

Chapter 19- The Rise of Christian Antisemitism and the Third Temple

Constantius Chlorus died in office and his men proclaimed his son Constantine as Emperor in 306CE.

This flew in the face of the rules established by Diocletian because it implied the very same hereditary connection to power which he had tried to avoid.

The heir of Constantius according to the rules of the Tetrarchy was Flavius Severus so an uneasy compromise was enforced by Galerius which involved Constantine being politely demoted to the role of a Caesar instead of an Augustus.

A long civil war ensued in which several Emperors made their claims and died. The last man standing was Constantine the Great.

During the crisis of the 3rd Century Hebrew as a common language died off.

The revival of the Hebrew language in modern Israel is a

phenomenon unseen in any other instance. Usually when a language dies it stays dead.

It was still used for liturgical purposes but in practice people didn't speak Hebrew for general purposes like trade or communication. They wouldn't speak Hebrew until it became modern Israel's official language and was taught to students in Israeli schools.

In modernity Hebrew is a renewed language and spoken by the Israeli population, but even now it has had to borrow missing pieces from English, French and Arabic to make it into a workable language of common speech. Modern Hebrew differs from its ancient roots but not very significantly.

Constantine was a Christian and officially legalized Christian worship in the empire. His position was secure enough to do this because the civil war had effectively killed off anyone with any connection to the imperial office.

Anyone with a capacity to try and launch a coup had already tried and failed. People were sick enough of fighting that they chose to just leave Constantine where he was.

Constantine was the undisputed master of Rome by 324CE. By 312CE he was an established ruler, but it was only in 324CE that he was able to defeat his main rival Licinius.

In the context of Jewish history much of the third century is not very important. Judaism underwent slow and subtle changes, but it was Constantine who was the most consequential leader of this period for the Jewish world.

It would somewhat be expected that the liberation of the Christians would help the Jews, but it actually did the opposite. Without Christians as an easy scapegoat Rome needed to find a new one.

The persecution of Christians by the Roman empire had to be reconciled with the fact that Rome was now a Christian state.

Not only was the Emperor of Rome the primary arbiter of Christianity, but he was also distantly responsible for the persecution of

Christians. Constantine didn't persecute Christians, but inherited guilt was and is quite a significant theme in Christianity.

He had inherited a position which was used in the past to oppress the Christians so he needed to figure out how such a history could coexist with the present situation.

This created a paradox in Roman Christianity which had to be resolved at a series of ecumenical councils. Ultimately the Church revised Christian sources and teachings to blame the Jews (as has already been discussed) for Yehoshua's murder.

Rather than accepting responsibility the Roman state simply blamed Jews for having crucified Yehoshua. To this day the anti-semitic notion that 'the Jews killed Jesus' is used against Jews in a racist context.

The group of people Yehoshua hailed from, and the same group which comprised his followers were now the ones who killed him in the eyes of the Christian authorities.

Rather than ending Roman antisemitism Constantine simply reimagined it in an entirely new and arguably even more virulent context.

The apostle Paul for instance seems to have been entirely mis-interpreted by the Roman Church and many scholars even believe this passage was written directly by Constantine's cronies.

"For you, brothers and sisters, became imitators of G-d's churches in Judea, which are in Christ Jesus: You suffered from your own people the same things those churches suffered from the Jews who killed the Lord Jesus and the prophets and also drove us out. They displease G-d and are hostile to everyone in their effort to keep us from speaking to the Gentiles so that they may be saved. In this way they always heap up their sins to the limit. The wrath of G-d has come upon them at last."[176]

Considering the fact that Paul was Jewish and a member of the Zealot party this passage seems to make absolutely no sense.

There are many more instances of this sort of forgery, and it is highly likely that seemingly antisemitic passages from the New Testament were simply inserts like this.

Although Paul tried to remove Judaism from Christianity he did so in a more delicate way and did not attempt to alienate the largely Jewish followers of Yehoshua.

By now Christianity had become far less Judeo-Centric so this need was removed, and it became easier to simply appeal to Hellenists.

It is hard to say whether Christianity killed Rome or Rome in fact killed Christianity. I like to imagine that they entered a sort of suicide pact.

When Rome adopted the Christian religion it lost its sense of direction, it lost its identity and values and tried and failed to reconcile its Pagan past with its Christian future.

So too did the Romans colonize Christianity, sapping it of any of the Jewish thought that had once created it. There is no better example of this than that to this day the seat of Christian power is at Rome, and the chief Church of Christianity is called the Roman Catholic Church.

Constantine was harsh towards the Jews and so was his son Constantius II.

Constantine's first choice for heir was his son Crispus, but he had Crispus strangled to death in 326CE when he was accused of sleeping with Constantine's wife Fausta.

Fausta was later killed as well for lying about this. Efforts were made to erase Crispus from history which not only illustrates Constantine's cruelty, but his desire to revise history in ways which benefitted him.

In his mind truth was whatever he happened to desire it to be. This is the same dangerous rationale that underpins all historical revisionism.

When Constantine died, he split the empire between his three remaining sons and his nephew Dalmatius.

Dalmatius was given dominion over Greece. Constantius II was given control over the East.

Constans was given control of Italy and Constantine II was given the west.

This odd split was likely a result of the brutal death of Crispus. Constantine just decided to give his relatives the chance to fight it out among themselves.

In the following civil war Constantius II came out on top. He ended up purging almost all of his relatives including his brothers, cousins and nephews.

The only ones he spared were Gallus, Nepatianus and Julian because of their youth.

Constantius was cruel to the Jews and sanctioned violence against them. We know this because Emperor Theodosius II later codified his religious laws in his codex.

"On the Lord's day, which is the first day of the week, on Christmas, and
on the days of Epiphany, Easter, and Pentecost, inasmuch as then the
[white] garments [of Christians] symbolizing the light of heavenly
cleansing bear witness to the new light of holy baptism, at the time also of
the suffering of the apostles, the example for all Christians, the pleasures
of the theaters and games are to be kept from the people in all cities, and
all the thoughts of Christians and believers are to be occupied with the
worship of G-d. And if any are kept from that worship through the mad-
ness of Jewish impiety or the error and insanity of foolish paganism, let

them know that there is one time for prayer and another for pleasure.

And lest anyone should think he is compelled by the honor due to our

person, as if by the greater necessity of his imperial office, or that unless

he attempted to hold the games in contempt of the religious prohibition, he

might offend our serenity in showing less than the usual devotion toward

us; let no one doubt that our clemency is revered in the highest degree by

humankind when the worship of the whole world is paid to the might and

goodness of G-d. Theodosius Augustus and Caesar Valentinian."[177]

This in effect made Judaism illegal in most cases and seriously restricted the religious freedom of Jewish people in the Roman Empire.

There are many instances of antisemitic policies taken up by the Roman state in this codex and the fact that they were written down just goes to show how ingrained and impactful they were on the Jewish population in Syria Palestina, which by now had declined to a shadow of what it had been.

In 351CE Gallus the cousin of the Emperor was appointed to oversee the eastern provinces. It was while he was there that the last great Jewish revolt began.

It is in the midrash that this rebellion is recounted in Yalkut Shimoni's commentaries on the Torah.

It is said that Isaac of Diocaesarea and Patricius led this uprising and managed to take Tiberias along with most of the Galilean region.

Both of these men were killed, and the revolt was put down very quickly. There simply weren't enough Jews left or enough will among them for this revolt to take off like the others.

The Sanhedrin was also abolished and had its final meeting in 358CE although it nominally survived until the 5th century. They used this final meeting to sort out some important problems which the Jewish faith would face without a Sanhedrin.

The Jewish calendar had always been inconsistent. The Sanhedrin had been relied on to artificially add extra months to the year to avoid confusion and keep them in line with the seasons.

Because so many Jews now resided away from Israel, and because the Sanhedrin could no longer set the calendar artificially Judaism needed to change.

The biggest issue was that Shabbat often interfered with Jewish holidays. If Shabbat happened to align with a Jewish holiday, then the holiday would be disrupted, or Shabbat would be disrupted.

For instance, Jews must fast for Yom Kippur. If Yom Kippur conflicted with Shabbat (a day on which you cannot cook) then Jews would be forced to go without food for 2 days.

A religion that is excessively difficult to keep up with is not one that tends to survive long so the Sanhedrin had to adjust the calendar as to avoid this sort of issue.

Through a complex use of arithmetic, the Sanhedrin was able to determine a system which would avoid holidays overlapping with Shabbat. It is difficult to even describe the arithmetic in question but essentially the months were realigned so that they skipped through Shabbat when it was necessary.

This change allowed Judaism to be practiced from anywhere without the Sanhedrin having to constantly interfere.

With this the Sanhedrin was abolished and apart from a few spurious revivals it never resurfaced.

Napoleon Bonaparte attempted to create his own French Sanhedrin and some modern religious Jews have tried establishing one in Israel but none of these attempts held any water.

Because of how long Judaism had survived without a Sanhedrin these efforts were widely mocked and given little attention.

It was only when Constantius II died in 362CE that Julian became Emperor and eased the woes of the Jews.

Julian was Constantius' cousin and also a pagan. He had been a Christian in his youth but converted to the pagan religion of Greece. For this he was branded Julian the Apostate by Christian historians.

Constantius had given Julian command over the western legions but when he died Julian was actually in open rebellion against him. Normally Constantius would have been harsh to a rebel but since he was dying anyway it is likely that he named Julian as his heir to avoid more conflict and strife.

The transition of power was therefore smooth and peaceful. Despite being opposed to Christianity Julian gave his predecessor a Christian burial. He treated his predecessor with respect despite the cruel way he had treated his relatives.

Julian was something of a renaissance man, he believed in returning to the old style of religion and government which he saw as more stable than Constantine's chaotic Church-dominated system.

He tried to reinvigorate the Senate and decreased his personal powers in favour of a more oligarchic early-Roman model of government.

Much like most restorationist movements Julian's died with him because there was no one left to propagate it after him and Christianity had just become too powerful to be stopped.

It was simply impossible to weed the Church out of the affairs of the state. They owned too much land, had too many important administrative roles and were given command over large aspects of domestic life.

The collection of Alms for the poor for instance was under the charge of the Church. Most hospitals and places of education fell under the Church's responsibility as well.

Much like today the Church was fused with the life of the community as a whole, it couldn't simply be removed or uprooted without decades of work and a ruthlessly effective plan for their removal.

Simply killing them all didn't work. Diocletian and his successors had brutally slaughtered the Christians, but they just came back in greater numbers.

In modernity the influence of the Church was only removed gradually and even now in many countries Christianity is still a force to be reckoned with. This was simply a challenge Julian was not up to.

In any case, Julian did not want to oppress Christians. He saw them as overly powerful and wanted to crack down on them because they were. They were not just free but given more freedom than other religious groups.

For Julian's pagan faith to have any chance of surviving he had to take the Christians down a peg. He wanted a plurality of religions to exist in Rome and for all of them to be held in equal regard by the state.

Julian's conversion to paganism was most certainly earnest because of this. He brought himself no advantages by abandoning the religion which most of his subjects practiced. He lost friends and allies and essentially pitted the Church against the state.

By this point in time the Church was hugely interlinked with the running of the empire and an Emperor with a civil service that hates him is from the start prevented from carrying out the functions of state.

This is not to say that he was inept, just that he made a personal religious choice that made governing much harder.

This illustrates an aspect of Julian's character that is vital to understanding why he ruled as he did. Julian had integrity.

Even when it was hard Julian used his intellectual gifts to come to a decision and stuck by it in times of ease and of woe. Yet he never despised anyone for coming to a different conclusion.

His family were largely Christian, his soldiers were largely Christian, his friends and intellectual contemporaries were largely Christian. Julian's reign marked a period of true and earnest toleration in the context of religion.

Rome became something of a meritocracy (relatively speaking) during Julian's reign. A Christian could advance just as high as a pagan and vice versa.

To the Christians this was threatening because Julian revoked their special favours and put them on an equal footing with everyone else.

What had been an act of egalitarianism was portrayed by later Christian sources as an act of persecution.

Christians had once been persecuted by previous pagan Emperors; this cannot be denied.

But in the context of Julian the Christians exploited this history to portray themselves as victims even as they became the oppressors.

Even as Christian armies ransacked Africa, Asia and the Americas during the era of colonialism they held high the symbol of the cross, an emblem of their self-perceived martyrdom.

This is less a point about Christian theology and more about the practical implications of Christian history.

By using martyrdom, persecution and suffering as a source of strength Christians have been able to deflect criticism and convert most of the planet to their faith.

The Christians of the past became what they had once hid from, they became Romans.

This is the real root of colonialism. The reason Christian nations have largely been responsible for colonialism is because they believed (in the same way the Romans did) that everyone else was simply a 'barbarian' or a 'savage' and that they needed to be saved from this perilous state of being.

Christian colonialism was even more successful than Roman colonialism because (unlike the Romans) the Christians could claim that they were the ones being oppressed even when this dynamic had shifted completely.

In many ways the condemnation of Julian was an early example of this line of argument. The Christians could demand special treatment and the persecution of pagans by merely claiming that not doing these things would be an act of oppression against the Christians in and of itself.

This was also partly why Julian favoured the Jews, because he knew that he needed allies anywhere he could find them.

As Edward Gibbon relates Julian wanted to rebuild the temple and return to the Jews their ancient rights. For this he was held in high regard by them.

> "While the devout monarch incessantly labored to restore and propagate the religion of his ancestors, he embraced the extraordinary design of rebuilding the temple of Jerusalem. In a public epistle to the nation or community of the Jews, dispersed through the provinces, he pities their misfortunes, condemns their oppressors, praises their constancy, declares himself their gracious protector, and expresses a pious hope, that after his return from the Persian war, he may be permitted to pay his grateful vows to the Almighty in his holy city of Jerusalem."[178]

Julian not only promised this, but he also met with the Rabbis of the empire to discuss how the project should be undertaken.

It is hard to determine how much of this endeavour was brought about by Julian's desire to decrease the power of Christianity and how much he honestly saw Rome's role in oppressing the Jews as wrong.

The only realistic view one can hold is that Julian desired to do it both out of self-interest and out of sincerity.

Another thing that endeared Julian to the Jews was his rebellion against Constantius. Julian was in a religious minority; he had been an underdog from the start.

This religiously diverse orphan had ended up becoming an Emperor, that was a story the Jews could relate to. Julian saw the misery of the Jewish people and spoke to them like a human being.

Even an aristocrat like Julian could channel a uniquely common touch that made him beloved by many.

The Emperor was also something of a libertarian and made it his mission to grant more rights to local authorities which decreased the power of the Church in government

After Julian's death this had the opposite impact because local Church authorities gained even more of a monopoly on the running of cities and towns.

He also made efforts to disrupt the Christian monopoly on education and went as far as banning them from teaching classical texts.

Although this was not a severe imposition it was done in the hopes that Christians would not be able to infest academic circles. This also failed as soon as Julian died because for millennia the Church had primacy in universities and all other forms of education until the modern period.

Even now Christian schools are a commonality and religion often plays a part in the education systems of the world.

Another great ambition of Julian's was ultimately what thwarted all of his other endeavours.

He invaded Sassania in 363CE and attempted to attack Ctesiphon. This was another reason he tried to rebuild the temple, because he expected Sassanid Jews to be more loyal to him than to the enemy if he did something grandiose in their favour.

Rather than marching directly there he marched further south then diverted his men by boat to a river adjacent to the city. This move caught the Sassanids off guard and by all probabilities should have ensured his victory.

Though Julian's planning was very good he did not account for the fact that one of his generals refused to reinforce his men. Procopius was Julian's cousin on his mother's side, and he refused to aid Julian when he was attacking Ctesiphon, he just left his cousin to die.

Julian was therefore surrounded in enemy lands with no hope of salvation. The Romans were forced into a humiliating retreat.

Julian was stabbed in the gut by a spear during the heat of battle. He lived for some days but died of his wounds. He was quickly replaced by a Christian named Jovian who immediately reversed most of his anti-Christian policies.

The reason Julian's vision never materialised was that he died unexpectedly. Had he lived the temple probably would have been rebuilt as the contemporary historian Ammianus Marcellinus testified.

"And although he weighed every possible variety of events with anxious thought, and pushed on with burning zeal the many preparations for his campaign, yet turning his activity to every part, and eager to extend the memory of his reign by great works, he planned at vast cost to restore the once splendid temple at Jerusalem, which after many mortal combats during the siege by Vespasian and later by Titus, had barely been stormed. He had entrusted the speedy performance of this work to Alypius of Antioch, who had once been vice-prefect of Britain. But, though this

Alypius pushed the work on with vigour, aided by the governor of the province, terrifying balls of flame kept bursting forth near the foundations of the temple, and made the place inaccessible to the workmen, some of whom were burned to death; and since in this way the element persistently repelled them, the enterprise halted.[179]

Julian's death snuffed the hopes of the Jews, and they were never fully rekindled. Julian was the last non-Christian Emperor and his successors cracked down on the Jews and introduced harsh laws to restrict their rights in the empire.

But it wouldn't have mattered if Julian lived for half a century, he was simply trying to force an old style of government on the Romans that they didn't want. The notion of an Emperor governing with the Senate was so remote to the Romans that it felt like a display of weakness.

The autocratic militaristic style of imperium was so deeply ingrained that even if Julian had lived much longer none of his attempts to restore the Senate's relevance would have lasted.

Trying to undo Christianity was impossible. Undoing Christianity would have undone Rome and alienated its largest religious group. Even though he was killed by a foreign enemy Julian's reign was something of a political suicide.

It was still possible that the temple could have been rebuilt, were it not for poor omens and a complete lack of political will from his successor Jovian.

As this excerpt also states the temple was stopped by natural disasters. The Christians interpreted this as a sign that their religion was more favourable to G-d than Judaism.

"*An earthquake, a whirlwind, and a fiery eruption, which overturned and scattered the new foundations of the temple, are attested, with some variations, by contemporary and respectable evidence.*"[180]

One piece of evidence Gibbon refers to is the line from Marcellinus above. It was seen as a supernatural event that the construction was stopped by such a disastrous set of calamities.

The Christians could feel a certain amount of vindication seeing their self-created enemies suffer such ills.

The Lord had seemingly spoken. The temple would not be rebuilt any time soon. Julian was the last Roman who ever tried.

Why would the Christians want to rebuild the temple of the people who killed their prophet?

This is not to say that the effort was pure folly, or that it achieved nothing. As Edward Gibbon relates, it was actually a very well-funded and enthusiastically supported project.

"The vain and ambitious mind of Julian might aspire to restore the ancient glory of the temple of Jerusalem. As the Christians were firmly persuaded that a sentence of everlasting destruction had been pronounced against the whole fabric of the Mosaic law, the Imperial sophist would have converted the success of his undertaking into a specious argument against the faith of prophecy, and the truth of revelation. He was displeased with the spiritual worship of the Synagogue; but he approved the institutions of Moses, who had not disdained to adopt many of the rites and ceremonies of Egypt. The local and national deity of the Jews was sincerely adored by a polytheist, who desired only to multiply the number of the g-ds; and such was the appetite of Julian for bloody sacrifice, that his emulation might be excited by the piety of Solomon, who had offered, at the feast of the dedication, twenty-two thousand oxen, and one hundred

and twenty thousand sheep. These considerations might influence his designs; but the prospect of an immediate and important advantage would not suffer the impatient monarch to expect the remote and uncertain event of the Persian war. He resolved to erect, without delay, on the commanding eminence of Moriah, a stately temple, which might eclipse the splendor of the church of the resurrection on the adjacent hill of Calvary; to establish an order of priests, whose interested zeal would detect the arts, and resist the ambition, of their Christian rivals; and to invite a numerous colony of Jews, whose stern fanaticism would be always prepared to second, and even to anticipate, the hostile measures of the Pagan government."[181]

Julian wanted to outshine the Jerusalemite Christians by building a temple more splendorous and magnificent than anything else anyone had ever seen before.

He was also not a monotheist, so it was easier for him to regard Hashem as an extension of the deities he worshipped. He wanted to respect all the G-ds of his empire which set him apart from the monotheistic Christians who regarded their way as the only way.

The Jews were evidently overjoyed at the notion of a rebuilt temple and thanked Julian with funds and praises.

"At the call of their great deliverer, the Jews, from all the provinces of the empire, assembled on the holy mountain of their fathers; and their insolent triumph alarmed and exasperated the Christian inhabitants of Jerusalem. The desire of rebuilding the temple has in every age been the ruling passion of the children of Isræl. In this propitious moment the men forgot their avarice, and the women their delicacy; spades and pickaxes of silver were provided by the vanity of the rich, and the rubbish was

transported in mantles of silk and purple. Every purse was opened in liberal contributions, every hand claimed a share in the pious labor, and the commands of a great monarch were executed by the enthusiasm of a whole people.[182]

The desire to rebuild the temple was a distant pipe dream but a dream, nonetheless. It had been destroyed 291 years before Julian took the throne, so the main aim of the Jewish faith was to interpret and cope with the temple's destruction.

It was about figuring out what Judaism actually was if the Jews couldn't even enter the city or worship in their temple. Without a sense of Jewish nationhood Judaism had to find something else that made it cogent and meaningful.

In the end Judaism found an escape from the pain within the pain itself. It was through holidays such as Tisha B'av that the Jews discovered how to express their pain without losing the real point of their religion.

It wasn't about some notion of self-pity or fear. Jews mourn on days of mourning because we know full well that we must stick to our identity even in times of woe.

Every Shabbat dinner, every game of spin the dreidel, every funny hat on Purim is made that much sweeter knowing that we can enjoy these despite (and because of) the suffering of our ancestors.

All those poor souls King Antiochus force-fed pork, all those who died in the revolts against the Romans, they died for a reason.

They died so that we could live as we do now. Our suffering represents our endurance. Surely that is worthy of celebration?

This is what the Jews figured out from the most unobservant right to the Rabbis, that even if Judaism had lost a great deal, it was not dead and never would be.

In some ways they did rebuild the third temple. In some ways the temple never left our hearts or our actions.

In some ways it will stay standing for as long as we do. Evermore.

20

Chapter 20- How the Byzantines Lost the Holy Land

Julian was succeeded by a Christian called Jovian in 363CE and no pagan would ever hold the imperial office again.

The new Emperor had to cede land to the Sassanids and died after he left a candle burning in his chambers.

The candle ignited the fresh coat of lead-based paint, and this suffocated him in his sleep. From here a series of Emperors both capable and poor rose. Valentinian I for instance carried in his retinue two pet bears who would maul his enemies to death.

By 380CE Emperor Theodosius I had made Christianity the official religion of the Roman empire. Fortunately for the Jews most of his persecutions impacted pagan worshippers rather than them.

Due to Christianity's similarities to Judaism the Jews saw a greater degree of toleration than the pagans. The pagans had their temples destroyed and worship of the ancient G-ds was outlawed.

It was also Theodosius who formally split the Roman empire. His sons Arcadius and Honorius split the empire in half.

To the Romans this was normal. All of the co-Emperors of the preceding century had ruled separate parts of the empire, but it stayed together as one nation.

No one would have fully been aware that this split was permanent. Honorius was succeeded in the west by a series of weak Emperors who ultimately became puppets of the gothic hordes that infested the Western Roman Empire. The decline of the west was rapid because a great number of tribesmen were able to infest the Roman government.

The tribes would often choose Roman Emperors based on their pliability. They chose many child Emperors and allowed the empire's institutions to fall into disrepair and ruin.

In 476CE the West finally fell when Romulus Augustus (a child Emperor) was deposed by Odoacer the first Germanic King of Italy. Although the west formally remained under the authority of the Emperor in the east, this was the moment that western Emperors stopped being crowned.

When the West fell Odoacer nominally recognised the Eastern Emperor Zeno as his master and senior but in practice this was the point where the West was no longer governed by Romans and was instead formed in a more medieval image.

The east meanwhile survived under Arcadius and his successors and even thrived without the liability of the West. The west was not worth keeping anymore, it was an economic and defensive sinkhole.

The East was economically powerful and easier to defend than the West. Losing Rome was mostly a symbolic defeat as the main capital of the empire had been Constantinople for some time.

Arcadius' successor Theodosius II was married to a non-Christian wife by the name of Aelia Eudocia. She was known as a patron of the Jews and wanted to allow them access to the city of Jerusalem.

Barsauma the Bishop of Nisibis at the time was fiercely antisemitic and attempted to persecute the Jews which pitted him against Empress Eudocia.

When she was banished by Theodosius II for alleged adultery she moved to Jerusalem and patronised people of all faiths for the rest of her life. Although she tried to restrict Barsauma and his followers they were too powerful and violent for her to stop them.

She in died in Jerusalem and was buried there in 450CE.

Barsauma was also intently focussed on persecuting the Samaritans who by now outnumbered the Jews in the region and had more power and rights.

Barring what came next the Samaritans probably would have become the dominant ethnic group in Palestine, but for reasons which will be elaborated on they would almost face extinction.

Even today there are only a few hundred Samaritans left. They are a tiny ethnic minority in the state of Israel, and it is highly unlikely that their numbers will swell anytime soon.

The Samaritans are the descendants of the northern tribe of Israel whilst the Jews are descended from the southern tribe of Judah. The Samaritans had their own temple and practiced a similar religion to Judaism with only slight alterations.

They had been an oppressed minority in the ancient Jewish Kingdom and once the Jews had been sufficiently suppressed the Roman empire desired to be rid of the Samaritans as well.

Zeno made it his mission to persecute the Samaritans and ended up starting a set of rebellions similar to those the Jews had mounted. The Emperor demanded that the Samaritans become Christians which led them to fight back fiercely.

According to a later historian this is why the first Samaritan rebellion took place.

"There is a city in Palestine named Neapolis, which is overhung by a lofty mountain named Gerizim.This mountain was originally held by the Samaritans, who ascended it at all seasons in order to pray, not that they had ever built a church there, but worshipped and reverenced the summit of the mountain above everything else. Jesus, the Son of G-d, when in the flesh, went amongst these people, and held a conversation with one of the women of the country. When she inquired of Him about the mountain, He told her that in future times the Samaritans should not worship in this mountain, but that the true worshippers should worship Himself there, alluding to the Christians. In process of time this prophecy came to pass, for it was not possible that the true G-d should lie. It came to pass in the following manner. In the reign of the Emperor Zeno, the Samaritans suddenly collected together, and fell upon the Christians in Neapolis, who were keeping the feast called Pentecost in their church, and killed many of them, while they struck with their swords the Bishop, by name Terebinthius—whom they found standing before the holy table, engaged in celebrating the sacrament—so as, amongst other wounds, to cut off the fingers from his hands, while they insulted the holy mysteries in a manner fit indeed for Samaritans to do, but not fit for us to speak of. This priest shortly afterwards came to Byzantium, into the presence of the then Emperor, to whom he showed what he himself had suffered, described what had taken place, and begged the Emperor to avenge what had been done, reminding him of the prophecy of Christ. The Emperor Zeno, much moved at what had taken place, without delay inflicted a full measure of punishment upon those who had been guilty of this outrage. He drove the Samaritans out of Mount Gerizim, handed it over to the Christians, and

built upon the summit a church which he dedicated to the Virgin, which he enclosed with what was indeed called a wall, but which in truth was a dry stone fence. He placed a sufficient number of soldiers as a garrison in the city below, but in the church and its fortification not more than ten. The Samaritans, enraged at these proceedings, were filled with anger, and remained sulky and dissatisfied, though, through fear of the Emperor, they kept silence. In process of time, however, in the reign of Anastasius, the following event took place. Some of the Samaritans, at the instigation of a woman, climbed unexpectedly up the steep face of the mountain, for the road which leads up it from the city was strictly guarded, so that it was impossible for them to ascend by it. Falling suddenly upon the church, they killed the guards who were posted there, and called with a loud voice upon the Samaritans in the city to join them. They, however, fearing the soldiers, were not at all willing to join the conspirators; and not long afterwards the governor of the province (he was named Procopius, of the city of Edessa, an eloquent man) captured those who had been guilty of this outrage, and put them to death. Yet even then the Emperor did not bestow any attention or care upon the fortification; but in our own time the Emperor Justinian, although he has for the most part converted the Samaritans to a better religion, and rendered them Christians, yet, leaving the old wall round the church upon Gerizim in its former condition of loose stones, as I described before, he enclosed it within a second wall, and rendered it altogether impregnable. In this place he also rebuilt five Christian churches which had been burned by the Samaritans. These were his works in this country."[183]

In 484CE the first Samaritan revolt (Justa uprising) took place, the name of this revolt comes from the King the Samaritans selected to lead them.

King Justa managed to take Caesarea and a string of other important cities in the north of Judaea. The rebellion ended in bloodshed and Zeno placed a tomb for his deceased son on the site of the Samaritan temple.

This meant that the worshippers would have to pray in front of a Christianized Roman monument if they wanted to worship in their ancient way.

The next rebellion took place later and they became a sustained problem for the Byzantines.

In 495CE under Anastasius I a similar rebellion was launched and ended in the same way.

The Samaritans were slaughtered, they lost more rights and their numbers started diminishing even more.

This new Eastern Roman Empire (commonly called Byzantium) was very different to what the old empire had been.

The official language was Greek, the East was much wealthier without having to subsidise the west and most importantly this new empire operated on an Autocratic model of government more similar to medieval feudalism.

Diocletian had started the process of creating a feudal society, but it took centuries for the Romans to fully adopt it.

The Emperor was an all-powerful monarch with a lower tier noble class to support him and a peasant class to provide soldiers, labour and resources.

The Church was also at the peak of its power and the Emperor was seen as being responsible for Church affairs to some extent. The Emperor was supposed to intervene in matters of the Church and set the legal standards for religious practice in the empire.

The Byzantine empire was a complex beast, and it obviously differed from the empire it claimed to be a reimagining of in a lot of ways.

This does not mean that the Byzantines were not Roman at all. They saw themselves as Romans, they identified with Roman ideals, history and culture. They referred to themselves entirely as Romans and would continue doing so even after the collapse of the Byzantine empire in 1453CE.

As Byzantine history progresses it becomes ever harder to justify calling it an extension of Rome. But for the purposes of discussing Jewish-Roman relations (considering the fact that Byzantium's true decline came long after they lost Syria Palestina) the Byzantines are still relevant.

Much like a medieval Kingdom the Byzantine empire brutally repressed all religious minorities including the Jews. In fairness they spent far more time oppressing other Christian denominations that ventured away from the Catholic (Orthodox) Church, but this does not detract from Byzantine antisemitism.

At this time the Orthodox and Catholic Church were one entity, their schism took place in 1054CE, which is slightly later than the scope of this text.

Before further alluding to the cruel fate the Samaritans and Jews endured under Byzantium Emperor Justinian must be discussed.

He was the architect of much of their suffering in this period.

Justinian had started life as the son of a pig farmer in modern Macedonia. His uncle was a highly regarded soldier and took Justinian under his wing from a young age once his father died.

Justin was the commander of the imperial guard and when Anastasius I died Justinian managed to threaten, cajole and bribe his way into guaranteeing that Justin would take his place.

During Justin's reign Justinian was an important figure in administration. He was so valued and loved by his uncle that he even had the law preventing nobles from marrying the lower classes so that he could marry the love of his life Theodora.

Theodora had been an actress (a profession which often also involved prostitution) and was seen as too lowly for Justinian, but he loved her anyway. He loved her so much that he refused to marry anyone else and in the end his uncle relented.

Theodora would prove to be an important influence on Justinian when he took the throne. She often defended him when he was too weak to defend himself and she also guided key policy decisions with her strength of character.

Justin ruled for about a decade and gave the throne to his nephew in 527CE, who he trusted and admired.

For all his faults it must be said that Justinian knew how to get things done. He was ruthless and hard-working in every aspect of his administration.

He hired some of the best and brightest to run his empire including Belisarius, Narses and John the Cappadocian.

In 532CE a riot broke out in the Hippodrome (chariot racing venue) and the people tried to overthrow Justinian. They burned much of the city down and killed many of Justinian's men.

Right as he was about to flee his wife convinced him to stay and fight. Her famous speech gave Justinian the resolve to win.

He had the rioters killed by his general Belisarius and an army was drafted to cut down 30,000 of them.

In 542CE the Justinian Plague broke out and killed so many of Constantinople's citizens that the city walls had to be filled with the corpses. Justinian himself contracted the plague and because he had no heirs Theodora had to step in and keep the empire running while her husband was comatose.

Although Justinian lived, his wife was the only reason that the royal family weren't simply executed and replaced.

What Justinian is best remembered for is his attempt to restore the empire's former glory.

One of the chief aims of Justinian's reign was to retake the Western portion of his empire. He saw it as his patriotic duty and the ultimate assurance of his legacy.

He sent Belisarius first to make war on the Vandals (who controlled North Africa) and retake Roman possessions in the region.

The Vandals were German but had migrated to Africa and took it from the Romans in 435CE.

Belisarius was very successful despite wildly poor odds. The details of the Vandalic wars are complex, but the most relevant piece of information is that Belisarius won the war and was rewarded with a triumph.

The Vandals had also sacked Rome in the previous century and took many treasures including the menorah.

When Belisarius defeated the Vandal King Gelimer he carried both him and the menorah back to the east.

"Belisarius, upon reaching Byzantium with Gelimer and the Vandals, was counted worthy to receive such honours, as in former times were assigned to those generals of the Romans who had won the greatest and most noteworthy victories. And a period of about six hundred years had now passed since anyone had attained these honours, except, indeed, Titus and Trajan, and such other Emperors as had led armies against some barbarian nation and had been victorious. For he displayed the spoils and slaves from the war in the midst of the city and led a procession which the Romans call a "triumph," not, however, in the ancient manner, but going on foot from his own house to the hippodrome and then again from the barriers until he reached the place where the imperial throne is. And there was booty,—first of all, whatever articles are wont to be set apart for the royal service,—thrones of gold and carriages in which it is customary for a king's consort to ride, and much jewelry made of precious stones, and

golden drinking cups, and all the other things which are useful for the royal table. And there was also silver weighing many thousands of talents and all the royal treasure amounting to an exceedingly great sum (for Gizeric had despoiled the Palatium in Rome, as has been said in the preceding narrative), and among these were the treasures of the Jews, which Titus, the son of Vespasian, together with certain others, had brought to Rome after the capture of Jerusalem. And one of the Jews, seeing these things, approached one of those known to the Emperor and said: "These treasures I think it inexpedient to carry into the palace in Byzantium. Indeed, it is not possible for them to be elsewhere than in the place where Solomon, the king of the Jews, formerly placed them. For it is because of these that Gizeric captured the palace of the Romans, and that now the Roman army has captured that the Vandals." When this had been brought to the ears of the Emperor, he became afraid and quickly sent everything to the sanctuaries of the Christians in Jerusalem. And there were slaves in the triumph, among whom was Gelimer himself, wearing some sort of a purple garment upon his shoulders, and all his family, and as many of the Vandals as were very tall and fair of body. And when Gelimer reached the hippodrome and saw the Emperor sitting upon a lofty seat and the people standing on either side and realized as he looked about in what an evil plight he was, he neither wept nor cried out, but ceased not saying over in the words of the Hebrew scripture: "Vanity of vanities, all is vanity." And when he came before the Emperor's seat, they stripped off the purple garment, and compelled him to fall prone on the ground and do obeisance to the Emperor Justinian. This also Belisarius did, as being a suppliant of the Emperor along with him. And the Emperor Justinian and the Empress Theodora presented the children of Ilderic and his offspring and all those of the family of the Emperor

Valentinian with sufficient sums of money, and to Gelimer they gave
lands not to be despised in Galatia and permitted him to live there to-
gether with his family. However, Gelimer was by no means enrolled
among the patricians, since he was unwilling to change from the faith of
Arius."[184]

Justinian decided to accept the return of the menorah to Jerusalem but was cruel to the Jews by placing it in one of his Churches.
He did this as a mockery of the Jews and to prevent them from
having access to their sacred treasure.

Justinian is also praised for building the Hagia Sofia in Constantinople and for codifying the laws of the empire so that all localities
would have to follow the same rules.

Although this was necessary for avoiding corruption and unfair-
ness in the justice system it did not help the Jews or Samaritans.

Procopius relates just how harsh Justinian was when it came to
finding legal routes towards attacking the Jews in just about every
way possible.

"If ever the time of Paschals is celebrated before Christians, the love of
fortune, It is in this time of the Judaeans that they are in the midst of
their duty, and what is the power of g-d is accomplished by in the tighten-
ing of the law. many of them who have been ordered by the rehearsals of
the year, the state of illegality who have suffered a great deal of money. I
have worked with me, and with all the other things that Austinianus
have been reflected in the number of things that have been believed in,
and that he has come to an end to the word. it is necessary for the sake of
it, and through it that the human being is marked."[185]

In simpler terms Procopius is saying that antisemitism was enshrined in the Roman legal system by Justinian's revered law code.

A document which inspired countless future states, and which is arguably the foundation of the modern legal system was also used as an antisemitic tool not just to suppress the Jews, but to legally justify and enforce this suppression.

Similar things happened to the Samaritans which is why the Jews and Samaritans ended up joining in common cause.

Julianus ben Sabar was of Samaritan extraction and declared himself to be both the rightful King of Israel and the messiah in 529CE. The Jews and Samaritans had joined forces which made two fledgling minorities into a force to be reckoned with.

This revolt did not last long but was very successful. Justinian was forced to use a great number of soldiers and resources to put it down. It is said that 100,000 Samaritans including their leader were put to death.

In 556CE a similar rebellion occurred, and a similar number were killed. It was this final blow that killed the Samaritan identity. Though there are still some Samaritans their population has never recovered, and it isn't likely to.

The Jews survived for multiple reasons but one of these was that they lived in diaspora, so it was harder to attack them all at once.

It was because of these brutal reprisals that the Jews and Samaritans began to loathe the Romans so much that they would willingly help foreign enemies.

In later conflicts the Jews often allied themselves with whoever Rome happened to be fighting against in the hopes of better treatment.

If a horde of foreign soldiers marching into your towns is seen as 'better treatment' then the conditions you're experiencing are clearly horrendous.

Justinian's greatest blunder in his policies against the Jews was that he oppressed them so much (even making reading Jewish texts in Hebrew a crime) that he made them fear him and his empire more than the possibility of a new ruler.

If anyone sent a force to Syria Palestina in the future the Jews would probably not be much inclined to support their empire.

When Khosrow I of the Sassanid empire made war with Justinian he was helped by the fact that he was tolerant of the Jews in his empire. Though there was no particular love for him among the Jews he was easily preferred to Justinian.

This gave Khosrow a much greater rate of success when it came to invading the Roman East.

Although Justinian was never beset with a full invasion of the Roman east this new dynamic did put a lot of strain on his successors. It put them on the backfoot when it came to foreign policy and forced them to become even more defensive of the eastern border.

The rest of Justinian's reign was reasonably successful, he had his good moments and his poor ones.

He tried to create Christian unity in the empire but failed, he successfully took Spain, Africa and Italy back as Roman provinces and he managed to see Rome through the Justinian Plague which killed over ¼ of the population.

Justinian's successors would lose a lot of what he had gained in the following years. His nephew Justin II was mentally unstable and ended up having to rely on his wife and his co-Emperor Tiberius II to run the empire.

Justin was so severely ill that he had to be put under a form of house arrest, he was even rumoured to be a cannibal because of his penchant for biting people that approached him.

It was during these years that much of Africa, Italy and Spain was retaken by other nations.

Justinian had been ambitious, but his folly was in the fact that he didn't see the bigger picture. Belisarius was arguably the most exceptional general of his time or perhaps of all time.

If a conquest couldn't be sustained by men of similar or greater capacities than their predecessors, it would inevitably be lost.

Anything that wasn't attached directly to the coast (so as to be easy to reach by boat) was lost to the Lombards gradually. There was not very much that could be done about this. A smaller empire also commands less resources, so as Rome shrunk its capacity for expansion shrunk equally.

Tiberius II chose Maurice as his successor because of his military skill and general good character. He was also Tiberius' son-in-law.

Maurice was a capable and successful Emperor for some years but when he attacked the Slavs the Roman army mutinied in favour of a man called Phocas.

Maurice was forced to flee the capital as Phocas acclaimed himself Emperor. Once Phocas entered Constantinople it was over.

Maurice along with his entire family were killed horrifically. Maurice had to watch his sons die one by one before the usurper finally finished him off.

In 602CE Justinian's dynasty officially came to an end and Phocas the Tyrant began his rule.

The death of Maurice triggered a war between Rome and the Sassanids, Rome's enemies smelled blood in the water and came for their piece.

Heraclius the Elder, the Exarch (governor) of Africa launched a rebellion with his son of the same name against Phocas in 608CE.

The drawback of usurping power is that you become an example of the benefits of usurpation. A successful usurper is a good target for usurpation because they have proven the effectiveness of it just by virtue of their existence.

Phocas was known for his cruelty and incompetence. He was hated by the population who saw Maurice as their true ruler.

Heraclius the Younger was far more popular and his rebellion which started in Egypt was largely backed by the populous and the nobility. Heraclius the Younger took the throne instead of his father because he was too old. He knew that his son would do a better job and died soon after the revolt ended.

Phocas' war with Sassania was so disastrous that the enemy reached all the way to Chalcedon (opposite Constantinople across the Bosporus Straight) and sacked most of the Roman East.

The regime Phocas had tried so hard and so violently to create was crumbling at the smallest sign of decline.

As Heraclius reached Constantinople Phocas was betrayed by his own men and brought before the new Emperor to be killed. He killed Phocas in a violent display of wrath, he cut off his limbs and then his head. Unlike most imperial murders this one was done by Heraclius himself.

Heraclius had now avenged Maurice and was acclaimed Emperor in 610CE. The war with the Sassanids went far better with Heraclius in charge.

By now the new Sassanid King Khosrow II dropped the pretext of invading to avenge Maurice and just continued the conflict anyway because he perceived the Byzantines to be weak.

This view was entirely justified but Heraclius had a funny way of defying expectations. From 602CE to 628CE the war raged on.

The two powers fought fiercely in the hopes that one would establish dominance over the other. Rome was at a serious disadvantage because it had lost its western half and lacked the same vigour and resources of the old empire.

The Empress Fabia Eudokia died in 612CE, and the following year Heraclius married his niece, Martina. Their children were

382 | ANDRÉ NICE

largely born with sicknesses and most died young because of the incestuous nature of their birth and the obvious genetic frailties that incest can cause.

Heraclius sent capable generals to the front, but it was pointless. The Sassanids cut off the middle east and threatened Anatolia as well as Egypt.

They captured Antioch and Jersualem with relative ease and even when they had to fall back Antioch and Jerusalem remained in their hands.

This source which is attributed to Bishop Sebeos of Armenia describes the fall of Jerusalem.

"Then the entire country of Palestine willingly submitted to the king of kings. The remnants of the Hebrew people especially rebelled from the Christians and taking in hand their native zeal wrought very damaging slaughters among the multitude of believers. Going [to the Iranians], [the Jews] united with them."[186]

The reason the Sassanids were able to capture Jerusalem so easily was that the Monophysite Christians (a middle eastern form of Christianity which saw Yehoshua as having one unified nature rather than two distinct ones) had helped the foreign invaders.

Christians at this time often fought over petty differences in semantics which made them weaker politically and religiously.

The persecution of the Monophysites became so severe that when Shahrbaraz was intent on taking Antioch and Jerusalem in 614CE the Jews and Monophysites willingly helped the foreign armies and even rose up in rebellion to support them.

National loyalties were crushed by the desire for autonomy and fair treatment. The Sassanids brutally raided Jerusalem and killed many of the Romans living there, they went so far as to take ancient relics such as the spear St. Longinus used to kill Yehoshua and the 'true cross' back to their empire as tokens of Rome's defeat.

Shahrbaraz was also aided by two prominent Jews who accompanied him on the campaign.

Benjamin of Tiberias was a wealthy merchant who successfully gathered the forces of the Galilee and marched them south to help the Sassanids take Jerusalem.

Nehemiah ben Hushiel was a messianic claimant who was given governmental control of the city of Jerusalem by the Sassanids.

Together with Benjamin of Tiberias they made plans to rebuild the temple and even resumed sacrifices at the temple mount.

A few months in the new Jewish government faced a rebellion and was forced to seek Sassanid assistance to retake the city.

"Now first [the Jerusalemites] voluntarily submitted, offering the general and the princes very great gifts, and requesting that loyal ostikans be stationed with them to preserve the city. However, several months later the entire mob of the city's young braves united and killed the Iranian king's ostikans. Then they rebelled from his service. After this a battle took place among the inhabitants of the city of Jerusalem, Jew and Christian. The multitude of the Christians grew stronger, struck at and killed many of the Jews. The remainder of the Jews jumped from the walls, and went to the Iranian army." [187]

After this the Sassanids realised that the Jews were not the majority group in the region anymore and decided to ally themselves with the Monophysite Christians instead.

Nehemiah also died in battle shortly after this trying to take the city of Tyre, so the Jews quickly outlived their usefulness and started being persecuted by the Sassanids as well. In 617CE the Sassanids drove the Jews out of Jerusalem.

Beyond the practical worries of losing one of the most economically important regions of the empire this was a massive symbolic blow to Heraclius, and it made his administration look exceptionally weak.

If he couldn't even protect the sacred relics of the son of G-d he could hardly be trusted to protect his subjects from the enemy at the gates.

The war escalated when Heraclius fundamentally changed his strategy to one where he led the soldiers directly. There was a strict law which prohibited people with disfigurements or disabilities from being Emperor which was why Emperors would not normally risk losing their position by going off to fight.

And since the paradigm had shifted from Senatorial oligarchy to military dictatorship right through to aristocratic oligarchy again it was not common for an Emperor to have incredible military skills.

Usually, a more capable general would be sent instead but, in this case, Heraclius had sent Rome's best and brightest and they still hadn't gained any ground.

In 619CE the city of Alexandria fell to the Sassanids as well. Around 625CE Khosrow II wrote a humiliating letter to Heraclius which is detailed by Sebeos.

"From Xosrov (Khosrow), the honored of the g-ds, lord of every country and king, born of the great Aramazd, to Heraclius, our stupid and useless servant."You did not want to give yourself into our service, but rather, you call yourself lord and king, and those treasures of mine which are with you, you spend, and you deceive my servants. Furthermore, having assembled troops composed of brigands, you give me no rest. Did I not, truly, exhaust the Byzantines? You claim confidence in your G-d, yet how was it that your troops did not save Caesarea, Jerusalem and

*great Antioch from my hands? And could it be that even now you do not
know that land and sea has been made obedient to me. Now it is only
Constantinople which I have been unable to dig up. Yet, I will forgive all
your faults. Bring your wife and children and come here, and I shall give
you fields, vineyards and olive-trees by which you may live; and we shall
look upon you affectionately. Do not deceive yourself with your vain
hopes, for how can that Christ who was unable to save himself from the
Jews (but was crucified instead) save you from me? For [even] if you
descend to the bottom of the sea, I shall stretch forth my hands and seize
you. And then you will see me under circumstances which you would
rather not."*[188]

This letter was so offensive that it is said that Sergius the Patriarch of Constantinople wept on hearing it. This was clearly a power
move aimed at killing Heraclius' spirit, but it did the complete
opposite.

Heraclius had nowhere else to go, the Egyptian grain supply was
gone, so he went about recruiting every man he could for the war.

In 622CE he left for the final campaign with almost every man
from every legion in the empire. His army was quite literally the last
Roman army left, if they were defeated no reinforcements would
be coming.

The main source available on Heraclius' reign is the Chronicle
of Theophanes the Confessor.

Theophanes was born over a century after the war took place so
some events may well be fabricated or exaggerated.

The Chronicle is mostly a timeline of events rather than the
traditional format of historical narrative. In a sense this makes it
more reliable as it is harder to falsify events when you are not at
liberty to provide long, flowery summations of events.

The Chronicle largely paints Heraclius in a positive light but in reality, it must be kept in mind that he was a harsh and cruel military leader.

Every Roman Emperor would probably be considered a war criminal in a modern context.

Cruelty was an inevitable responsibility of Roman Emperors, but this does not excuse it.

Heraclius had good traits and was evidently skilled. But viewing his legacy in black and white does little service to the painting of a meaningful historical picture.

Rome was in a dire position and Heraclius chose to take the ultimate gamble in the hopes of preserving his empire. He merged all of his legions into one single army. He would use every man available to him, if they lost Rome would be no more.

Initially Heraclius went to Armenia because the mountains were a good natural defence. He had many successes in battle but briefly had to return west to deal with the Avars, a tribe who had invaded much of the interior of Greece.

In 622CE Heraclius took the Persian city of Ganzak and destroyed the sacred temple of Zoroastrianism housed there. This was likely an act of retribution for the fact that Khosrow had taken the 'True Cross' from Jerusalem previously.

He also destroyed the birthplace of Zarathustra, the founding prophet of Zoroastrianism.

Today Persia is mostly Muslim, but Zoroastrianism is still a major religion in the region.

This win was both proof of Heraclius' strength and an act of revenge which gave the Christians of Rome a sense of absolution.

Theophanes the Confessor recounts Heraclius' skill in warfare in a slightly farcical way.

*"A giant of a man confronted the Emperor in the middle of the bridge
and attacked him, but the Emperor struck him and threw him into the
river. When this man had fallen, the barbarians turned to flight and,
because of the narrowness of the bridge, jumped into the river like frogs,
whilst others were being killed by the sword. But the bulk of the barbarians
poured over the river bank: they shot arrows and resisted the passage
of the Romans. The Emperor did cross to the other side and bravely
opposed the barbarians with a few men of his guard. He fought in a
superhuman manner so that even Sarbaros was astonished and said (to)
one Kosmas (a runaway Roman and an apostate) who was standing close
to him:'Do you see, O Kosmas, how boldly the Caesar stands in battle,
how he fights alone against such a multitude and wards off blows like an
anvil?"*[189]

This feels less like a historical account than some sort of bizarre
tributary piece of fiction. This is probably a made-up anecdote or
a massively overexaggerated one. But what it does illustrate is that
Heraclius was a good general and the enemy now knew about it.

After Heraclius beat back the Sassanids the Avars sieged Constantinople.
Heraclius could do nothing to help defend his capital,
they were on their own.

On one side of the city were the Sassanids, and on the other
were the Avars. The city was besieged in 626CE by two powers.

The city was fairly unlikely to fall considering how impossible
it was to siege. The fact that the city was perfectly positioned to
receive supplies, that it had its own water source, and that it had
the Theodosian walls and highly advanced defensive fortifications
meant that it was not realistically possible for any foreign army
to take it.

The number of resources which needed to be spent on a siege were so exorbitant that more often than not sieges fell apart because the defenders outlasted the attacking forces. The pressure of trying to take Constantinople was so great that it made it impossible to sustain such an operation.

The city's defence involved sinking ships that tried to attack the coast whilst also successfully attacking the Slavic attackers trying to scale the walls.

There were multiple walls with moats and anti-siege weapons. Often if one wall was breached the invaders would be pushed back at the next one. The Romans also utilized a form of Phosphorus known as Greek Fire.

This substance was the napalm of antiquity, it would still burn under water and once launched at an enemy force it was universally fatal.

Patriarch Sergius and Heraclius' deputy Bonus successfully repelled the Avars and Sassanids and in the end they had to give up.

In the same year as the siege was lifted one of Khosrow's top generals Shahin was defeated in battle. Khosrow was so angry about this that he had the corpse of his fallen ally taken back to his palace and mutilated it with blunt force.

The war took a turn for the worst when the Khazars allied with Heraclius and began raiding the Sassanid empire. The war had turned. The Khazars to the north and the Romans to the west put too much pressure on Khosrow. He started cracking and went mad with rage and distrust.

Khosrow demanded the execution of Shahrbaraz because he thought the general was plotting against him, but the Romans found the letter on its way and gave it to Shahrbaraz instead.

This forced Shahrbaraz to mount an open rebellion against his King. He convinced his soldiers that many of them were also set to be executed so they joined Shahrbaraz in his revolt.

In 627CE Heraclius faced Rhazadh. He was drafted to stop the
Romans from reaching Ctesiphon (the Sassanid Capital) and was
their last line of defence. Defeating this general was Heraclius' final
hurdle in the way of victory.

It was at the city of Nineveh that the final battle commenced.
The battle initially went better for the Romans than for the Sassanids so in a desperate last stand Rhazadh challenged Heraclius to
single combat.

This was it. Whoever won this fight would win the entire war.
Heraclius and Rhazadh ran at each other and with a single blow
it was over. With a single swing of the sword the winner of this
seemingly endless war was decided.

Heraclius killed his enemy. The Romans won. The Sassanids lost
morale and fled the field after Heraclius had butchered their general
and many of his officers.

After the war ended Khosrow II died. Shahrbaraz overthrew the
ruling dynasty briefly and from there the Sassanid empire fell into
decay and collapse. Many of its lands would be absorbed by the
Islamic conquests not long after they lost to Heraclius.

The final war between the two great powers of the middle
east ended up wiping them both off the map. If a winner is to be
announced then it was of course the Byzantines, but their victory
came at a serious cost.

Compared to the total destruction of the Sassanids the Byzantines got off easy, they were only reduced to something of a third-
rate power in the region.

Towards the end of the war Benjamin of Tiberias met with
Heraclius and they made a deal.

*"When he had come to Tiberias, the Christians there accused a certain
man called Benjamin of oppressing them. For he was very rich and*

received the Emperor and his army. The Emperor censured him, saying: 'For what reason do you oppress the Christians?' He replied, 'Because they are enemies of my faith.' For he was a Jew. Then the Emperor instructed him and, after converting him, had him baptized in the house of Eustathios of Neapolis, a Christian who also received the Emperor. On entering Jerusalem, the Emperor reinstated the patriarch Zacharias and restored the venerable and life-giving Cross to its proper place. After giving many thanks to G-d, he drove the Jews out of the Holy City and ordered that they should not have the right to come within three miles of the Holy City."[190]

Heraclius would spare the Jews if Benjamin converted to Christianity, he did this to save his people from Heraclius' wrath.

The fact that even Theophanes admits that Heraclius broke his oath is a clear indication that he actually did this and wilfully lied to Benjamin.

The Emperor immediately went back on his word and launched a pogrom against the Jews, forcing them all to convert and massacring thousands. He also returned the 'True Cross' to Jerusalem and extracted many treasures from the Sassanids in the peace settlement.

Fortunately for the Jews Heraclius' control of Israel would only last another 4 years. In 634CE the Rashidun Caliphate under Muhammad's successor Abu Bakr would successfully take Egypt and the Levant.

This spared the Jews of Heraclius' harsh policies and was mostly welcomed by the religious minorities living there.

The new governing power over the region chose to be magnanimous and for many years demographics didn't really change.

Although Jews were an oppressed minority, they weren't treated any more harshly than the Christians which relatively speaking was a step up from their time under Roman rule.

From 63BCE all the way to 634CE the Jews had been under Roman rule. This was precisely why the Muslims took the region so easily, because the Jews held such contempt for the Romans that they were willing to risk war and toil and a new oppressor just to be relieved of some of their hardships.

697 years of oppression came to an end when the Islamic armies marched through everything south of modern Turkey.

The wealthiest and most prosperous region of the empire was gone. The main area of trade and agriculture was gone. Rome still technically existed, but now it had lost its empire.

The hopes for a Jewish temple to be built where the previous ones had been was snuffed out in the latter part of the 7th century when Al-Aqsa Mosque was built.

It was originally built where Herod's marketplace had been so its existence didn't intrinsically come into conflict with the existence of the Jewish temple. Jews could still visit the temple mount and in theory there was nothing physically preventing them from rebuilding it at this point.

In 691CE the Dome of the Rock was built exactly where the Jewish temple had been, this expansion onto a Jewish site created tensions so severe that they continue even today. The Al Aqsa Mosque had already been built so this was clearly a move made purely to enhance the prestige of Islam and further suppress the Jews.

It has since become a very contentious issue in relations between Israel and Palestine because both Jews and Muslims regard it as theirs by right.

What is certain is that the construction of the Mosque prevented and still prevents the notion of a restoration of the temple.

Apart from this issue Judaism has also evolved to the point that it no longer needs a temple to function.

Unlike when the Babylonians destroyed the temple Judaism has evolved in the time since the second temple was destroyed. This evolution has made having a temple almost redundant.

A new temple is commonly associated with Jewish eschatology and Jewish messianism.

Rather than seeing the reconstruction of the temple as a pervasive and relevant issue most Jews consider it an integral part of enabling the end of the world in accordance with Jewish theology.

A religious concept and a practical desire are two different things, but in the case of the temple the line does begin to blur.

After the Muslim invasion of Persia, North Africa, Spain and the former Eastern Roman Empire most of the world's Jews ended up under Muslim control which in a sense means that the dynamic shared by Rome and the Jews was inherited by the Islamic empires.

Though Islamic nations were fairly tolerant of the Jews compared to Christian ones the basic animosity and present territorial disputes were caused indirectly by the legacy of Rome.

This is not to say that modern Palestinians are Romans, but the fact that the most antisemitic states in the world today are Muslim and most Jews living in Muslim countries were expelled after Israel was founded does seem to indicate that the Muslim world took on the Roman mantle when it came to antisemitism.

The Muslim world is not the sole historical oppressor of the Jews or even the main one, but it does go to show that even if Rome died, some of its antisemitic legacies survive today in the form of modern antisemitism.

Blaming Muslims as a general group for this would be a foolhardy and bigoted endeavour but much like the subjects of the Roman empire a lot of people living in Muslim-majority countries have been fed lies similar to those of Apion such as the idea of blood libels and a 'global Jewish cabal' who secretly run the world.

This is precisely why this book ends here, because Rome no longer had any relations with the Jews once they lost their southern holdings. They were replaced in their position of power and religious repression by the Rashidun Caliphate which was comparatively tolerant.

The Rashidun Caliphate was replaced by a series of other Islamic empires and (minus some short-lived Crusader states) the Jewish holy land stayed under Muslim control until the end of the First World War.

With the 1913 Balfour Declaration promising a Jewish homeland in Israel and the later 1948 declaration of independence the dream so many fought and died for was achieved.

After more than 1000 years a sovereign Jewish state was reborn.

The best possible summation of Jewish-Roman relations is that one group lives on and the other is long-dead.

The Romans were victims of their own success, the Jews were victims who made a success of themselves.

Though beaten and bereft of happiness the Jews were and remain today thoroughly unbroken.

References

1.   ^ The Histories of Polybius 29.27.4
2.   ^ 2 Maccabees 5:11–14
3.   ^ The Antiquities of the Jews by Flavius Josephus XII.5.1
4.   ^ The Antiquities of the Jews by Flavius Josephus XII.6.1
5.   ^ The Antiquities of the Jews by Flavius Josephus XII.6.2
6.   ^ The Antiquities of the Jews by Flavius Josephus XII.6.3
7.   ^ 1 Maccabees 3:18-21
8.   ^ The Antiquities of the Jews by Flavius Josephus XII.9.2
9.   ^ The Antiquities of the Jews by Flavius Josephus XII.10.2
10. ^ The Antiquities of the Jews by Flavius Josephus XII.10.6
11. ^ The Antiquities of the Jews by Flavius Josephus XII.10.6
12. ^ The Antiquities of the Jews by Flavius Josephus XIII.2.2
13. ^ The Antiquities of the Jews by Flavius Josephus XIII.6.4
14. ^ The Antiquities of the Jews by Flavius Josephus XIII.7.4
15. ^ The Antiquities of the Jews by Flavius Josephus XIII.8.1
16. ^ The Antiquities of the Jews by Flavius Josephus XIII.8.2
17. ^ The Antiquities of the Jews by Flavius Josephus XIII.9.1
18. ^ Book of Numbers 27:18-21
19. ^ The Antiquities of the Jews by Flavius Josephus XIII.10.5
20. ^ The Antiquities of the Jews by Flavius Josephus XIII.11.1
21. ^ The Antiquities of the Jews by Flavius Josephus XIII.11.2
22. ^ The Antiquities of the Jews by Flavius Josephus XIII.11.1-2
23. ^ Jeremiah 52:1-11
24. ^ The Antiquities of the Jews by Flavius Josephus XIII.12.1
25. ^ The Antiquities of the Jews by Flavius Josephus XIII.15.4
26. ^ The Antiquities of the Jews by Flavius Josephus XIII.14.2
27. ^ The Antiquities of the Jews by Flavius Josephus XIII.15.5
28. ^ The Antiquities of the Jews by Flavius Josephus XIII.16.4

29. ^ The Antiquities of the Jews by Flavius Josephus XIV.1.3
30. ^ The Antiquities of the Jews by Flavius Josephus XIV.1.2
31. ^ The Antiquities of the Jews by Flavius Josephus XIV.2.3
32. ^ The Antiquities of the Jews by Flavius Josephus XIV.4.4
33. ^ SPQR A History of Ancient Rome by Mary Beard, Pg 273
34. ^ The Antiquities of the Jews by Flavius Josephus XIV.7.1
35. ^ The Antiquities of the Jews by Flavius Josephus XIV.9.4
36. ^ The Antiquities of the Jews by Flavius Josephus XIV.12.1
37. ^ The Antiquities of the Jews by Flavius Josephus XIV.16.2
38. ^ The Antiquities of the Jews by Flavius Josephus XV.1.2
39. ^ The Antiquities of the Jews by Flavius Josephus XV.3.3
40. ^ The Antiquities of the Jews by Flavius Josephus XV.6.2
41. ^ The Antiquities of the Jews by Flavius Josephus XV.6.4
42. ^ The Antiquities of the Jews by Flavius Josephus XV.6.6
43. ^ The Antiquities of the Jews by Flavius Josephus XV.11.3
44. ^ Deuteronomy 16:16
45. ^ The Army of Herod the Great by Samuel Rocca, Pg 15
46. ^A History of Israel from Alexander the Great to Bar Kochba by Henk Jagersma, Pg 107
47. ^ The William Davidson Talmud Yoma 35.b
48. ^ The William Davidson Talmud Shabbat 31a.6
49. ^ The Antiquities of the Jews by Flavius Josephus XVI.3.3
50. ^ The Antiquities of the Jews by Flavius Josephus XVI.4.3
51. ^ Saturnalia by Macrobius Ambrosius Theodosius. II.IV, verse 11
52. ^ King Jesus by Robert Graves, Chapter 5 pg 55-57
53. ^ The Antiquities of the Jews by Flavius Josephus XVII.6.5
54. ^ A History of the Jewish People in the Time of Jesus Christ, Vol. I, Herod the Great by Emil Schürer
55. ^ "Chronology of the Reign of Herod the Great" by W. E. Filmer
56. ^ The Antiquities of the Jews by Flavius Josephus XVII.9.6
57. ^ The Antiquities of the Jews by Flavius Josephus XVIII. 1.6
58. ^ The Antiquities of the Jews by Flavius Josephus XVIII. 2.3
59. ^ The Antiquities of the Jews by Flavius Josephus XVIII. 5.1
60. ^ The Antiquities of the Jews by Flavius Josephus XVIII. 3.3
61. ^ Matthew 2:16-18
62. ^ Where was Jesus born? By Aviram Oshri
63. ^ Jesus of Nazareth as Seen by Jewish Writers in the XX Century by Joseph Sievers
64. ^ Two ways of believing Vol 1 by Martin Buber pg 657

65. ^ Schalom Ben-Chorin, Brother Jesus. A Jewish point of view on Nazareth pg 41

66. ^ In self-testimonies and pictorial documents by David Flusser

67. ^ In self-testimonies and pictorial documents by David Flusser pg 279

68. ^ Ezekiel 37:1-14

69. ^ John 11:1-44

70. ^ Matthew 10:34-36

71. ^ Mark 11:15-19

72. ^ Luke 13:31-33

73. ^ Matthew 27:24=

74. ^ The Annals by Cornelius Tacitus, Book XV, Chapter 44

75. ^ Jesus Outside the New Testament: An Introduction to the Ancient Evidence by Robert E. Van Voorst pg 39-53

76. ^ Mark 14:61-65

77. ^ The Antiquities of the Jews by Flavius Josephus. XVIII.3.1

78. ^ Matthew 27:15-21

79. ^ Zealot: The Life and Times of Jesus of Nazareth by Reza Aslan

80. ^ Matthew 5:17

81. ^ Acts 10:9-15

82. ^ Acts 22:3-5

83. ^ Zealot: The Life and Times of Jesus of Nazareth by Reza Aslan

84. ^ The Lives of the 12 Caesars by Gaius Suetonius Tranquillus, LXII

85. ^ Roman History by Cassius Dio 48.44

86. ^ Roman History by Cassius Dio 53. 30.

87. ^ The Lives of the 12 Caesars by Gaius Suetonius Tranquillus, Tiberius 7

88. ^ Roman History by Cassius Dio 65. 10.

89. ^ Roman History by Cassius Dio, 57.18.

90. ^ The Lives of the 12 Caesars by Suetonius. Tiberius 24.

91. ^ The Annals by Tacitus III.65

92. ^ Claudius the G-d by Robert Graves pg 15

93. ^ The Antiquities of the Jews by Flavius Josephus XVIII. 6. 3.

94. ^ Roman History by Cassius Dio 58. 12-14.

95. ^ On the Firmness of a Wise Person by Seneca the Younger. XVIII.

96. ^ The Lives of the 12 Caesars by Suetonius. Caius Caesar Caligula. 9-10.

97. ^ The Lives of the 12 Caesars by Suetonius. Caius Caesar Caligula. 14.

98. ^ The Lives of the 12 Caesars by Suetonius. Caius Caesar Caligula. 15.

99. ^ The Lives of the 12 Caesars by Suetonius. Caius Caesar Caligula. XXIV.

100. ^ The Lives of the 12 Caesars by Suetonius. Caius Caesar Caligula. XXV

101. ^ The Lives of the 12 Caesars by Suetonius. Caius Caesar Caligula. XXX
102. ^ The Lives of the 12 Caesars by Suetonius. Caius Caesar Caligula. XXXII
103. ^ The Lives of the 12 Caesars by Suetonius. Caius Caesar Caligula. XXXIII
104. ^ The Lives of the 12 Caesars by Suetonius. Caius Caesar Caligula. XLV-XLVII
105. ^ Roman History by Cassius Dio. LIX. 28.
106. ^ The Lives of the 12 Caesars by Suetonius. Caius Caesar Caligula. LVIII-LIX
107. ^ The Lives of the 12 Caesars by Suetonius. Caius Caesar Caligula. XXX
108. ^ The Antiquities of the Jews by Flavius Josephus. XVIII. 7. 1.
109. ^ The Antiquities of the Jews by Flavius Josephus. XVIII. 7. 2.
110. ^ The Antiquities of the Jews by Flavius Josephus. XVIII. 8.7.
111. ^ The Antiquities of the Jews by Flavius Josephus. XVIII. 8.7.
112. ^ The Antiquities of the Jews by Flavius Josephus. XIX. 5.3.
113. ^ The Antiquities of the Jews by Flavius Josephus XIX. 8.2
114. ^ Roman History by Cassius Dio. LX. 2.
115. ^ The Lives of the 12 Caesars by Suetonius. Tiberius Claudius Drusus Caesar. II.
116. ^ The Lives of the 12 Caesars by Suetonius. Tiberius Claudius Drusus Caesar. XII.
117. ^ Roman History by Cassius Dio. LXI. 31.
118. ^ The Lives of the 12 Caesars by Suetonius. Tiberius Claudius Drusus Caesar. XLIV.
119. ^ Roman History by Cassius Dio. LXI. 35.
120. ^Roman History by Cassius Dio. LXII. 18.
121. ^ The Lives of the 12 Caesars by Suetonius. Nero Claudius Caesar. XXXV.
122. ^ Roman History by Cassius Dio. LXII. 27-28.
123. ^ Church History by Eusebius. II. 25.5.
124. ^ Apologeticum (Lost text) by Tertullian, quoted in Eusebius' Church History, II.25.4
125. ^ Roman History by Cassius Dio. LXII. 25.
126. ^ Roman History by Cassius Dio. LXIII. 14.
127. ^ The Lives of the 12 Caesars by Suetonius. Nero Claudius Caesar. XLIX.
128. ^ The Antiquities of the Jews by Flavius Josephus XX. 5. 4.
129. ^ The Antiquities of the Jews by Flavius Josephus. XX.7.3.

130. ^ The William Davidson Talmud. Nazir 19b. 8.
131. ^ The Antiquities of the Jews by Flavius Josephus XX. 2. 5.
132. ^ The Jewish War by Flavius Josephus. II. 14. 6.
133. ^ The Jewish War by Flavius Josephus. II. 21. 2.
134. ^ The Jewish War by Flavius Josephus. III. 7. 35.
135. ^ The Jewish War by Flavius Josephus. III. 8. 3.
136. ^ The Jewish War by Flavius Josephus. IV. 3. 7-8.
137. ^ The Jewish War by Flavius Josephus. IV. 5. 5.
138. ^ The Jewish War by Flavius Josephus. IV. 9. 3.
139. ^ The Lives of the 12 Caesars by Suetonius. Sergius Sulpicius Galba. XII.
140. ^ The Lives of the 12 Caesars by Suetonius. A. Salvius Otho. XI-XII.
141. ^ The Lives of the 12 Caesars by Suetonius. Aulus Vitellius. XIII.
142. ^ The Lives of the 12 Caesars by Suetonius. Aulus Vitellius. XV.
143. ^ The Jewish War by Flavius Josephus. V. 1. 4.
144. ^ The Jewish War by Flavius Josephus. V. 9-10. 3-4, 1.
145. ^ The Antiquities of the Jews by Flavius Josephus. XX. 8. 5.
146. ^ The Jewish War by Flavius Josephus. VII. 8. 6.
147. ^ Roman History by Cassius Dio. LXVI. 14.
148. ^ The Lives of the 12 Caesars by Suetonius. T. Flavius Vespasianus Augustus. XXIII.
149. ^ Roman History by Cassius Dio. LXVI. 19.
150. ^ The William Davidson Talmud. Gittin 56b. 9.
151. ^ The William Davidson Talmud. Gittin 56b. 15.
152. ^ Roman History by Cassius Dio. LXVI. 26.
153. ^ The Lives of the 12 Caesars by Suetonius. Titus Flavius Domitianus.
154. ^ Roman History by Cassius Dio. 67. 4.
155. ^ The Lives of the 12 Caesars by Suetonius. Titus Flavius Domitianus. XVI.
156. ^ The Lives of the 12 Caesars by Suetonius. Titus Flavius Domitianus. XVIII.
157. ^ Roman History by Cassius Dio. LXVIII. 5.
158. ^ Roman History by Cassius Dio, LXVIII. 7.
159. ^ Church History by Eusebius. IV. 2. 2.
160. ^ Roman History by Cassius Dio. LXVIII. 32.
161. ^ The William Davidson Talmud. Nedarim 5a. 4.
162. ^ The William Davidson Talmud. Makkot 24a 33, Makkot 34b 1-4.
163. ^ The William Davidson Talmud. Kiddushin 27a. 9.
164. ^ Against Apion by Flavius Josephus. I. 2.
165. ^ Against Apion by Flavius Josephus. I. 8.

166.   ^ Against Apion by Flavius Josephus. II. 8.

167.   ^ Roman History by Cassius Dio. LXiX. 13.

168.   ^ Roman History by Cassius Dio. LXIX. 17.

169.   ^ Roman History by Cassius Dio. LXIX. 22.

170.   ^ Against Apion by Flavius Josephus. II. 42.

171.   ^ The William Davidson Talmud. Pesachim 112a. 12.

172.   ^ The William Davidson Talmud. Shabbat 33b. 5-6.

173.   ^ The William Davidson Talmud. Avodah Zarah. 10a. 15.

174.   ^ The William Davidson Talmud. Avodah Zarah. 10b. 2.

175.   ^ The Chronicon by Jerome.

176.   ^ 1 Thessalonians 2: 14-16.

177.   ^ The Codex Theodosianus. XV.v.1.

178.   ^ The History of the Decline and Fall of the Roman Empire Volume 2 by Edward Gibbon. Chapter XXIII – The Reign of Julian Part II.

179.   ^ Res Gestae by Ammianus Marcellinus. 23.1.2–3.

180.   ^ The History of the Decline and Fall of the Roman Empire Volume 2 by Edward Gibbon. Chapter XXIII – The Reign of Julian Part III.

181.   ^ The History of the Decline and Fall of the Roman Empire Volume 2 by Edward Gibbon. Chapter XXIII – The Reign of Julian Part III.

182.   ^ The History of the Decline and Fall of the Roman Empire Volume 2 by Edward Gibbon. Chapter XXIII – The Reign of Julian Part III.

183.   ^ The Buildings of Justinian by Procopius. IV. VII.

184.   ^ The Vandalic Wars by Procopius. IV. IX.

185.   ^ Historia Arcana by Procopius. 28. 17-19.

186.   ^ The Armenian History by Sebeos. 24.

187.   ^ The Armenian History by Sebeos. 24.

188.   ^ The Armenian History by Sebeos. 26.

189.   ^ The Chronicle of Theophanes the Confessor. AD. 623/4.

190.   ^ The Chronicle of Theophanes the Confessor. AD. 627/8.

Lightning Source UK Ltd.
Milton Keynes UK
UKHW020952201022
410792UK00006B/21